Transatlantic Obligations

Transatlantic Obligations

Creating the Bonds of Family in Conquest-Era Peru and Spain

JANE E. MANGAN

OXFORD
UNIVERSITY PRESS

Oxford University Press is a department of the University of
Oxford. It furthers the University's objective of excellence in research,
scholarship, and education by publishing worldwide.

Oxford   New York
Auckland   Cape Town   Dar es Salaam   Hong Kong   Karachi
Kuala Lumpur   Madrid   Melbourne   Mexico City   Nairobi
New Delhi   Shanghai   Taipei   Toronto

With offices in
Argentina   Austria   Brazil   Chile   Czech Republic   France   Greece
Guatemala   Hungary   Italy   Japan   Poland   Portugal   Singapore
South Korea   Switzerland   Thailand   Turkey   Ukraine   Vietnam

Oxford is a registered trademark of Oxford University Press
in the UK and certain other countries.

Published in the United States of America by
Oxford University Press
198 Madison Avenue, New York, NY 10016

An earlier version of Chapter 2 appeared as "Moving Mestizos in Sixteenth-Century Peru:
Spanish Fathers, Indigenous Mothers, and the Children In Between," *William and Mary
Quarterly*, Vol. 70, No. 2, April 2013, pg. 273-294.

Library of Congress Cataloging-in-Publication Data
Mangan, Jane E., 1969–
Transatlantic obligations : creating the bonds of family in conquest-era Peru and Spain /
Jane E. Mangan.
    pages cm
Includes bibliographical references and index.
ISBN 978–0–19–976857–8 (hardcover : acid-free paper) — ISBN 978–0–19–976858–5
(paperback : acid-free paper) 1. Families—Peru—History—16th century.   2. Mestizaje—
Peru—History—16th century.   3. Spaniards—Peru—History—16th century.
4. Transnationalism—Social aspects—Peru—History—16th century.   5. City and town
life—Peru—History—16th century.   6. Peru—Social life and customs—16th century.
7. Peru—Ethnic relations—History—16th century.   8. Imperialism— Social aspects—
Peru—History— 16th century.   9. Peru—Relations—Spain.   10. Spain—Relations—
Peru.   I. Title.
HQ605.M36 2015
306.85—dc23
2015016977

9 8 7 6 5 4 3 2 1
Printed in the United States of America
on acid-free paper

In memory of
Lewraine Magee Buckingham and Delia Varley Mangan

Contents

Acknowledgments

GIFTS OF MANY kinds have helped me write this book. The support of a Charles A. Ryskamp Award from the American Council of Learned Societies was of singular importance for research trips and teaching leave. My home institution, Davidson College, has also provided generously in the form of sabbatical, a Faculty Study and Research Grant from the office of the VPAA, and a faculty travel grant from the Dean Rusk International Studies Program. I am grateful for this financial investment in my historical research and writing.

The research for this project took me to Peru and Spain many times where archivists and librarians toil daily to preserve and organize documents for researchers like me. For their expertise with locating documents, efforts carting heavy *legajos*, and energy making reproductions, I am grateful to the employees of the Archivo Regional de Arequipa, the Biblioteca Nacional del Perú, the Archivo General de la Nación–Perú, the Archivo General de Indias, and the Archivo Histórico Provincial de Sevilla.

Friends and fellow historians made research trips delightful. In Seville, I greatly enjoyed the company of David and Sasha Cook and shared archive time with Sarah Chambers, Kaja Cook, Sara Vicuña Ginguerich, Luis Miguel Glave, Nancy van Deusen, and Michael Francis. In Lima, Augusto Chian made a wonderful companion and guide. Lucy Cáceres Ojeda was invaluable on my first foray into the regional archives in Arequipa and has been a good friend to my family on many visits to the city. Professor Rubén Pachari facilitated a wonderful audience of history students at the Universidad Nacional de San Agustín that asked probing questions about this project at an early stage.

Gifts of time from colleagues provided the intellectual support necessary to complete this project. Critiques by student and faculty at several institutions have made this a better final product. In particular, I would like to thank the history departments of Florida International University, the University of South Florida, Rutgers University, Ohio State University, and Concordia University, Canada, for invitations to lecture on this topic. Workshop settings for various iterations of this book also provided invaluable feedback. The conference "Centering Families in Atlantic Worlds, 1500–1800," sponsored by the Omohundro Institute of Early American History and Culture and University of Texas at Austin's Institute for Historical Studies was especially edifying. Suggestions from colleagues at the Triangle Early American History Seminar, the Tepoztlán Institute for the Transnational History of the Americas, the TePaske Seminar at the University of South Carolina, and the University of North Carolina at Chapel Hill conference "Global Encounters: Legacies of Exchange and Conflict (1000–1700)," influenced my analysis in chapters 1 and 2. A workshop on child removal in colonial settings at the 2014 Berkshire Conference on the History of Women helped place my work in global context. An unexpected and joyful by-product of this project was my collaboration with Sarah Owens on the volume *Women of the Ibero-American Atlantic, 1500–1800*, after a College of Charleston conference of the same name. Sarah combines intellectual curiosity with incredible organization skills; I wish I could have imitated her work ethic in my solo project.

In addition to these formal presentations, chance conversations in archives, at conferences, and by email with other historians have provided invaluable leads, criticism, and support. For all these things, I thank Ida Altman, Jodi Bilinkoff, Adriana Brodsky, Kathryn Burns, Paul Charney, Matt Childs, Suzanne Cooper-Guasco, Nicanor Domínguez, Alcira Dueñas, Ruth Feldstein, Karen Graubart, Karl Hele, Renzo Honores, José Carlos de la Puente Luna, Kimberly Gauderman, Lyman Johnson, Cynthia Radding, Rachel O'Toole, Frances Ramos, Ella Schmidt, Elvira Vilches, Ben Vinson, and Zeb Tortorici. I am especially grateful to colleagues who have given of their precious time to critique chapters of the manuscript, namely Kris Lane, Bianca Premo, Anadelia Romo, and Joanne Rappaport. Nancy van Deusen generously read a late version of the manuscript in its entirety and offered incisive feedback. I would like to thank the anonymous readers for Oxford University Press whose extensive comments shaped my work significantly. Any errors, of course, are mine alone.

Working with Oxford University Press has made for a great publishing experience. My editor Susan Ferber offers sharp criticisms in good measure with encouragement. She wields a pen to make corrections; her personal attention to authors and manuscripts is uncommon in the editorial world these days. I am grateful for her patience with my schedule and her commitment to seeing this project through to completion.

Many in the Davidson College community have given of their energy to move this book forward. My former chair in the history department, Sally McMillen, was an excellent model for being a teacher-scholar at Davidson. Colleagues in many departments at Davidson offered support including Vivien Dietz, Mike Guasco, Magdalena Maíz-Peña, and Matt Samson. Joe Gutenkanst in the Interlibrary Loan Office is an unsung hero. My Davidson College writing group has read chapters, listened to talks, and provided ongoing moral support; Patricio Boyer, Melissa González, and Trish Tilburg, I am so glad to have gone through this process with your input and your good humor.

All of my family members may not read this book, but I hope they will see its dedication to the memory of two remarkable women, my grandmothers, Lewraine Magee Buckingham and Delia Varley Mangan. The former entered an Ivy League university when female students were a rarity and the latter boarded a ship as a teenager, on her own, to cross the Atlantic. During my childhood, these women were the twin pillars of my family. As I migrate through the challenges of life, they emerge as models of extraordinary character. Moreover, the families they nurtured have filled my rich life through time shared with several generations around tables (kitchen tables, dinner tables, card tables) on Midland Avenue and North Harlan Street, Springettsbury and Lambeth Walk, as well as countless locales on the Delaware Shore.

My deepest debt for gifts given is to my *familia chica* who has lived with this book for so many years that they have stopped asking when I would finish. Years ago, my young daughter famously told friends that her mom "only has to write two more chapters and the concussion" to finish the book. As the process wore on my son was more philosophical asking, "But why do you have to write this book?" My husband stoically weathered my many comings and goings over the ten years during which I researched this book. Rob, Nicholas, and Caroline, if my words could lift up off these pages, they would embrace you with fierce love. May I be as generous in supporting your passions as you have been with mine.

J.E.M.

Transatlantic Obligations

Introduction

IN MAY 1593, a llama caravan loaded with 1,692 bars of silver destined for Spain made its way from Potosí, Peru, to the Pacific port of Arica (figure I.1). The silver cargo was then conveyed to Lima's port at Callao, and onward to Panama where mules carried it to Nombre de Dios on the other side of the isthmus. Once the silver reached the Atlantic port, workers reloaded it for travel to Seville. Such shipments were common in the sixteenth century during Potosí's heyday of silver production. What makes this shipment particularly interesting is that along with those 1,692 bars of silver went a modest inheritance of 823 silver pesos due to two girls from their recently deceased mother, the indigenous Isabel Tocto.[1] When Tocto had made her last will and testament, she had tallied up her debts owed and debts owed her, and then she had ordered her belongings to be sold. Whatever proceeds remained from her estate Tocto ordered them to be sent to "my daughters María Ortiz and Francisca Ortiz who are in the Kingdoms of Spain." The girls had traversed the same route to Spain some twenty years earlier with their father, Spaniard Baltasar Ortiz. Tocto remained in Peru while the girls' father traveled around Spain's empire. The two Ortiz daughters, mestizas, resided in Spain with their paternal aunt.

The record is silent on many points. What relationship did Tocto have with the Ortiz daughters' father? Was she his servant as well as something more? Did she want to accompany him to Spain? Did she agree to have the girls leave Potosí? Finally, did she want to leave her estate to the girls or did Spanish officials or Baltasar's relatives prompt her to do so? The challenges of trying to read this record pointed to the complexities of family in an era of conquest at the same time it hinted at the legal and cultural understandings of obligation through family roles.

FIGURE I.I Drawing by Pieter Vander Aa (1706) depicts a llama train in Peru like the one that would have carried Isabel Tocto's inheritance from Potosí to the Pacific Coast

Source: Courtesy of the John Carter Brown Library at Brown University.

That sixteenth-century case inspired this book about family—family as it existed within emerging colonial structures, over distance, and through cultural mixing. From its pages spring the themes of obligation, mobility, and surrogacy that bound together families in this era of colonial expansion. Its subjects are those who knew each other as spouses, lovers, sexual partners, mothers, fathers, sons, daughters, sisters, brothers, aunts, uncles, and fictive kin. Its narrative exposes scenes of colonial families from the 1530s through the end of the sixteenth century in distinct but related spaces in Peru, in Spain, and aboard the ships that sailed between them. The subject of family when parsed into categories of race, class, and location reveals only fragments; yet for the individuals who lived in this era, such pieces were but a part of a holistic experience they knew as family. Viewing family as a whole allows for the imagining of colonial patterns as well as networks that crossed the Atlantic.

Transatlantic Obligations revisits the colonial encounter's impact on definitions of family and negotiations of race and blood in order to link processes of family creation of the 1530s to the emerging colonial society in Spanish America.[2] Conquest and colonial expansion were synonymous with violence, disease, and mobility, factors that prompted the destruction of family units, the loss of loved ones, and prolonged separation that weakened family ties. Indigenous–Spanish pairings produced family ties outside of marriage, which were forged in new colonial settings. Even for those who held the greatest political, social, and economic power in colonial Latin America, conquest signalled challenges for family relationships. The disruption of marriage and domestic life by transatlantic travel profoundly influenced the lives of women and children in Spain.[3] Though many factors seemed to hinder family structure, it remained the institution at the center of the colonial world. Instead of seeing family as peripheral, when placed at the center of indigenous–Spanish relations, conquest, and colonial life, family networks and obligations serve as the pulse for moving people and goods over oceans and from generation to generation.

Historians of colonial Latin America have identified the fundamental role of family connections in transatlantic expansion and the operation of empire.[4] This book pushes these connections further by looking at multiple locations and a variety of historical actors. In addition to those at the top levels of the social hierarchy, illegitimate children and abandoned wives play a role in the history of family and empire, too.[5]

Transatlantic Obligations maps family onto empire, not in the interest of tracking lineage, status, and prestige, but to understand what actions cemented ties of blood and, to a lesser extent, fictive kin, and considers the place of emotion therein. Actions and words make up the analysis in these pages: actions through which individuals experienced family connections, as well as the words and phrases people used to speak about family. If the archival record coats any "tender ties" of these relationships in layers of bureaucratic language, the documents themselves yield more tender scenes in households or on voyages where people negotiated the rules of family.[6] Even those rules that seem black and white (such as laws) were in ink that faded with time and might obscure the malleability of the sixteenth-century definition of family. Unscripted situations prompted people to explain what it meant to be a spouse hundreds of miles from home, a mother separated from a child, or part of a family of mixed Spanish, indigenous, or African descent. In short, the lives of family and kin woven between conquest-era Peru and Spain affirm that definitions of family have always been complicated, contested, shirked, or embraced outside of, but in dialogue with, the Church and the State. In this way, *Transatlantic Obligations* argues that colonial families actually challenged the very caste and class structures of the sixteenth-century world instead of being units determined by those structures. The dichotomies of married/unmarried and legitimate/illegitimate create false divisions that obscure how family operated for many people in sixteenth-century Peru. The children born to Isabel Tocto and Baltasar Ortiz point to a process of *mestizaje*, or mixture, well beyond biological reproduction, as unprecedented types of mixing redefined the colonial family.[7]

Ultimately, families habituated to the extraordinary circumstances that arose in the sixteenth century. The very flexibility of institutions, even Church and Crown, incorporated the extralegal (illegal or illegitimate) situations that arose. Yet they did so in uneven fashion and created a more expansive form of family that helped allow slavery, discrimination against indigenous peoples, and the imperial system to function. In their roles as parents or spouses, individuals used laws and decrees in their interest when possible, yet they also demonstrated an ability to negotiate between prescription and practice to nurture relationships. People met their family obligations in this space, some with gusto and others begrudgingly, setting patterns that had long-term implications for Andean society.

The family in the sixteenth century is a challenging subject given its many potential definitions. Scholars acknowledge that family was defined simultaneously on several different levels: by family tree and by blood lines, as well as by kinship ties, godparenthood, and household.[8] Although the nuclear family was important, it excludes too many of the relationships that were critical to the function of family to be a working model for this study. Moreover, it privileges legitimate births in a society where illegitimacy was commonplace.[9] So, a consideration of family as based on household is imperative. This presents challenges, as well, though because law and custom cemented family connections even when people did not live under the same roof. Household models, however, are of utmost importance to consider how daily lived experience shaped intimate bonds or fictive kin.[10] This book emphasizes blood relations, both legitimate and illegitimate, but also considers household members in order to fully account for the complexity of what family meant in this era. This expansive definition reveals how sixteenth-century people understood relationships to one another and enacted them, highlighting those families affected by transatlantic historical currents.

This "family" in the transatlantic arena between the Andes and Iberia in the mid- to late sixteenth century was defined, imagined, lived, and enacted. Family practices, such as childrearing, religious education, rituals of marriage, and inheritance, evolved from pre-conquest traditions as well as the historical process of conquest and its related themes: political alliance, demographic imbalance, labor needs, cultural and sexual mixing, and religious and legal parameters.[11] This book confronts the contradictions that arose in this particular historical context: how could Spanish males be both conquistadors and concerned fathers?[12] How could indigenous women be both victims of colonial power and active mothers? Ultimately, these dichotomies limit defining units that were both pieces of an expanding colonial system as well as of families.

Individuals, in particular, husbands, wives, fathers, mothers, and lovers, appreciated their obligations to other members of their family. Some people used the word "obligation" to describe what they did for spouses and children. Others took action that represented a perceived obligation. Some obligations were legally required, such as parents bequeathing inheritance to their children; under Spanish law, Isabel Tocto had to leave her estate to her children.[13] Laws that dictated marriage practices, property, and inheritance collectively influenced how families lived and created legacies. Yet custom interacted with the interpretation and application of the law. Both Iberian laws, well recorded, and Inca rules of law, less easy to decipher from the sources at our disposal, mattered in sixteenth-century Peru. Scholars of Iberian law emphasize that those who applied law, mainly judges and courts, weighed local tradition alongside legal code when arbitrating justice. In Spain local customs often conflicted with standard law as codified in the Siete Partidas, for example. This balance between local custom and the ideas of law influenced practice in the Andes, as the Spaniards there respected the importance of respecting Inca traditions so long as they did not conflict with Catholic doctrine.[14]

In analyzing how obligations were culturally informed, this book focuses on fathers. Rather than dwell on lineage, this book studies the role of fathers and their obligations, allowing them to emerge as multidimensional, both responsible and irresponsible, violent and affectionate. It was expected that fathers would provide for their children.[15] We already know that European men had children with indigenous women in various parts of the Americas during conquest whether or not they were married, whether or not they were in a casual relationship, whether or not they had any intention of raising the children, whether or not these episodes of *cuenta carnal* (carnal knowledge) were accompanied by emotion or executed in violence. Those accused of neglecting family obligations are predominantly male: fathers who did not raise their children and husbands who left their wives. In some cases the abandonment was intentional; in other cases, it was accidental, a result of the demands of life in the service to the Crown. Some Spanish fathers failed to carry out paternal responsibilities for mestizo children.[16] Other fathers died in battles for the Spanish Crown.[17] Another group of fathers claimed their children and in doing so incorporated them into their family networks. This does not mean they were claiming them on equal footing, but the children—once paternity was identified—were then a part of a web of obligations, expectations, and responsibilities that determined how social status was maintained, how trade functioned, how economies expanded, and how political factions emerged in the sixteenth-century Andes. While historians of the family have focused on marriage alliances as the key to understanding these themes, further analysis of fatherhood and children reveals the varied roles of father's actions as forces shaping the construction of colonial society.

Fathers often used surrogates to shoulder obligation. Siblings played an important role as surrogate parents when fathers or mothers traveled around Spain's empire, as the case of the Ortiz girls shows. Examples of surrogate parenting spread beyond blood relatives as well because Spaniards in Lima often served as surrogate parents to mestizo children. Spousal surrogates emerge, too, for transporting letters and money and as travel companions. The use of surrogacy highlights how families functioned through vertical and horizontal ties, both parent to child ones as well as sibling relations.[18] Brothers gave away sisters in marriage; siblings provided financial support and helped one another emigrate.

Surrogacy was necessary due to separation over great distances for significant blocks of time. Thus, mobility emerges as another key factor for understanding family during the first century of Spain's presence in the New World. Families in Spain had experienced travel and separation before but the opening of the Atlantic changed the degree of its impact. Mobility now produced more extreme challenges. Some Spanish wives sought to track down husbands "absent in the Indies." Some fathers provided for their children but never lived with them in the same household. Yet travel was not only negative in its impact. The connections among family members across the Atlantic had an important economic component. Family ties prompted and supported voyages. Exchanges of property, from large amounts to token objects, functioned as one means to unite relatives who were geographically separated. The economic ties between relatives in Peru and Spain were continuous and imbued with significance. In this way, the family links between metropole and colony were about personal, economic, and legal obligations. As different as life was in Spain and Peru, many individuals experienced the two spheres connected by family members.

Isabel Tocto and her daughters had a connection across oceans despite the fact that they did not see each other for years. The Tocto case has important links to existing scholarship on indigenous women. By analyzing indigenous women's experience squarely through the lens of family, however, this work raises new questions. When scholars have investigated the experiences of indigenous peoples under colonialism, indigenous strategies about marriage, children, and other family interests became evident, even when they were not the focus per se of the research.[19] Historians of indigenous women's experience have given more detailed analysis of how these women accumulated earnings and used inheritance strategies in urban settings.[20]

Sixteenth-century indigenous women, recent work has emphasized, created families and networks with deep economic and emotional ties even within the frameworks of vicious oppression they experienced.[21] Indigenous mothers were sometimes identified by name, but often only as *india* (indigenous woman) in a telling stroke of anonymity reflective of their social status. Father Juan de Vivero wrote of Peru, "'As the land is such that men give themselves to the vice of sensuality, a great many mestizos are born, many of whom turn out badly among mulattos and Indians.'"[22] In his sweeping pronouncement, Vivero completely removes the indigenous women who gave birth to the children, and he emphasizes the "vice of sensuality" to obscure the multiple reasons ranging from human nature to political alliance for sixteenth-century Spanish–indigenous unions. By reintroducing Isabel Tocto and many other indigenous women of her generation into this history, with an explicit eye on family structures, this book dismantles rigid dichotomies of legitimate/illegitimate and married/out-of-wedlock to show the centrality of indigenous women to the colonial family structure with its blended indigenous, Spanish, and sometimes African members.

One does not have to scratch far below the surface of labels such as indio, mestizo, or Spaniard to see that their official and generic uses differed.[23] Mestizos were, in the words of chronicler Guaman Poma de

Ayala, "bad people, and very damaging to the royal crown and to the poor Indians," since they took after neither their Spanish fathers nor their indigenous mothers.[24] The decade of the 1560s has been viewed as a watershed moment for mestizos because of Jesuit debates that ultimately forbid mestizos to enter the priesthood and Toledan mandates that discriminated against mestizos.[25] This work focuses in great detail on the childhood oversight of these mestizos as well as their day-to-day life as adult family members in the 1570s and 1580s.[26] The issue of mestizos' social experience has been raised in important works on Cuzco and, more recently, Nueva Granada.[27] In particular, scholars have argued that the gender of a child born to Spanish father and indigenous mother had a significant impact on his or her ability to rise in colonial society. In Cuzco, mestizo sons fared poorly in comparison with their sisters.[28] Herein I explore mestizos' experiences by studying them as members of a family rather than as a category of unrelated people with mixed ancestry.

Like most other historians, I employ the term "mestizo" throughout this book to refer to children of indigenous mothers and Spanish fathers. Yet much evidence suggests that these children were not thought of as "mestizos" when they were born. In fact, in the 1530s and 1540s the label was used only rarely. While it is true that many Spanish fathers abandoned them to live among their indigenous relatives, a smaller subset of these mestizo children were claimed by Spanish fathers who oversaw their upbringing.[29] One contribution of this book, then, is to reveal how the discourse of families about identity differed markedly from that of royal decrees. Even as the Crown or priests assigned children to categories of lineage, the fathers and mothers who cared for them had another set of priorities.[30]

For some scholars mestizos were not born, but they were created as a social construct.[31] This book applies categories such as mestizo, indio, and Spaniard in their early modern context.[32] Often these labels appear more significant as legal categories used by the Spanish Crown than they do as racial categories according to a modern definition of race.[33] Because the Crown established clear legal categories for indigenous peoples and for Spaniards, the mestizo category proved problematic. The individual of mestizo heritage might integrate into either group depending on the situation.[34] This nebulous situation was a thorny issue in legal cases, but was not always an issue for mestizos as they went about their lives. In colonial Mexico the labeling of individuals created "genealogical fictions" that were not connected to biological family trees.[35] Much social history, including my own, has documented the variability of such labels.[36]

The emergence of a generation of mestizo children in the immediate decade or two after Spanish arrival prompted debates about issues such as paternal love, child abandonment, and children's education. This historical moment then, when new kinds of families were in formation, is of utmost importance for understanding the colonial family.[37] Like the mixture of peoples from different backgrounds, the entire creation of family units in the sixteenth century was itself a process of *mestizaje*, or mixture. Family construction, legal as well as lived-in-practice, is a vessel through which to read the impact of conquest expansion in Spain and in Peru.[38]

To focus on that moment of emergence, this study covers Peru and Spain between the 1530s and the 1590s.[39] This period encompasses the decades directly after Spanish arrival in Peru as well as the first and second post-conquest generation that were critical in the emergence of colonial family patterns. Through this period, violence and accommodation comingled as factors in colonial life.[40] Actions of conquest happened simultaneously with the creation of family, and the violence inherent in colonial life continued to affect families, Spanish, indigenous, or mixed race, in the late sixteenth century. While previous studies have focused on family life or related topics for the seventeenth and eighteenth centuries, this study centers on the sixteenth century.

This study moves along a Lima-Seville axis, with connected sites in the Andes and Spain contributing to the web of family in both directions (see figure I.2). It is urban-centered, with the viceregal capital of Lima and the emerging economic axis of Arequipa as the main sites of research and analysis. Seville, the gateway to the Indies, is the most important site in Spain for seeking out connections between Peru and Spain. Other locations within the Viceroyalty of Peru and within Iberia are highlighted, including Potosí and La Plata. Numerous Spanish towns dot the narrative, especially from the Andalucía region, which was the birthplace of the majority of those who emigrated to Peru. If we think of how circuits of commerce moved in the sixteenth century, the transatlantic route moved from Seville through Panama to Lima. The primary Andean circuit in existence at this moment was a triangular one that linked Cuzco, Potosí, and Arequipa. Arequipa and Lima, the two sites of my research, were thus the connector route of the transatlantic circuit and the Andean one.[41] Given the significance of these sites in terms of moving goods and money, they were home to people and families who were at the heart of colonial

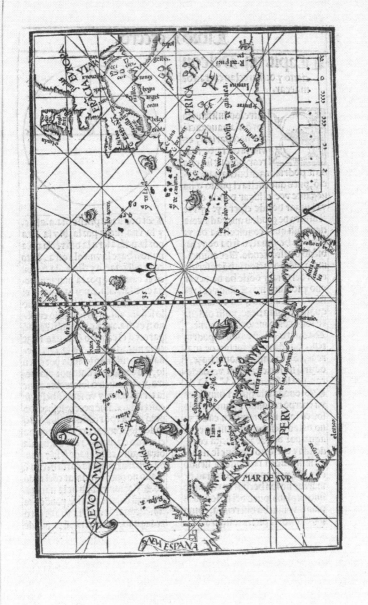

FIGURE 1.2 The 1545 *Carta de Navegar* by Pedro de Medina illustrates a sixteenth-century understanding of the route families traveled between Spain and Peru

Source: Courtesy of the John Carter Brown Library at Brown University.

change in the 1500s. The multiplicity of places acknowledges how events of the sixteenth century had a direct impact on the movement of people, which in turn drove the creation of families.

Migration also moved along the lines of expansion from Central America toward Peru. The foundation of Spanish urban centers in Lima and Arequipa and Potosí attracted people from Cuzco. Migration from Spain, especially Andalucía, to Peru spiked during the 1550s. Because mobility was dramatic during this period, people were natives (*naturales*) of one place and lived in another. While Seville was a sending location for emigrants to the New World, many came from smaller towns or other regions of Spain before making the trip to the New World, just as many indigenous men and women noted in the records of Lima (founded 1535) and Arequipa (founded 1540) were from central America, mainly Nicaragua, Cuzco, and many other provinces/towns of the Andes. The focus on elite indigenous families necessitates particular attention to people from the city of Cuzco, along with the growth of Lima and Arequipa in the 1540s. Lima and Arequipa, locations with excellent extant documents for the 1540s and 1550s, served as the main sites of research and analysis for the early decades of colonial rule.

Research into the family hinges on finding the interstice between prescription and lived practice. Little of a visual record of non-elite families remains for the sixteenth century, and precious few descriptions of physical appearance still exist.[42] What was left behind is language of familial responsibility and legal obligation and affective ties. And therein lies the space between the letter of the law or Royal Decrees and the practice of daily life in an emerging colonial society in the sixteenth century. The prescriptions are found in Iberian laws, Royal Cédulas, and church doctrine. The clues to lived practice, often in tension with prescription, emerge in notarial documents, records on licensing and travel to the Indies, and judicial cases about inheritance.[43] The Spanish documents come from the Archive of the Indies and the Seville archive of Protocolos, and the Peruvian ones from the National Archive in Lima as well as the regional archive of Arequipa. Wills, donations, and dowries drawn from notarial records in Lima and Arequipa constitute the most important body of documentation for this study. My sample of these volumes yielded 416 wills for Lima and 114 for Arequipa. I also consulted the notarial archives of Seville for evidence of connections to Peru. Occasionally relevant cases are drawn from other Andean archives, specifically those in Sucre and Potosí. Documents generated from judicial cases about inheritance, *vida maridable,* and *probanzas* formed another important group of sources.[44] The availability of documents influences the chronological emphasis of the study. Specifically, for the 1530s, the first decade of Spanish presence in Peru, applicable royal decrees or Iberian laws exist; however, only a handful of notarial records and court cases are extant. Thus, the heart of the analysis about families focuses on the 1540s through the end of the sixteenth century. This timeframe reveals both family structure and actions in the immediate post-conquest era as well as the coming of age of another generation.

Using this type of local source creates a fine-grained analysis of a range of historical actors who are participating in transatlantic networks. Yet these "local" sources, to quote historian Alejandro de la Fuente, are "local only in the sense that they were produced in a given administrative unit within the Atlantic, but their very existence and configuration were part of the process of imperial expansion and the creation of the Atlantic as a historical space."[45] Looking at families' actions in a local space highlights a fundamental interconnectedness between relatives in Lima and Seville and how this shaped the development of colonial society in Peru. These same people were actively integrating family into native Andean networks as well. This interconnectedness was not the sole domain of former Spanish conquistadors, but rather one of men, women, and children whose relationships in a family network moved them between one site and another.

The process of mining the notary's final product for the actual experiences of historical actors can be challenging. For all the unusual family structures on display in colonial documents, some individuals nonetheless held back and did not reveal children born out of wedlock or the names of the children's mother. Documents reveal hesitations through words written in the margins, inserted between lines, or added later in a distinct hand or with different ink. These additions are particularly revealing when it comes to issues of family structure.[46] When Luis de Tapia acknowledged his natural daughter Isabel Vázquez de Tapia in his 1552 will, the original scribe left a blank space for the name of the girl's mother.[47] Eventually someone filled in the blank, albeit in different handwriting, with the name Francisca López. Was the initial space left because Tapia forgot her name or because he needed to check with someone before listing it or because he was unsure if he should publicly acknowledge the mother of his out-of-wedlock daughter? These kinds of changes to the records might be intentional or innocent. Either way, they highlight common expectations about family structure and written representation that dominated the culture of Peru and Spain and the notary's office. This book draws attention to such notarial "cut and paste" moments for the clues they reveal about ideal family roles and the reality of sixteenth-century family life.

In addition the book analyzes actions, focusing on the verbs that pulse through the documents on family: fulfill (*cumplir*), reform (*remediar*), recognize (*reconocer*), and oblige (*obligar*). Husbands and wives had duties to one another; parents had obligations to children. The absence of such responsibilities was often written about as "freedom," as in single men were "free" from obligations. Was the language in notarial records telling of what happened? Could it reveal emotional ties? Yes and no. The records might not tell exactly what happened yet the script was a powerful indicator of how society perceived the roles of family should be carried out.

Certain populations are underrepresented in the text. While Afro-Peruvians formed families in this era, the documentary record on those families is slim. Demographics, slavery, and bias in the record make for far fewer examples of African fathers, mothers, and children. Studies that cover African and Afro-indigenous families in Peru focus on Lima and Trujillo and treat a slightly later chronological period when the Afro-descended population in some parts of Peru expanded greatly.[48] Thus, this book makes use of anecdotal evidence about these populations but draws on the much greater source base for Spaniards, indigenous men and women, and mestizos.

The book begins with the Spanish arrival in Peru. Its gaze moves, like its subjects, back and forth across the ocean. Chapters shift between Spain and Peru, as did boats, people, and the thoughts of those who lived on one side of the ocean but had been born on the other. The availability of sources, indeed the very production of sources in the sixteenth century, privileges certain groups over others and leads to an uneven narrative, especially in the case of Afro-Peruvians. Connections linking indigenous and Spanish families through relationships of blood, marriage, and kin are more the focus than an imagined maintenance of indigenous family or Iberian family. It is the points of contact, friction, and affection borne of colonial contacts, pressures, and opportunities that underscore this analysis.

The organization of the book is at once thematic and chronological. The entrance of the Spanish to Peru and the changes in emerging colonial rule, specifically demographic shifts and the growth of colonial urban centers, propels the work forward. Generally speaking, chapters 1 and 2 focus on the 1530s to 1550s. In chapters 3 and 4, the primary chronological emphasis shifts forward slightly to acknowledge the desire for family settlement and the accompanying demographic shift as more Spanish women reached Peru. This is a significant chronological moment, for Spanish women served as the traditional foil for complicating family-like relationships between Spanish men and indigenous or casta women. Chapters 5 and 6 focus primarily on the late 1550s through 1590s, a period with growth of colonial urban centers, the arrival of viceroy Francisco Toledo, and the Council of Trent. These chapters identify family makeup to develop the notion of a blended colonial family shaped by urban experiences, and to trace those through dowry and inheritance.

In chapter 1, family traditions of Inca and other Andean groups enveloped arriving Spaniards in 1532. Inca ruler Atahualpa gifted an Inca princess to Pizarro. Family relationships within the indigenous population and between newly arrived Spaniards and indigenous women are central to the events of the 1530s. Family ties continued to play a central role in how indigenous elites represented themselves to the Spanish Crown. In this chapter both the changes to the "real" Inca family tree and the written representations of such in judicial cases come under scrutiny. Famous examples such as El Inca Garcilaso de la Vega and Francisca Pizarro introduce larger themes of the book involving marriage, parenthood, *mestizaje*, and mixed families in sixteenth-century Peru.

Whether in marriage or cohabitation, Spanish and indigenous unions produced a new generation of children known as *mestizos*. Chapter 2 addresses the treatment of those children born outside of marriage. Many of the children of these first Andean–Spanish sexual unions were removed from their indigenous relatives.[49] This chapter examines this process, with a focus on the power and interests of the Spanish father. When fathers removed children, the action simultaneously represented a legal process, a colonial act, and a paternal obligation. Boys and girls moved about within Peru from the care of indigenous mothers to the care of Spanish others, and in many instances traveled from the Andes to their fathers' homeland of Spain. Paternal power over mestizo children aimed to maximize their cultural capital by raising them with Spaniards. Fathers had a variety of objectives, but in the main they wanted their offspring to be raised as Christians among people they considered their kin.

Were these mestizos an elite minority?[50] On the one hand, many mestizos, like the great majority of non-literate people, men and women, Spanish, African, and indigenous, did not form part of the historical record. Yet the mestizos I study were a varied group which included a few daughters of princesses and Spanish nobles but many others whose economic status was less lofty. Moreover, the patterns of their lives reveal important trends in the emergent colonial society as well as a glimpse into early ideas about racial identity. This chapter uses extant information about mestizo children from various locales in Peru to reveal the development of *mestizaje* in the sixteenth century as well as the historical experience of mestizos.

Since most did not claim their offspring in order to raise them personally, where did fathers move their mestizo children? Some placed them in convents.[51] But most fathers transferred their children into households run by Spanish women, preferably married ones. Spanish women were few in Lima, Cuzco, and Arequipa in the 1530s, but their numbers increased beginning in the 1540s. Trends in Crown rulings forced married couples to unite, bringing Spanish women to Lima, especially. As Peru's fame grew as a good place for a woman to marry with a modest dowry, it became a more desirable location for women to migrate. The number of female passengers to Peru, especially from Andalucía, jumped by mid-century. For indigenous families, economic pressures and urbanization began to increase by the 1550s, which heightened pressure to "lose" children to Spanish labor forces in cities. These trends furthered mobility for both Iberian and Andean families, as women left home in search of opportunities.

Chapter 3 focuses on Spanish couples separated by imperial motives. In the late sixteenth century, Luisa Pendones gave her husband Manuel Hernández permission to travel from Spain to the Indies for three years. When seven years later, in 1591, Hernández remained in his New World home of Peru, Pendones petitioned the Crown to force her husband to return to Spain or, if that was impossible, to send financial support.[52] In 1528 the Crown ruled that married men had to return from the Indies to be with their wives or bring the women to them. The ruling exposes the complexity of marriage in the era of transatlantic conquest. The family dramas that emerge from personal letters and legal petitions reveal lovelorn spouses and abandoned wives.[53] Abandoned wives often filed petitions with the King of Spain seeking to discover the whereabouts of their husbands and trying to hold them responsible for their financial obligations to the family.

Transatlantic voyages came to form an intimate part of family life, especially for people in southern Spain, in the sixteenth century. Chapter 4 analyzes the space between the worlds of Peru and Spain. This voyage across one ocean, a land bridge, and another ocean took months and was costly. The trip was a major focus of letters between relatives, a reference point for all sorts of business, financial and legal; it signified dreams and hopes for people in Lima and in Seville. While a voyage could put miles between one family member and another, its more typical role was that of connecting family members.

Chapter 5 is situated back on land in Peru, and it opens with a study of urban indigenous families. The source base for this chapter comes primarily from 1550 to 1590, though the sources frequently refer to family relationships begun in the 1530s or 1540s, and these reveal that indigenous families adapted in significant ways to emerging colonial structures. Dowry was an important practice for families, and it marks the efforts of relatives and surrogate relatives to help move young women into marriage. Indigenous men and women dowered daughters, but Spanish men and women also dowered indigenous women who had served as their employees. Men and women, Spanish and indigenous, frequently had children before marriage, and this occasioned numerous blended families joined by obligation. Thus, following practices such as dowry in addition to premarital relationships, this chapter argues that many mid- to late sixteenth-century families merged indigenous and Spanish people and traditions in modes that were bicultural.

One critical question in this book is how the colonial family, molded by transatlantic experiences, looked to its next generation. Chapter 6 focuses on inheritance as a key piece of the answer. First, it considers how and why fathers recognized children born outside of marriage. Next, by analyzing inheritance with attention to race, gender, and birth status, this chapter shows how the desire to fulfill family obligations and create firm foundations for the next generation drove bequests to out-of-wedlock children. Parents, especially fathers, did not give equally, but they created a web in which all offspring inherited. Most often this meant that legitimate children were privileged over those born out of wedlock. However, some individuals challenged colonial hierarchies and traditional legal practice in episodes of willful unlawfulness that sought to care for all their children, regardless of status, on equal terms.

In the second half of the sixteenth century, father Baltasar Ortiz chose a Spanish future for his daughters and took them an ocean away in order to live it. Yet Isabel Tocto's death in Peru produced a final maternal obligation, a claim on those girls as hers through the act of giving. The girls had not seen their mother in many years, but her devotion to them in the testament is striking. Despite the distance, despite the differences in lifestyle, her final act honored a family tie. In the end an amount of 823 pesos was packed onto a llama train with 1,692 bars of silver and wended its way from Potosí to the port at San Marcos de Arica and north to Lima. After crossing the ocean, it finally arrived at the Casa de la Contratación in Seville. Isabel Tocto's experience, her children's birth, their departure, and her transatlantic bequest suggest the complicated emotional and physical depths of family relationships in Spain's "New World" empire in its first century. Like the tides that moved people between Peru and Spain, waves of family connections moved people together and apart across lifetimes.

1

Matchmaking

LAW, LANGUAGE, AND THE CONQUEST-ERA
FAMILY TREE

THE FAMILY TREE of the Andes grew new branches in the sixteenth century. In 1532, Atahualpa was a contender for the title of Inca when the Spanish captured him at Cajamarca. He orchestrated many actions during his imprisonment, one of which was to give his sister, Quispe Sisa, to Pizarro. The action was in keeping with Andean customs that united men and women to create and strengthen political alliances. Of course, in this instance, acts of violence between Pizarro and Atahualpa preceded the gift of Quispe Sisa to the Spanish conquistador and the eventual birth of their children.

Over the sixteenth century, the written representations of Andean families revealed an experience of conquest that paralleled their physical lives. This is not to say that the extant documents reveal precisely what happened to these families, but rather how family structures changed with conquest. As individuals encountered the emerging colonial presence of Spaniards, they also witnessed the colonization of the family tree as reinterpretations or silences in documents of colonial bureaucracy that challenged the Andean meanings of family. Inca elites had to prove the legitimacy of family, and often dynastic history, in written requests to the Spanish Crown for recognition or reward. Sixteenth-century Andeans and Spaniards who commissioned or wrote documents that described family ties had to define Inca families to Spanish rulers.

When people created a narrative of Andean family history for a legal process, the daily lived experience of Andean structures might be obscured in the accounts that were notarized folio after folio. Spaniards tried to assert power and affect cultural change in the sixteenth century, yet did so through the very structures of Andean society on which they depended for arranging marriages and labor.[1] The Andean motives, meanings, and consequences of marriage and other domestic unions inform the arrangements worked out in the documents. While many native Andeans were victims in this era, some elite Inca maintained control over family structures in the immediate conquest era.

The foundation of Iberian colonialism was inherently violent, so family and violence operated together within this superstructure on a day-to-day basis. This chapter considers how the violence of conquest threatened the culture of family at the same time that family formation occurred in a new context. Forced sexual unions had political goals at this moment. Language that obliterated pre-conquest ideas of family wrought another kind of violence. The first decades of indigenous–Spanish encounter were critical to how the processes of family unfolded. The examples discussed here, primarily involving elite Inca families, reveal how pre-conquest ideas of family in the New World and Iberian notions from the Old were woven together in texts of the colonial empire at the same time the first generation of colonial-era families was born. Given the context, violence was never far removed; it occasioned marriages, created children and orphans, divided relatives over political alliances, prompted lawsuits, politicized genealogies, and, ultimately, became part of how family history was told.

Inca Family Structure

The family tree of the Andes is not exclusively Inca, but it is associated very closely with the Inca because of their imperial role.[2] The best known Inca families from the colonial period are well known because they intermarried with the Spanish, resisted the Spanish, or used their Inca heritage to negotiate with the Spanish Crown. Francisco Pizarro and Quispe Sisa famously formed political and cultural ties between the Spanish and Inca through their children. Manco Inca and those who succeeded him in Vilcabamba were of special interest as resistance fighters. Finally, those children born to Inca elites/rulers just before conquest used the Spanish legal system to seek reward from the Crown.[3] Analysis of the *probanzas* (a proof of merit document that includes narrative family histories) has shown the political power balance as more of a see-saw between

Spaniards and indigenous peoples than a ladder with the Spanish atop. Inca leaders such as Paullu maintained authority in the political realm well after 1532.[4] This "double recognition" in the political realm also existed in the interrelated arena of family where family networks had a particular and heretofore unexamined significance in light of conquest and the emerging colonial state. A full discussion of family structure and marriage in the Inca empire is therefore a fundamental starting point.

Beginning with the general Andean customs, society was based on the kin-unit called the *ayllu*. All members of an *ayllu* could trace their ancestry back to the same couple. The *ayllu* functioned as a way to link and reproduce kin, to structure labor, and to foster community. When marriage occurred in this society, members of *ayllu* groupings tended to marry each other rather than marry outside their kin unit. The Andean ritual of marriage marked the passage to adulthood for men and women. The marriage ceremony celebrated the man and woman who came together as different but equal beings; through speeches and ritual gift-exchange the couple acknowledged that both must play a role to ensure the function of their household. Within the *ayllu*, men plowed fields, herded animals, and fought. Women wove and made clothing for families, cooked, brewed, farmed, and raised children. The labor of each was a contribution not to the family per se, but to the *ayllu*. The intertwined relationship of family and *ayllu* is a critical underpinning to the concept of family in Andean society.

Several hallmarks of marriage in the pre-Columbian Andes include trial marriage, Inca state rituals of marriage, and polygamy. In the tradition of trial marriage known as *sirvanacuy*, a young man and woman lived together prior to a formal marriage ceremony to determine if the union was suitable.[5] Should the couple decide to break apart instead of marry, no formal mark of shame would follow the woman or man. If the couple had children, those children were accepted into society without the mark of illegitimacy that was such a heavy burden to bear in Iberian society. Once a couple did marry through a formal ritual, it was expected that they would remain monogamous.

While *sirvanacuy* was a common practice at the local level, marriage rituals and one's status as married had direct connections to the Inca empire. For commoners, marriage was the moment at which one began to pay tribute to the State. The Inca empire drew on the labor of its subjects in gendered fashion. Men served as soldiers and planted fields. Women wove textiles and brewed *chicha*, the corn beer that was a fundamental part of the exchanges between ruler and ruled. When men fought in battle, the Inca acknowledged their service through *chicha*. If men planted their fields, celebrations also utilized *chicha* provided by the Inca state and brewed by female labor of the *acllas* (chosen women designated to leave home and serve the empire). The Inca claimed desirable young women from each community for the *acllawasi*, or houses of the chosen women.[6] After service to the *acllawasi*, women emerged expert in brewing *chicha*. The *aclla* functioned at the local level as well as the imperial, so all women likely spent some time in the *acllawasi* as a sort of finishing school.[7] Most women ultimately left the *acllawasi*, emerging as adults ready for marriage. The Inca officials presided over mass marriages in which the rituals gave the impression of Inca rulers "gifting" women to men, for which the men thus owed them tribute.[8] Tribute status has as its basis a nuclear family unit: husband, wife, and children. Larger kin units were critical in the Andean world, but tribute designations came from the nuclear family, which highlighted the significance of marriage.

Marriage was also mediated by class status (commoner vs. elite). Marriages among the Inca elite had distinct roles related to the continuation of imperial rule and strengthening the power of the state. They enjoyed polygamy and arranged matches to preserve royal blood lines, known as *panaca*, or noble Inca lineage.[9] Thus, the son or daughter of two Inca parents had a different and higher status than a child born to an Inca man and a non-Inca woman.[10] The Inca used the practice of sister marriage whereby the Inca ruler would marry his own sister to ensure that blood lines remained intact. In fact, a major concern of Catholic priests in the post-contact era was the degree of relatedness of potential indigenous couples, which suggests these practices of kin marrying kin existed not only at the imperial level.[11] "Mixed" marriages were important as well. The Cuzco resident Juan Betanzos wrote extensively about Inca history and customs and, according to anthropologist Catherine Julien, Betanzos "alludes to marrying Inca daughters to provincial lords as a means of subjecting them to Inca authority."[12] As the husband of doña Angelina Yupanqui, an Inca princess, Betanzos was privy to information about these practices. Doña Angelina was in a marriage-like relationship with Francisco Pizarro before she married Betanzos. Theirs was a post-conquest mixed marriage. Yet examples of mixed indigenous couples exist for this era; don Felipe Guaman Poma is a famous example of a child from an Inca–provincial marriage in the Lucanas province, south of the city of Huamanga.

The idea of pure and mixed marriages in pre-Columbian Peru high-lights how class and gender informed the relationship between marriage and kinship structures in the Andes. As historian Silvia Rivera Cusicanqui writes, the use of kin metaphors "allowed the Inka to codify not only its social organization but also military and administrative into a system in which there was a place for the recognition of the dominated, as well as the most ancient pueblos or ethnicities."[13] Kin structures also helped the Inca (or any *ayllu*) integrate what was foreign. The Inca integrated a community they dominated; an *ayllu* integrated a marriage partner from a distant *ayllu*. This integration happened in gendered fashion; it was women who maintained the links to their mother's family through bilateral inheritance. The tragic irony, concludes Rivera Cusicanqui, is that "this egalitarian conceptualization converted itself into an authentic suicide at the hour of encounter with other foreigners, arrivals to the Andes in 1532."[14]

This book sees the "hour of confrontation" playing out as a process rather than a single event. Family formation in the presence of Spanish conquistadors drew upon Andean traditions even as it innovated in the face of conquest. Inca rulers gave their sisters to Spanish men in order to promote the same type of relationship that subjected any foreign man to Inca authority. Even as they gave the women in marriage, they anticipated the women would continue to perform their complex family obligations in Inca society. Although Spaniards were well acquainted with the practice of domestic union and marriage for political purposes, they may have understood only pieces of the Inca cultural landscape of the households into which they moved. For instance, Inca women in Cuzco, including Marca Chimbo, the sister of the Inca ruler Manco Capac, accused the Spanish of stealing cloth (likely the *cumbi* textiles highly valued in Andean society).[15] Here sisters acted as both potential sources of information and elements of developing a network of Spanish–indigenous relations. These actions were post-conquest, yet fully informed by pre-conquest kin networks.

Inca families maintained further continuities during the 1530s even as conquest battles occurred. For instance, not every Inca princess was being married to a Spanish soldier. While the business of Spanish conquest spread throughout the Andes, as noted by notary Pedro Becerro who recorded the sale of indigenous slaves or conquistadors' wills in town after town, Inca marriages continued apace with Inca leader Manco Capac arranging or presiding over ceremonies. In 1534 Vispla Ocllo was married to don Gerónimo Guacra Paucar of Jauja at the behest of Manco Capac.[16] Guacra Paucar received her from the Inca leader in a ceremony that honored his power in Jauja and rewarded his loyalty with a royal Inca woman. In another case of indigenous marriage, Pedro Pizarro was used as an intermediary to arrange a marriage in Cuzco between a captain of Manco Inca and a noblewoman. Pizarro was shocked to realize he was expected to "speak" to ancestor mummies to receive their approval for the marriage.[17] The new arrival, the Spaniard, had a role in the continuation of Inca practice that merged family and imperial dynasty. Sometimes Spaniards were not being given the elite woman they had requested, but rather a substitute bride, suggesting that the Inca perpetrated a bait and switch in the realm of matchmaking.[18]

Given demographics of the early conquest era in Peru, elite indigenous–indigenous marriages continued apace in the 1530s. Those Spanish men who gained elite women as gifts were being "fitted into" indigenous family structures rather than the other way around. The written record of this era, however, emphasizes Iberian norms of family. As power increasingly rested with the Spanish Crown over Inca nobility or Andean elites, this produced complex interplay between individuals as well as ideas about family, legitimacy, and responsibility. Arranged marriages, between the arrival of the Spaniards in 1532 and the fall of Vilcabamba in 1572, played an important role in Spanish–indigenous politics.

Arranged Couples and Conquest Politics

Between the early 1530s and the early 1550s, violence in the Andes was constant. As one conflict simmered down, another erupted. The first conquest battles began in 1532. The pretenders to the Inca Crown, half-brothers Atahualpa and Huascar, fell quickly, one at the hands of the Spanish and the other at the hands of Atahualpa. Yet battles ensued. In 1535, the native Andeans launched an effective campaign of rebellion against the Spanish led by Manco Capac. This rebellion led Inca elites to flee to the highland locale of Vilcabamba and relocate the center of their falling empire while the Spanish controlled Cuzco. Grumbling among Spanish factions over the spoils of conquest had begun even as the Inca retreated into the mountainous region. Native allies also showed division. Thus, during the Civil War period (1537–42) between Francisco Pizarro and his onetime partner Diego Almagro, native soldiers and elites positioned themselves on both sides of the battle with their own motivations. Yet marriages and

FIGURE I.I This eighteenth-century image entitled "Pizarro entertain'd on shore by a Peruvian lady" emphasizes a European perspective of gifting women over the notion of Andean political alliance

Source: From *The World Displayed* (London: J. Newbury, 1760). Courtesy of the John Carter Brown Library at Brown University.

births continued and thus created a colonial tapestry of relations even before Peru was through this almost twenty-year period of warring.

The opening example shows Quispe Sisa being given in marriage to a Spaniard by her brother Atahualpa in 1532 (figure 1.1). His gesture came after the Spanish attack on his troops. This was a dramatic act, but by no means a unique one. Inca women were objects of potential alliance for their Inca kin at the same time they were objects of desire for Spaniards.[19] Both groups were familiar with marriages being used to foster political alliance, but after 1532 many of these unions were not official marriages. In 1534, Manco Capac followed in the pattern of Atahualpa and offered Ynguill to Juan Pizarro.[20] Ynguill, eventually baptized as doña Francisca Coya, was one of the most elite women of the Inca dynasty at the moment of Spanish conquest, because she was descended from the Inca dynasty on both maternal and paternal sides. Spanish men who had observed the house of the couple in Cuzco noted that Pizarro kept her well-guarded and that Incas came to the house to worship her as a coya (queen).[21] The daughter of Juan Pizarro and Ynguill, named Francisca Pizarro, never received his legal acknowledgment. Juan Pizarro dictated a will wherein he acknowledged the "services" of an indigenous woman (name withheld) who had a daughter. Although Pizarro's will never acknowledged Francisca as his daughter, he did bequeath her 2,000 ducats for exclusive use as a dowry.[22] If the goal of uniting this Spanish–indigenous couple was one of strengthening alliances, it failed. Despite uniting Ynguill with Pizarro, Manco Capac led indigenous troops into rebellion against the Spanish in 1535. Juan Pizarro died while fighting the rebellion (started by the man who "gave" him his "wife").[23] Not all indigenous–Spanish alliances failed, though. Francisco Pizarro was the beneficiary of his indigenous mother-in-law's troops from Huaylas when Lima was under attack during this same rebellion.

It is worth emphasizing that both marriage and non-marital domestic unions were used for political ends from 1532 through to the Inca state at Vilcabamba that would last until 1572. Although the Vilcabamba Inca state was a weakened relic of the Cuzco-centered Inca empire, marriage and family legacies continued to serve as critical links from past generation to future generation, and power alliances between groups. Spaniards found the existence of the Vilcabamba state a thorn in their side, and they envisioned numerous ways to bring about its downfall, one that included a marriage proposal. As an infant, Beatriz Coya (who was the daughter of the elite Inca couple Sayre Tupac and Coya Cusi Huarcay [baptismal name doña María Manrique]) became part of a plan to pacify the violent neo-Inca state at Vilcabamba by having her marry the son of an equally elite Inca child. Sayre Tupac, brother of Titu Cusi Yupanqui, negotiated with the Spaniards in order to received status and benefits. He left the neo-Inca capital at Vilcabamba as a gesture of support for the Spanish and, in return, he was awarded an encomienda. When Sayre Tupac died in 1560 or 1561, his daughter Beatriz Coya was an infant. Both her bloodlines and her material situation (she was heir to the large encomienda) made her eligible for a political and economic alliance through marriage.

In 1565 Licentiate Lope García de Castro was in negotiations with the Incas at Vilcabamba. His "Capitulations of Acobamba" included a proposed marriage between the young Beatriz Coya and Felipe Quispe Titu.[24] The birth of Felipe Quispe Titu, a full-blooded noble Inca born some two decades after conquest, facilitated the existence of Vilcabamba. His very existence was a potential threat to Spanish rule. He was raised in the company of his parents from an early age. With the negotiations around pacification of the Vilcabamba rebels, however, he was brought in from the wilderness—both in the physical sense, as he was brought to a Spanish town, but also in a spiritual sense. Father Antonio de Vera baptized Quispe Titu in the town of Carco, province of Vilcabamba.[25]

This noteworthy proposal tried to use pre-conquest family lines within Inca culture to bring about a union that would serve the political goals of Spanish conquest. It also aimed to strengthen a line of Inca nobility through the encomienda, land viewed by the Spanish as their gift, but most likely understood by the Incas as theirs since the Spanish had taken it from them. In the Capitulations of Acobamba, one sees the discussion of family relationships move among Andean pre-Columbian realities, Spanish documents, and colonial discourse. For instance, the negotiations recognize Inca heritage even as they promote a Christian marriage. The son of Titu Cusi, Felipe, was supposed to marry Beatriz, the daughter of Sayre Tupac, brother of Titu Cusi. This constituted a call for first cousins to marry, as they might have done in Inca times, to produce pure lineage for the Inca line of ascendancy. The capitulations stipulated this marriage (as well as the property Felipe would gain from it). Yet, the marriage was proposed only with the assumption that Pope Julius III would give a dispensation for the marriage of the relatives. Interestingly the plan also clarified that Titu Cusi himself, and no other representative, would be the guardian for the children Beatriz and Felipe. Instead of appointing a Spanish guardian, this proposal reiterated elite indigenous control for the family.[26] It acknowledged both indigenous family networks and traditions but did so in a uniquely Spanish colonial context, given the required dispensation from the Pope.[27]

Part of the documentation from this case draws a picture of Titu Cusi's family tree in order to prove his pure Inca lineage. The interrogatory asks if he is "married according to law and custom of the Incas, who were rulers of these kingdoms, with a sister of his named Coya Chinvo Ocllo, legitimate daughter of her father Manco Ynca Yupanqui in who he [Titu] had a son named Quispe Tito of ten years of age."[28] The legitimacy of his marriage and the status of the children of that marriage are critical for who would inherit rulership. When one witness was asked he responded that yes, "the said Chimbo Ocllo Coya is his [Titu Cusi] legitimate wife according to their laws and customs and his sister."[29] With specific attention to family structures and relationships, the Spanish document uses words laden with legal and cultural significance in the Spanish context and transfers them to a colonial context in such a way that a marriage between a brother and a sister is normalized; a daughter born to a ruler who has children born to many women is still a legitimate daughter. In terms of Felipe and Beatriz, the Spanish documents confirm that the young son Felipe was a true-blooded Inca with potential to rule and bring rebel Indians under the sway of the Spanish, especially in the company of Beatriz Coya, his cousin and another member of the Inca elite. Felipe's pure Inca lineage legitimated him as an envoy for the Crown in this matter.

Despite the use of family ties as a central piece of trying to end Inca resistance, the plan failed. By 1572, Tupac Amaru was captured and executed. And in the 1560s, shortly before the final downfall of Vilcabamba, doña María Manrique, the mother of Beatriz Coya, now widowed by the death of her indigenous husband Sayre Tupac, took actions that seem to turn on the unstable context in which she and other indigenous women found themselves in this era. Ultimately, she conspired with or was forced by Spanish men to turn over the nine-year-old Beatriz for marriage. Sources differ over whether the marriage was consummated.

The ensuing years for doña Beatriz reveal the Crown's interest as marriage broker and Manrique's counter-interest in her daughter's marriage alliance. Earlier, Manrique had placed Beatriz in the Santa Clara convent in Cuzco and arranged with Arias Maldonado to bring her to him when Beatriz reached eight years of age. Local *corregidor* Juan de Sandoval gave his approval of the arrangement. Arias (and others) planned to marry doña

Beatriz to Cristóbal Maldonado to bring together landholdings from both sides of the family and create a powerful union. Royal officials opposed the plan, and Ldo. Castro prohibited the marriage. The Crown's concerns had more to do with power-brokering than they did with the young age of doña Beatriz. But, the objection came too late as Manrique had already removed Beatriz from Santa Clara. In the city of Cuzco, rumors flew that a secret marriage had been performed and that the nine-year-old girl had been physically claimed by Cristóbal Maldonado.

Manrique was left in a delicate legal position, and she had to submit testimony on the matter. Her answers emphasized her rights as a mother and her devotion to the girl. She claimed that she placed Beatriz in the convent so she would "learn prayers." She said she visited her frequently.[30] Removing Beatriz from the convent on January 14, 1565, was necessary because her daughter was extremely ill. She brought the girl to Maldonado's house so that doctors could treat her. Manrique objected to the charge of a conspiracy with the Maldonado brothers. Manrique stated that she as the "legitimate mother" of her "legitimate daughter" had the right to decide the fate of her daughter.[31] Namely, she wanted Beatriz to be cured and then raised in the house of Arias Maldonado and his wife doña Isadora. The use of legitimate in reference to both mother and daughter highlights, as Manrique surely wished to do, the power of an Andean family structure from which doña Beatriz was born and its legitimacy in the 1560s' Andes. In this case, however, Manrique lost the right to raise Beatriz in a Spanish household of her choosing. The young girl returned to Santa Clara, the convent that had failed to protect her in the first place. It was, however, viewed as the safest place for her to remain until her future was sorted out. The Maldonado brothers received a sentence of banishment, though in contrast to the typical banishment to places of isolation, they were sent directly to the center of the empire—Spain. Their punishment highlights the value of the young elite doña Beatriz in the matrix of colonial politics. The Maldonados paid a price for crossing those men who meant to protect her for other purposes.

In 1572, when Beatriz was fifteen, viceroy Toledo sent word to the prioress of the convent to ask the young lady if she wished to take her vows or to marry. She chose marriage. Toledo arranged a union with Captain María García de Loyola, who married her to serve the King, in his words, "even though she was Indian in her dress."[32] In this colonial society, one's dress reflected much about how people lived, what they ate, how they worshipped, what language they spoke, and a host of other intimate customs associated with family life and raising children. This comment in the historical record framed the silent Beatriz as different, as an outside of sorts, even though it was Martín who was the outsider. He received an enormous gift with this marriage: a *repartimiento* in the valley of Urubamba close to the city of Cuzco. Sources recall him as a power-hungry man who eventually served as Governor of Chile. Doña Beatriz followed him to Chile. Once envisioned as half of a post-conquest Inca power-couple, doña Beatriz lived out her life as a widow in Concepción with her sister doña Melchora de Sotomayor Coya, far from the heart of the Inca world.

Chile was not known as a peaceful region in this era, but violence was part and parcel not only of the world into which Beatriz was born but also the family structures that emerged during her lifetime. Her family of birth made her a pawn in a plot to halt violence before she had reached the age of five. The failed plan to use her in a marriage of convenience to consolidate Spanish–indigenous political and economic power in Cuzco made her a potential victim of sexual violence before the age of ten. Until the fall of Vilcabamba, native elites still might use marriages as a way to stem the tide of physical or cultural violence but the negotiations entailed risks and women, particularly, might suffer.

Legitimate Daughters, Loyal Servants, and the Colonization of the Family Tree

The life of Beatriz Coya shows that legal battlegrounds increasingly hosted debates about families, lineage, and legitimacy. The Church is usually thought to influence ideas about family, especially with regard to native families in the era after conquest. For example, priests suppressed traditions of multiple wives, marrying cousins, or premarital sex. Yet Andean and Iberian family norms influenced representations of family roles in the legal arena, too. Notary offices and court rooms were sites of contestation about family definition and family structure. Spaniards in Peru during the early years after conquest felt the power of Andean families and family rituals. Further, the Crown ordered that native elites be protected in order to retain their markers of nobility, either lands or offices.[33] Andeans and, in some cases, their Spanish husbands also learned they needed to manipulate representations of family to successfully represent their family trees in Iberian institutions in order to argue for those protections. Moreover, they grasped the Spanish power to shape Inca history; when Pizarro claimed Manco Inca, and not Atahualpa, was the heir to the royal line, this interpretation of Inca royal lineage spread to Spain.[34] Quite soon Inca families would "refashion" their discussions of themselves (willingly or under force) in Spanish terms. This created a "genealogical fiction" based on family structure and ideas of legitimate marriage.[35] To make one's case to Spanish courts, then, those who inter-married with Spaniards and those who were of pure indigenous blood-lines used terms like "legitimate" and *"vida maridable"* to prove their ties to one another in ways the Spanish system found palatable. Language and ideas of family from legal cases about two children of Huayna Capac, his daughter Quispe Sisa and his son Paullu, and their families reveal how legitimacy, as defined in Iberian terms, came to dominate colonial discourse.

Quispe Sisa was born around 1516 to the supreme Inca ruler Huayna Capac. (See Inca rulers in figure 1.2.) Her mother, Contarguacho, was from a high-ranking family in the province of Huaylas and received land and some 300 servants when she became one of Huayna Capac's wives.[36] Her life course shifted when Atahualpa gave her to Pizarro. By 1534 Quispe Sisa gave birth to a daughter, Francisca, and she would have a son, Gonzalo, with Pizarro in 1535. If indigenous women were going to marry Spaniards in this era, they needed two things: baptism and a dowry. Quispe Sisa received both of these. By 1537, after baptism, she was known in documents as doña Inés Huaylas Yupanqui. While Pizarro did not marry her, he did provide her with a marriage partner and a dowry.

Within several years Quispe Sisa married Francisco de Ampuero.[37] Ampuero would eventually make an appeal to the Crown on her behalf that she was a "legitimate" daughter. Ampuero served as a page to Pizarro, and the conquistador gave Ampuero the encomienda of Chaclla at the time of his marriage to Quispe Sisa.[38] While Pizarro married off his former lover with a nice dowry, he did not send her children along; Francisca and her brother stayed with their father. In essence, her mar-riage to another man or transfer to a household headed by another man signaled a loss of control over the children. Quispe Sisa went on to have two sons with Ampuero, Martín and Francisco, and one daughter, Inés.

Eventually, Ampuero sued to retrieve property that had been awarded to Francisca by Pizarro. Ampuero's connection to Quispe Sisa was neces-sary to reclaim the province of Huaylas, allegedly given to Contarguacho from Guayna Capac, as befitting the wife of the Inca ruler. Ampuero, stepfather of Francisca, argued that Pizarro did not have the right to take the land, as Contarguacho would have passed it on to her daughter Quispe

FIGURE I.2 This eighteenth-century drawing represents an Inca royal couple in traditional dress and surrounded by, among other objects, drinking vessels or *queros*

Source: From Amédée François Frézier, *Relacion du voyage de la mer du suc aux cotes du Chily et Perou* (Paris: Chez Nyon, Chez Didot, Chez Quilllau, 1732). Courtesy of the John Carter Brown Library at Brown University.

Sisa. Quispe Sisa, then, would have had the sole power to bequeath it as she wished. Presumably, for Ampuero, this would lead to reclaiming it from his stepdaughter, Francisca Pizarro, and having it in his power through his marriage to Quispe Sisa.

Ampuero made the case at the court in Madrid. His testimony focused on representations of legitimacy in Quispe Sisa's family tree. The case stretched out over years. The elements of family history (indeed, dynasty) formed part of numerous requests to the Crown and lawsuits during the sixteenth century. Spaniards in Peru during the early years after conquest felt the power of Andean families, as Andeans learned to argue those elements of Spanish family such as legitimacy that held sway in court. Ampuero specifically drew attention to his wife's parents and claimed that she had been "a legitimate daughter according to the custom of the country."[39] A "legitimate" child referred only to the offspring of a married Catholic couple. Yet, despite its legal basis, the term had distinct implications for one's acceptance into society and household. For Ampuero or others who tried to make claims about indigenous families, winning the point on legitimacy was key, notwithstanding the fact that legitimacy in the Spanish sense was impossible to achieve prior to Spanish arrival, since no Catholic sacrament of marriage existed. The "custom of the country" to which Ampuero referred was Inca, and it would have been the dominant mode of operation for families at the moment of Spanish conquest in 1532, one that was still respected by the Spanish because of their protection of certain elements of Inca rule. Spaniards, such as sixteenth-century jurist Francisco de Vitoria, observed that Inca society maintained clear marriage rituals, one sign of rulership among indigenous societies.[40] These marriage practices differed from European custom, and thus as Spanish legal decisions proved ever more important for indigenous elites or mestizo children, their language about family clouded Inca complexities in order to represent a more palatable and legally viable family to the courts.

An elaborate discussion of family structure emerged as Ampuero struggled in court to obtain the *repartimiento* of Huaylas for himself, albeit in his wife's name. The generations of family being discussed encompassed all the transitions of the 1500s. The original family was Inca. The next generation was of conquest: Pizarro and Quispe Sisa. The parallel relationship that emerged after Pizarro moved on was the marriage to Ampuero.[41] The next generation, doña Francisca Pizarro (daughter of Quispe Sisa and Francisco Pizarro) did not remain in Peru but moved to Spain. One issue that spans the pre-Columbian family unit, the conquest unit, and the emerging colonial unit across all three generations is legitimacy. In this transition period between Inca rule and Spanish colonial rule, the legitimacy of pre-conquest Inca norms were not called into question per se. First, Quispe Sisa was called a "legitimate daughter." This language was amplified in the interrogatory, which asked witnesses "if they know that Huayna Capac and Contarguacho his wife had and procreated the said doña Inés Yupanqui [Quispe Sisa] for their natural and legitimate daughter according to the custom of the land and in such veneration and esteem and reputation it was understood by all the principal caciques of these kingdoms."[42]

Even in a Spanish arena, Ampuero had to merge Andean concepts of family and legitimacy with Spanish ones to narrate Quispe Sisa's family tree. He also hoped to establish her as the only person with this legacy in order to legitimate his wife's right to inherit land and any other privileges accorded her by the Spanish Crown. In doing so, he had to rely on both Spanish and indigenous witnesses, some of whose responses he could not control.

Witnesses were asked "if they know that in these kingdoms and provinces at present there is not nor is there known another daughter of the said Huayna Capac and the said Contarguacho except for the said doña Inés their only daughter and heir."[43] To complete Ampuero's family narrative, it was not enough to have witnesses testify to the legitimacy of his wife's birth and parents' marriage, as well as her status as the only daughter of the royal Inca pair. Given the colonial Spanish context in which Ampuero maneuvered, he had to justify his marriage as well. Thus, witnesses who just had testified to the legitimacy of a marriage by the custom of the country in the Andes were then asked to testify to the legitimacy of the marriage between Ampuero and Quispe Sisa. "And if they know that the said Francisco de Ampuero is married and wedded and blessed in the face of the holy mother church with the said doña Ynés Yupanqui [Quispe Sisa]."[44] This language is standard from legal documents of the era. Witnesses might be asked to verify the marriage of a couple for any number of judicial reasons, and the phrase used would be exactly the same. In this case, what is remarkable with regard to discussions of family relationships is that within one single interrogatory all parties utilized the same language to discuss differing family structures. Ampuero, his legal advisors, the scribes, and the witnesses amended phrases and shifted emphasis as to what constituted lawful marriage or legitimate children to fit a situation. This created a family fiction about the labeling of relationships. What goes unstated here in the attempt to normalize (and make linear) Quispe Sisa's family past and present (where she came from, where she had been, and where she was at the present) is that Pizarro was Quispe Sisa's first Spanish relationship and, while it did not receive legitimate blessing, it did produce a daughter, Francisca, who was legitimated by the Crown. Quispe Sisa's relationship with Pizarro might seem to qualify as a legitimate marriage in Andean terms "by the custom of the country," yet because it ended with Pizarro taking a new indigenous lover, it did not count.

With regard to the pre-conquest relationship between Contarguacho and Huayna Capac, the witnesses responded to questions in a variety of ways. Some agreed with all the information; some said they could not affirm it because they did not know. Others added their own interpretation of the family structures in play. Nicolás de Ribera, one of the first Spaniards to arrive to Peru, affirmed the question, but he could not remember the name of the mother (Contarguacho).[45] Gómez Caravantes de Maçuelas recalled he knew "an india of Guaylas" that was said to be the mother of Quispe Sisa. He went on to identify her as "the muger of Huayna Cava [sic], one of several that he had." Like some of the other witnesses, he confessed he did not know the name of Contarguacho, though he had seen this woman "obeyed and revered" by the *indias* of Huaylas.[46] He also referred to Quispe Sisa as the "hija natural" of Huayna Capac, omitting the "and legitimate" phrase suggested in the interrogatory.

The indigenous witness Antonio Poma, a cacique from Huaylas, described the relationship between Huayna Capac and Contarguacho in different terms. He stated that Huayna Capac "had fallen in love with her [Contarguacho] and she bore him a son who died and then [bore] the said doña Inés."[47] Poma, a nephew of Contarguacho through his mother's side, was the only witness to ascribe sentiment to the relationship between the two. Perhaps for him the expression of "falling in love" privileged Huayna Capac's tie to Contarguacho above others. Poma was also the only witness who mentioned the infant son born to the couple prior to doña Inés. His identity as a *natural* of Huaylas, her home province, and her relative created the only testimony which expressed emotion and added significant detail not present in the interrogatory.

In general, the witnesses agreed on the current marital status of Ampuero and Quispe Sisa.[48] One witness asserted that he knew the couple to be married because he had attended their wedding and had seen them in *vida maridable* together.[49] Testimony on the validity of the marriage between the two was ironic given that other documentation from the era suggests that Quispe Sisa had tried to poison her husband by the late 1540s.[50]

Quispe Sisa's conquest-era family history represents elements of a typical experience for elite Andean women. For elite Andean men, differences emerged in terms of representations of their families and their experiences. Consider the language in the family tree presented about

Paullu, son of Huayna Capac. Paullu's son, don Carlos Inca, married doña María de Esquibel, a noblewoman born in Spain. This arrangement of an Inca man marrying a Spanish woman was uncommon but Paullu had achieved important status through collaborations with the Spanish. The couple's son, don Melchor Carlos Inca, eventually travelled to Spain in 1602.[51] Melchor Carlos Inca represented the family of Paullu in his *probanzas* to seek remuneration and favors from the Spanish Crown. Documentation from his case is less rich than Ampuero's in terms of discussion of family, perhaps because Melchor was one generation removed as a grandson and as a petitioner to the Crown in the early seventeenth century. Still, the case highlights the dynamic representations of family at this moment where histories, bloodlines, and discourses from two sides of the Atlantic were in dialogue.

Incas themselves were using Inca ideas about family lines and succession as they presented themselves to the colonial state. These claims did not stand in the end because Francisco Toledo made the ultimate decision as to who the Spanish would regard as the legitimate Inca (and it was Huascar). Yet the actions show both understandings of how family lines and political status operated in both cultures, and in the new colonial context, notions of family were adapted to fit the needs of fathers, mothers, and sons. Paullu's strategy was not the same one his son Carlos would employ in the next generation.

While in Spain making his case for support, the grandson don Melchor highlighted the legitimately constructed family tree of Paullu, the "friend" of the Spanish, in order to gain favors from the Crown. He related his great-grandfather's allegiance to the Spanish Crown. Projecting an image of the couples in his life (his ancestors and at present) as having legitimate marriages was an equal component of his claims. When Paullu gave his support to the Spanish, he and his wife Toto Usica both became Catholics, as did Naz Colque, his mother ("wife in their law of said Huayna Capac").[52] They received new names: Cristóbal, Juana, and Catalina. Cristóbal married Catalina in a Catholic ceremony, after which they lived a legitimate married life. From this union, they produced a "legitimate, first-born son," the father of don Melchor.[53] He stated that his father's parents had "made vida maridable."[54] The Peruvian viceroy don Francisco de Toledo favored don Melchor, given his status as great-grandson of Huayna Capac and grandson of Paullu and paved the way for his marriage to doña Leonor Ardas Carrasco, granddaughter of an original conquistador of Peru.[55]

Don Melchor's legal case presents a narrative of legitimate unions begetting more legitimate children and so on. Note that in his presentation Paullu's mother Naz Colque was "wife in their law of said Huayna Capac."[56] In Ampuero's petitions, however, Contarguacho was the wife of Huayna Capac, not Naz Colque. Furthermore, Contarguacho and Huayna Capac, were, in the words of one witness, "in love." If Contarguacho was Huayna Capac's special wife, how could Naz Colque be his wife as well?

Don Melchor's representation of family in the probanza was not absolute. It was one construction of family that hinged on representing the Inca family to Spanish courts in an acceptable way. It tried to fit Andean family patterns and practices of the early conquest era into a Spanish framework that did not hold the same meaning for indigenous families and which many had actively resisted. At the same time as this representation of family structure was undergoing significant change to meet the demands of the colonial moment, the way of doing family business was changing. The Inca once used marriage to incorporate the unfamiliar and in turn to receive rewards.[57] After 1532, that calculus shifted. Increasingly the Spanish rules of incorporation and reward disadvantaged indigenous families. For elite women, marriages with potential political networks presented more of a possibility than what was available to non-elites, who served Spanish men in a variety of capacities with little legal recourse for compensation.

"For Services She Has Rendered Me": Indigenous Mothers as Objects and Actors

If legal documents changed the representation of elite indigenous Andean families in the wake of conquest, a parallel transformation occurred with the relationship between indigenous women, elite and non-elite, and their male partners. In the pre-conquest era, indigenous commoners married and then fit into a community structure that provided stability for the *ayllu* and tribute to the Inca. For elites, the Inca used marriages to incorporate newcomers or newly dominated subjects by, for instance, marrying Inca princesses to provincial rulers in order to cement ties to the empire or by allowing elite males to take secondary wives from ethnic groups under the control of the empire. The tradition of combining politics and marriage occurred within a new context after 1532. Indigenous women, as the proxy-wives awarded to Spanish men, experienced this shift in a particularly poignant fashion.

In the opening acts of conquest, indigenous mothers appear as powerless objects of Spanish male power. Likewise, they were frequently recipients of modest donations or bequests that did not sufficiently constitute respectful acknowledgements of their vital role in domestic comforts and bearing the children of the men who offered them money.[58] As Spanish men recorded the role of indigenous women in their lives, few acknowledged their physical unions and shared parentage, as did Juan Flores of Arroyo Spain who gave a donation to Isabel of Nicaragua "for being as she is the mother of *our* children."[59] The use of "our" in the phrase acknowledged a shared role, a connection between Flores and Isabel that was typically avoided in such documents by the use of "my" and not "our" to describe children.

The unions of Spanish men and indigenous women have often been portrayed in one-dimensional form, which obscures the lives of both parties as historical actors, along with the power implications inherent in such acts. The precedents for the sexual relationships between Spanish conquistadors and native women came from both sides of the Atlantic. On the Andean side, the exchange of women to cement political alliances was well established. From the Spanish side, men's cohabitation with native women "replicated the patriarchal pattern between the masculine head of family and the network of servants, where powerful men took sexual favors from servants."[60] The particulars of most of these relationships remain inaccessible. Historian Karen Powers spelled out a range of possibilities: "Though rape and betrayal probably represented opposite poles of the spectrum, in its interstices we are likely to find mutual consent, economic opportunism, physical attraction, political alliances, social mobility, genuine love."[61] Historian Nancy van Deusen advocates analyzing this spectrum in depth in order to redefine the relationship between violence and intimacy, especially during the 1530s to 1550s period when many indigenous women were captives and bought and sold as slaves.[62]

Although extramarital relationships dominated, it should be noted that the Crown did not oppose the marriage of Spaniards to indigenous peoples. In fact, the Crown passed a royal decree in 1514 that allowed such marriages between Spanish men and indigenous women. Moreover, the Crown hoped to promote Spanish-native marriage in order to cement military alliances with native chieftains and to quiet church voices that abhorred cohabitation. The 1514 law allowed for the possibility of legitimating what was already occurring in practice. In Mexico, for instance, the lord of the Tlaxcala gave numerous princesses to the Spanish conquistadors, including Hernán Cortés.

After their initial pairing with Spanish men, native women traveled along different trajectories that were often determined by class status. Quispe Sisa's noble Inca status positioned her to be sexual partner to Francisco Pizarro and, after bearing him two children, to be married to the aforementioned Francisco de Ampuero, originally a page to Pizarro.[63] For some, these marriages were paternalistic acts to control the indigenous women. Emma María Mannarelli argues that "lovers behaved like fathers" when they provided dowries so that their former lovers and the mothers of their children could be married to Spaniards of lesser social status.[64] Other scholars, however, have emphasized the potential for indigenous women to influence the choice of the marriage partner and even the dowry. Camilla Townsend challenged this analysis in her treatment of Malintzin, the indigenous translator of Hernán Cortés. Malintzin, who married Juan Jaramillo after her sexual relationship with Cortés ended, influenced not only Cortés's choice of her marriage partner but also her dowry of land in her native region of Mexico.[65] One significant difference in Malintzin's case is her role as Cortés's translator during the conquest of Mexico. Rather than being an elite woman accustomed to relative luxury, she was a slave who came into a position of leverage through her role as an ally to Cortés. In the Andean examples, then, ideas about family structure and marriage patterns were expressions of a collective response to the current situation, rather than individual negotiation. Further, an indigenous women's status was an important factor in her ability to influence her futures as did Malintzin.

Other examples suggest that indigenous women did not need to be elite to enjoy dowries and help with the marriage arrangements made for them by their former Spanish partners.[66] Moreover, rather than experience some kind of ostracism because of extramarital relationships, most indigenous women did marry later in their lives, sometimes to Spanish men or other times to indigenous men.[67] Even when former partners did not offer a dowry, many still made their own forms of acknowledgement of their indigenous lovers. No legal requirement compelled a man to make a donation to his child's mother, but it was an established customary practice in Spain. By the 1540s and continuing through the sixteenth century Spanish men routinely used a donation to offer some material provision for the women who satisfied their physical desires and frequently bore them children. The practice is suggestive of a pattern in Spain whereby men would pay women with whom they had children out-of-wedlock through a legal process known as *apartamiento*.[68] In Spain, a tribunal heard the cases, whereas in the New World the payment was given through a clause in a will or a donation. The idea of paying the mother of one's children when there was no intention to marry was well established in Spain; the process by which it happened may have changed in the colonies. This act was a practical way to ensure better sustenance for one's children. It also represented a spiritual obligation, as men cleared their consciences of adultery or cohabitation with money, land, or goods. The following examples demonstrate the range of gifts mothers received, as well as the relative significance of such gifts compared to those bestowed on loyal servants.

The most common bequest was a lump sum of silver pesos, and notaries dutifully recorded the reasons ascribed to such gifts. Such bequests related an understood obligation by these men to make some provision. In 1553, Diego Maldonado bequeathed fifty pesos to the indigenous Ana, mother of his daughter, "for the good service she gives me and for raising my said daughter."[69] One year later Merida native Juan Flores donated twenty-five pesos each to the two indigenous women with whom he had four children.[70] In 1560, Gonzalo Gutiérrez left a bequest of twenty pesos to Isabel, the mother of his natural son Juan, along with a strict order to "take care to look after my son."[71] Gutiérrez also granted one year of sustenance for Isabel, provided she live in the power of Pedro de Lupiana, a tutor of his son. Unlike many indigenous mothers, Isabel was ordered to stay close by the boy, perhaps still an infant, for at least one year.[72] These women received material acknowledgments for bearing children, in some cases the only heirs of these men, and for giving them round-the-clock care and sustenance as they grew from newborns to toddlers.

Some indigenous mothers received property bequests. Francisco Ramírez, a *vecino* (property holder) of Arequipa, ordered that 300 pesos from his estate be used to purchase a *solar*, or urban property lot, for the indigenous Ana, mother of his natural son Juan Rafael.[73] Ramírez acknowledged Ana's services to him and said that the bequest was made to relieve his conscience. The donation of urban property was especially valuable, since it could be rented for income. Ana received one of the more handsome material offerings in the archival record for her role in Ramírez's life.

Manuel de Herrera, a native of Valverde, Spain, lived for decades in Arequipa, Peru.[74] He had several children with two indigenous women: Francisco Martín, Alonso Martín, and Juana Pérez. Catalina was the mother of Juana and Alonso. Leonor was the mother of Francisco. Both women received urban property, bordering on "the lot of the indios," from Herrera. The women's relationships (kin or blood) are not specified but their receipt of adjacent plots of land would have tied them to one another after Herrera's passing. Both women also received clothing in the form of common *abasca* dresses typically worn by servants. Although the donation of clothing to the two women was equivalent to a servant's annual contract, the donation of the property to these women signified that this was much more than a donation to a worker. Moreover, Herrera favored Catalina with fifty pesos, much more than he gave to Leonor, and any clothing or linen of his that she wished to take after his death. People frequently resold textiles and clothes in urban settings or traded to gain additional goods, so the gift of any of Herrera's clothing or linen had financial potential for Catalina. Herrera did not offer any language of affection about either woman to his notary, but it is hard not to read some greater connection to Catalina than Leonor given the accumulation of gifts he made to her.

Many of the women who bore sons and daughters to Spaniards in the 1550s and 1560s also worked as their servants. This did not preclude the men from specifically acknowledging the son or daughter as the child of his servant. Sebastián Bernal gave a twenty-peso bequest to Angelina who was a Cuzco native and a long-time servant to Sebastián Bernal. The two had a daughter, Juana Bernal, who was named in her father's will. Bernal also recognized Angelina as his servant and the mother of this daughter and gave her a modest bequest of twenty pesos.[75] In the case of Bernal and many others, indigenous women received something of material value and occasionally words of praise or affection for overlapping labor, sexual, and reproductive responsibilities.

In Arequipa, women found themselves recipients of goods, primarily cloth or animals. Francisco de Quiroz had two daughters with the indigenous Isabel, a native of Arequipa.[76] He left her clothing in the form of a *cumbi* dress and two cotton dresses (dresses would have included both a lliclla and anaca), thirty pregnant goats, and a *fanega* of corn per month for fifteen months. Isabel's portion of his estate came her way "for services she has made me." He bequeathed clothing or goats to his other servants at the same time, though none received as many as Isabel and none received the added bequest of corn. In that sense, Isabel's treatment was special relative to other servants, a stratum in which he clearly placed her.

Imagine how these ties stretched on the path of transatlantic travel and then reemerged near death, when a person's will emphasized those who played a significant role over the course of a lifetime. Diego Alonso de Sotomayor was a merchant in Peru in the sixteenth century. In 1570 in Seville Sotomayor made a will in which he acknowledged his business ties to Peru, but also noted personal ties to an indigenous woman whom he never married and with whom he may or may not have had children. He ordered that ten ducats worth of masses be said for "a deceased india to whom I am indebted" and also for "the conversion of her children."[77] He made two additional donations in the name of the soul of the deceased woman, six ducats to the Hospital of the Poor and six ducats to two poor individuals. At the moment of making a testament, these donations were typically made for the souls of those closest to someone: a parent, a spouse, a child who had predeceased. Sotomayor's gestures through this will reiterate the way quotidian links born in colonial Peru created lifelong connections. Relationships that stayed close to the conscience prompted the gesture most representative of the sixteenth-century Iberian world: using one's money to help the salvation of a loved one even as it ensured saving one's own soul. The bond is less clear with regard to the children. It is reasonable to suspect they may have been his. Although a standard element of a will, the prayer for their conversion points to the desire to have them raised as Christian and, thus, able to enter into heaven. Sotomayor's ties to an indigenous woman during the conquest era weighed on his mind even as he made his will four decades later.

In the 1540s and 1550s, the indigenous women who were servants to and parents with Spanish men experienced the changing politics of the conquest era through their daily labors as well as their family role. The implications for their children were complex. These children were enmeshed in a world in which indigenous culture predominated but Iberian culture was gaining dominance in colonial life.

The First, and Famous, Andean Mestizos

A significant cultural realm of Hispanicization encompassed religion. Spanish fathers of children born to elite indigenous women felt a duty to raise them as Christians. By the late 1550s and the 1560s, this issue might not be as pressing because indigenous women would have increasingly been baptized and perhaps even active participants in Catholic practices. Yet few indigenous mothers in the 1530s and 1540s had been baptized, and indigenous women were not yet participants in *cofradías* (lay religious brotherhoods). Men turned to Spanish relatives to raise this first Andean generation of mestizos.

The baby girl born to Quispe Sisa and Francisco Pizarro in the turbulent early years of Spanish presence grew up in a world that was highly conscious of her family ties on both sides. Although Francisca was born in Jauja, the influence of her mother's family always competed with Spanish cultural influence. Her childhood overlapped with the rebellion of Manco Capac as well as the civil wars between Pizarro and Almagro. She lost relatives on her mother's side in the ongoing violence between Spaniards and Andeans, as well as members of her immediate family.

By 1536, Francisco Pizarro had taken the requisite steps to have Francisca legitimated by a royal decree.[78] After her mother married Ampuero, Francisca lived with paternal relatives, Francisco Manuel Alcántara, half-brother of Pizarro, and his wife Inés Muñoz.[79] Pizarro ordered that she learn to read and write, study music on the clavichord, and receive religious instruction, common for elite Spanish girls. When her father died in 1541, he named her uncle Gonzalo Pizarro as her tutor. Francisca remained in the physical care of Muñoz, after Alcántara died in the Civil Wars between the Pizarro and Almagro factions. At one point Muñoz attempted to travel with Francisca and her younger brother Martín toward Quito, allegedly fearing for the safety of the children at the hands of the Almagrists.

By the end of the decade, King Charles I decided that he did not want Pizarro's children to remain in Peru. Chief among his concerns was the amount of property controlled by those children and their eventual political influence as adults. He hoped to limit the potential power of the Pizarro mestizos by bringing them back to the metropole. In March 1550 Francisca Pizarro dictated her first will as she prepared to sail for Spain in the company of her half-brother.

Her will emphasized her ties to her uncle Gonzalo as well as provision for a 4,000 ducat-dowry for his daughter Inés. Her half-brother was heir to one-third of her estate. The remainder was to pass to her mother Quispe Sisa, though she used no words of affection or emotion for her mother in any portion of the will as she had for her uncle.[80] Ampuero, her stepfather, likely oversaw the will and could have influenced what was designated for Quispe Sisa.

The group traveling to Spain included seventeen-year-old Francisca, her half-brother Francisco, and her stepfather Francisco de Ampuero as their escort. Catalina Cueva, a native of Segovia who had been a governess to Francisca in Peru, also went with the group. Ampuero included his daughter Isabel on the trip to have her live in Spain. He reported to the Audiencia of Lima that he needed to take her so she did not have "poor care" while he was absent.[81] It is possible that Ampuero did not trust Quispe Sisa to raise the girl because he feared the potential impact of an Inca noble upbringing in matters of religion, politics, culture, and courtship on the young Isabel, half-sister of Francisca.[82]

On landing in Spain, Francisca was soon in the company of her uncle Hernando Pizarro. In the years prior, Hernando Pizarro had been imprisoned in a castle at La Mota where he lived with Isabel Mercado, a young Spanish woman who bore Pizarro four children only one of whom lived to adulthood. After Francisca's arrival, Mercado was sent away to a convent, Pizarro invited his niece to La Mota, and he married her in 1552. After ten years they left the prison and eventually settled on Pizarro family property near Trujillo. Francisca bore five of Hernando's children, two of whom died in infancy. When Hernando dictated his will in 1578, he wrote several clauses that indicated his affection and concern for his wife both in terms of expressing sentiment and meeting her material needs.[83] In addition, Hernando requested that Francisca never remarry. Three years after his death at age forty-seven, however, she married Pedro Arias Portocarrero, the brother of her son's wife.[84] She died twenty years later in Spain, having never returned to Peru.

Another Francisca Pizarro, the daughter of Juan Pizarro and Ynguill, and cousin to the daughter of Quispe Sisa, was not recognized officially by her father nor given legitimate status through a royal cédula.[85] Formal acknowledgment by her father notwithstanding, this Francisca's early life had parallels with that of her cousin. She was born and grew up during a time of tremendous instability in the Andes. In 1548, Diego Velázquez took her to the house of Francisco González, the elder, and his wife Cecilia Vázquez de Bribiesca. It is not clear where she lived between her birth and 1548. Was she with her mother, other indigenous relatives, or in another Spanish household?[86] In 1548, though, the daughter of Velázquez, Inés de Hortega was put in charge of Francisca.

Interestingly, when the Pizarro–Almagro conflict died down, this Francisca Pizarro did not cross the ocean to Spain. She remained in Cuzco where she married Gaspar López González and the couple had one daughter.[87] Her husband referred to her in legal documents as the *hija natural* of Juan Pizarro and doña Francisca Coya. No extant will has been found for this Francisca. She named her daughter Cecilia Vázquez Pizarro, drawing on the name of her father (who she never knew) and the Spanish woman in whose house she lived from 1548 until, presumably, her marriage to López González. While she never went to Europe, her life in Cuzco showed the Spanish structural control of her upbringing, household, and marriage partner.

Incorporating mestizo children into family had become a pattern by the time Pizarro and his men entered the Inca empire. Spaniards had been having children with indigenous women, elite and non-elite alike, for several decades. The experience of Inca nobles' mestizo children in the first generation after conquest certainly bore resemblance to what had transpired some ten years earlier in the case of Mexico. Martín Cortés, the son of Cortés and Malintzin, was taken to Spain at the age of six by his father and never returned to Mexico. He was legitimized by the Pope and fought for Spain, but he never again saw his mother.[88] María Jaramillo, the daughter of Malintzin and her husband Juan Jaramillo, was raised in Spanish fashion in the house of her father. Malintzin died when María was young, and Jaramillo remarried quickly to a young Spanish woman.[89] For the children of this important indigenous woman, Christianity, Spanish homes, and role models predominated.

The famed author El Inca Garcilaso de la Vega, born in Cuzco near 1539, moved to Spain in 1560, and never returned to Peru. His writing reveals how his indigenous family influenced his early life. His parents were Captain Sebastián Garcilaso de la Vega, a hidalgo from Extremadura, and Chimpu Ocllo, a direct descendant of the Inca. These two lived together for some time. In 1544, during the Pizarro—Almagro wars, Captain Garcilaso lived in Lima, and the boy was in Cuzco with his mother. About 1552 his father married Luisa Martel de los Ríos, a Spanish woman, and Chimpu Ocllo left their home. Garcilaso stayed in the home of his father, but visited the house of his mother. His father went on to have two daughters with Martel before he died in 1559. The marriage to Martel is in keeping with the pattern of the majority of fellow conquistadors. The Spanish—Spanish marriage also fit with the Crown's preference for the elite. To be clear, the Crown did allow Spanish—indigenous marriages as a last resort when a Spanish bride could not be found. Eventually Chimpu Ocllo was married to Juan del Pedroche.[90] Her marriage to a Spaniard of lesser means after having children with a Spaniard of high status replicates the pattern of many elite indigenous women including Malintzin.

Garcilaso did not legally recognize his son in his will, though he did leave him a bequest which supported the younger Garcilaso's voyage to Spain.[91] His well known writings reveal one perspective on Inca family history and include the memories, albeit distant, of his childhood. At least for part of his childhood, Garcilaso lived with his mother. Garcilaso recalls, in 1547, having don fray Juan Solano, then-bishop of Cuzco, in his father's house and that his mother "fed them."[92] His mother may have ordered servants to feed them, but the scene refers to both parents and their son being in the same household. There exists, then, a familiarity with both indigenous relatives and history through his mother as well as an introduction to local Spaniards and their customs. Was this typical for mestizo children? Was this more common in Cuzco than in other cities? Garcilaso recalls intimate details of indigenous life and customs. For instance, he describes in great detail how indigenous women in the Andes treat their hair with herbs and boiling water in order to keep it a pure black color. He claims he was "too young to notice how many or what herbs" went into the mixture, but that he "did not however fail to wonder at the ordeal, which seemed to me a severe one for those who submitted to it."[93] Did he see his mother do this? His indigenous servants? His observation of this process shows an intimate connection to indigenous daily customs as practiced in the 1540s and 1550s, which Spanish fathers would have witnessed as well.

He wrote in an effortless manner of being in the company of his mother. "I often heard as a child from the lips of my mother and her brothers and uncles" during weekly visits at her home in Cuzco of those "few relatives, both male and female, who escaped the cruelty and tyranny of Atahualpa."[94] His connections on his mother's side render him not only a voice of authority but also an interested voice in the interpretations of Inca history.[95] Consider for a moment the scene he paints: in a house in Cuzco were Chimpu Ocllo and relatives, and children including Garcilaso. Given the chaotic years of the 1530s and 1540s, they would have had much to talk about, and it is reasonable to think that these conversations would have had an impact on Garcilaso. And though he wrote of the memory in Spanish, he would have originally heard the discussions in Quechua.

Unlike Garcilaso, Francisca Pizarro left behind no recollections on how her indigenous family influenced her life. Perhaps Garcilaso enjoyed more freedom with his indigenous relatives because he was a boy. Yet the two shared education in a Spanish style, writing, and indoctrination into Christianity. Moreover, both would eventually leave their birthplace of Peru and their mothers' homeland to spend the rest of their lives in Spain.

FAMILY CONFIGURATIONS IN the mid-sixteenth century Andes layered complexity atop complexity. Given demographic realities and the strength of community at the local level, indigenous families were not on a path to total destruction, but rather reconfiguration. Indigenous couples and families continued to be an important presence in the Andean landscape, based in their ancestral homes and expanding to urban communities. After conquest battles ceased, the family tree of the Andes took on a new shape as it incorporated Spanish legal and religious roots. These changes demanded crafty legal representations of Andean families. On the one hand, the creative adaptation of a family history to suit a political purpose was familiar. After all, histories of Inca lineages were not impervious to fictive twists. Yet in sixteenth-century cultural interactions, rewriting the family tree for the colonial system foreshadowed not only change but loss. Both Inca and Spaniard had used marriage or marriage-like unions to forge political gains. Neither side fully grasped the other's cultural assumptions behind these unions of man and woman. When Inca rulers anticipated incorporation of the Spanish through gifting of women, they found instead that Spaniards expected to dominate politically and culturally. For some families, the offspring of these unions, the first generation of mestizo children in the Andes, were lost to indigenous families, a process that occurred in tandem with an increased focus on bringing Spanish women and children to Peru as building blocks of colonial society.

2

Removal

FOR THE LOVE AND LABOR
OF MIXED-RACE CHILDREN

ALONSO DE MESA moved in the elite world of the Pizarros and Garcilaso de la Vega in the early years of Spanish presence in Peru. Before he left Cuzco in 1542 to fight against Lope de Aguirre, he made a will in which he instructed his executors to send his son, Luis, and two daughters, María and Luisa, to his native Toledo, Spain. All three children had been born to indigenous mothers in Cuzco, but Mesa wanted his own mother, Lucía, to raise them. His legal wish was indicative of a larger pattern that sons and daughters be raised among Spanish kin. This pattern threatened to break limbs on the indigenous family tree. The indigenous mothers had no voice in Mesa's will. Even his naming of them hints at how much change some indigenous families endured in the 1530s and 1540s. His daughter Luisa, the notary's script declares, was born to "another *india* who is called Toctollo and her name in Spanish, Inés."[1] That she had a Spanish name suggests a baptism, but even if that was the case, a conversion to Christianity was not enough to convince Mesa to let Luisa grow up in her mother's care.

To be sure, many Spanish fathers abandoned their mestizo children and those boys and girls grew up among indigenous relatives. Yet extant historical records reveal that a subset of Spanish fathers of mestizos considered the upbringing of their children, both its material and cultural aspects, as part of their fatherly obligation.[2] Fulfillment of these obligations did not necessarily signify that the men were in close geographical proximity since enacting the responsibilities of fatherhood in this era did not require physically raising a child. Historians have long noted that

Spaniards sometimes placed their mestizo children in Spanish house-holds through legal or extralegal mechanisms.[3] Fathers took care with the choice of where to send children to ensure that their sons and daughters were with kin. In some instances, sending children away from their mothers or away from their birthplace to Spain was considered necessary for their well-being. Spanish fathers gave little if any value to the mother's role and denigrated the role of native Andean culture in the upbringing of these children.[4] That surrogates stood in for fathers and mothers, on both sides of the ocean, reflects the significant mobility of the time.

This chapter examines the relationships between fathers and children, as well as between parents, to fully explore paternal motives and the process by which fathers claimed mestizo children between the 1540s and the 1580s. By analyzing notarial legal documents and wills it shows how boys and girls moved within Peru from the care of indigenous mothers to the care of Spaniards and, in many instances, traveled from Peru to their fathers' homeland of Spain. Father's actions toward their children aimed to maximize their cultural capital by raising them with Spaniards. To those fathers who recognized them, the children were their responsibility. Yet the men exhibited a range of actions to fulfill that responsibility from raising sons and daughters in their homes to apprenticing them to other families. Raising them closer to Spaniards and in urban centers made it easier for the children to enter the worlds their fathers imagined for them as adults. Colonial households did not mimic their Iberian counterparts exactly, as indigenous servants, different foods, and new languages added to the children's experiences.

The focus, then, is on those fathers who not only recognized but also sought significant levels of control over their mestizo children. The largest demographic group to analyze in this period was the children born of out-of-wedlock unions between Spanish fathers and indigenous mothers. The notarial documents available give insight into families of lesser means, neither destitute nor elite. Looking at examples beyond the elite families of urban Lima or Arequipa is an important contribution of this study and a reminder that negotiations about family, legitimacy, and identity occurred throughout different levels of society with distinct consequences.[5]

For some scholars, mestizo identity and birth out-of-wedlock were synonymous by the mid-sixteenth century in Peru.[6] This has been cited as evidence that mestizos became increasingly marginalized in Spanish colonial society. This chapter argues that fathers in this era did not see "mestizos" but rather children, albeit ones born out of wedlock and known as *hijos naturales*.[7] In contrast to Crown or church officials, however, relatives did not typically use the terms "mestizo" and "natural child." Moreover, fathers' actions reveal what they envisioned for their children. The role of mestizo children as heirs could be a critical part of a father's rationale to acknowledge the child and have a concrete impact on the child's life. Further, some men wanted to incorporate those children into their families. In general, scholars view the early modern era as a time when the role of fathers included not only authority and power but also obligation and sentiment.[8] How and why some Spaniards did this unfolds in documents about the children's care. The actions by parents of mestizos, either *hijos naturales* (children born to an unmarried couple) or *hijos ilegítimos* also called *bastardos* (children born to a couple when one partner was already married), are key to understanding how family structures flexibly incorporated economic and other demands for women who were not spouses and children who were not legitimate in the early decades after conquest in Peru.

Some fathers acted out of moral, religious, or spiritual obligation. Others noted sentimental reasons. All emphasized acculturation on Spanish terms and within Spanish households. At this historical moment Peru had few convents and a small population of Spanish descent that strove to emphasize Iberian culture. These men wanted their children to speak Spanish and to eat wheat bread at a table, not seated on the floor. They assumed their children would dress in Spanish clothes, not indigenous attire. Further, these men viewed a Spanish home as the place to ensure their children would be raised as Christians. Spanish fathers relied on Spanish households or the option to send children to Spain in order to fulfill paternal obligations as they understood them.

Claiming Mestizo Children

Most mestizo children lived with indigenous mothers because Spanish fathers had abandoned them. These cases barely appear in the archives and for good reason. Sixteenth-century men and women in Peru lived within a legal and social structure that, generally speaking, empowered Spanish men at the cost of indigenous peoples, and women routinely adapted their circumstances to the expectations of male figures, both Spanish and indigenous. Thus, if an indigenous woman gave birth to a child of a Spaniard who did not wish to acknowledge the child, the detailed experiences of the woman and child are unlikely to appear in the historical record. However, many Spanish fathers did, in fact, acknowledge their sons and daughters born to indigenous mothers in the New World.[9] The Siete Partidas counseled that "although he [a father] may have natural love for it [his child] because it was begotten him, his affection for it increases much more by reason of the nurture which he affords it."[10] Law and custom, then, comingled to emphasize a father's obligation to nuture.

Such examples indicate how family responsibility included children who were illegitimate as well as from distinct racial backgrounds. Family patterns in Spain had long encompassed illegitimate children and incorporated them into family networks.[11] In sixteenth-century Iberia, children were regularly born out of wedlock, and many of the men who traveled to the Indies had children in Iberia without having married.[12] Rates of illegitimacy in Spain's empire were higher than those on the peninsula.[13] Take the example of Diego Francisco, a native of Portugal who had a son there with Catalina Luis in 1537.[14] In 1542, he married Isabel Martínez, with whom he never had children. He subsequently moved to the Indies. By 1554 he was making a will in Lima that focused on his connections to Portugal: bequests to his wife, his sister and her daughters, and his father as his heir. The will also named his seventeen-year-old son Tomás, gave him 200 gold pesos, and left a bequest to Tomás's mother. Thus, Spanish men who fathered children while engaged in the expansion of empire already had an Iberian precedent for dealing with children outside of marriage. Yet the historical experience in Peru meant greater mobility, longer distances, and increased power imbalances (between Spanish men and indigenous women) which highlighted the tensions of family structure and family roles.[15] From the 1540s forward, mestizo boys and girls born out of wedlock shaped Peruvian families and illegitimate children became an ordinary part of the colonial social fabric.[16]

Spanish soldiers' and adventurers' interest in their out-of-wedlock children was not new to Peru in the 1540s. Fathers endeavored to bring their mestizo children from one part of empire to another as they soldiered throughout the continent. Men who served Francisco Pizarro petitioned the Queen in 1534 about their children born to indigenous women of Nicaragua.[17] After the conquest of Peru, they hoped to bring the children to South America. In this instance, the Queen agreed that the children could travel freely to join their fathers. The rationale was cultural as well as personal. The result was that children moved about the Spanish empire like pawns on a chessboard: moved closer to their fathers; moved away from their mothers; moved to work in a Spanish household; moved to their father's birthplace in Spain.

From an institutional standpoint, the Crown desired paternal responsibility for mestizo children, since it was plagued by demands for those children who had been abandoned. The first attempt at explicit Crown bureaucracy on this matter was an office to oversee New World orphans decreed by Philip III in 1543.[18] Yet the issue of the well-being of orphaned mestizos did not get conveyed from Peru to the Crown's ears until 1551. Less than twenty years after Pizarro landed in Peru, the King heard that "there are many girls, mestiza daughters of Christians now deceased, who died in service to Your Mercy and because they have no one to protect them they are going about lost among the Indians."[19] These daughters of conquistadors presented a unique problem to the Spanish Crown.[20] The Santa Clara convent in Cuzco proved popular for fathers like Bartolomé Díaz, who lived in Lima but had left his mestiza daughter in the house of Joan Álvarez Maldonado and Barvola de Grado in Cuzco. In 1560 he asked the couple to place his daughter in the convent and promised a dowry of a farm, goats, pigs, and a male slave were she to take her vows.[21] One solution proposed in the Lima case of 1551 was to give a pension (in honor of the deceased fathers) and to make a special home for the girls in the city of Lima where they would be raised as Christians. In this case, the requests came in the names of fathers who had died fighting in the name of Spain and their orphaned daughters. Mestizo children in this first generation also presented challenges on an individual level to those Spanish fathers who survived the conquest of Peru and the ensuing civil wars. Few men wanted their children to be "lost among the Indians," to quote the petition to the Crown.[22] Nor did most want their progeny living among known indigenous relatives, such as their mothers.

Through *patria potestad*, or paternal legal rights, children constituted property of their parents, especially fathers, and Spanish fathers trumped maternal ties in the definition of family. To be sure, some fathers acknowledged their mestizo children and did not remove them from the day-to-day care of their indigenous mothers, as was the case with the mestiza Costanza who lived with her indigenous mother Barbola in Arequipa in the 1550s.[23] Age was a factor; men usually did not take children younger than two or three years from their mother's care.[24] This may be a behavior encouraged, if not completely prescribed by, Iberian law.[25] In these cases, however, parents had never married, so the father's decision to remove a child after age two or three to support him or her was seen as "courtesy rather than a responsibility, since he might never know if the child was truly his."[26] Often both the actions and the discourse around this practice denigrated native Andean culture and erased the role of a mother in raising a child.

The status of the indigenous mother was also a factor in a man's decision about whether or not to support a child. Both place of birth and elite or non-elite status could play into the social and material realities of mestizos. A noble indigenous woman with links to the Inca elite might have some clout in negotiations over her children's upbringing; moreover she might have political or economic networks to which her child's Spanish father wanted access. Many indigenous women in early Lima, however, were slaves from Central America.[27] These women were in a different situation as partners and mothers than women native to the Andes. Women from Nicaragua, for example, were already at least once-removed from their homes and had fewer kin networks to draw upon to accrue the social or economic capital to assist their sons and daughters. They might have been held in some esteem, however, because they were "foreign" to Peru.[28]

Gender is also a possible differentiating factor in the treatment of children who were acknowledged. In Cuzco fathers created a convent for their daughters. In other Peruvian cities, fathers used their wills in order to offer money to daughters to enter convents or marry.[29] Crown concern about mestizos grew with their coming of age; these young adults, especially those descended from nobility on the side of their indigenous mothers, held potential political power. For some, the experience of mestizo males was more challenging with regard to entrance into the upper echelons of colonial society.[30] The actions of non-elite Spanish fathers in the lives of their mestizo sons sheds light on how gender affected their treatment. At the same time the Crown policies sounded rhetoric of mestizo boys as potential trouble, individual fathers' initiatives showed a different approach. In Lima and Arequipa, fathers treated boys and girls as both responsibilities and assets, Spanish or mestizo, legitimate or out-of-wedlock. This did not signify equal treatment of sons and daughters, but rather a paternal responsibility to all offspring regardless of gender.

Most Spanish fathers did not use the term "mestizo" to describe their children before a notary scribe, just as the term was not used by Alonso de Mena or his notary. In most of the instances when Spanish men acknowledged their mixed-race children they did so with emphasis on the child's birth status as illegitimate, *hijo natural*, rather than with direct reference to their mestizo identity.[31] Mestizo was a term that described appearance as well as a category used for people whose ancestry was not completely Spanish or indigenous.[32] Indeed, in notarial documents during the 1540s and 1550s, what stands out is the absence of the term. The word "mestizo" was used sparingly in documents written in Peru and in Spain (with reference to Peru).[33] In these notary documents, then, the absence of a mestizo label suggests that where a Crown official might classify, a father might not—especially in the 1540s and the 1550s. Only when further context reveals the name of the parents does the child's mixed ancestry become clear to the reader. When Spanish men claimed their children in wills or donations, they used language that emphasized the ability of their children to inherit by calling them "natural" children.

Living with Spanish fathers provided a measure of cultural legitimacy for natural, mixed-race children in their communities and, potentially, under the law. For instance, the law provided avenues for natural children to become legitimate. In the case of a mestizo child, his cultural upbringing would be scrutinized by the judicial system if he were to undergo that process of legitimation. The significance of an upbringing with his father's influence, and not his mother's, was emphasized in the case of Juan de la Peña. Born in Lima to Francisco de Arébalo, a conqueror and *poblador* of the city, and the indigenous Catalina, he requested legitimation from the Crown upon reaching the age of twenty-two in 1570. Like other *hijos naturales*, mestizo or otherwise, who hoped to gain legitimate status, de la Peña cited his desire to "enjoy the superiority that all the other legitimate sons and daughters enjoy."[34] He gathered witnesses, all labeled as Spaniards, who attested to the honorable status of his father. They clarified that Arébalo had no other children, legitimate or natural. Moreover, de la Peña's indigenous mother had died. They explained that his father raised him in his home and the young man was "able and productive." The fact that he had been raised by Spaniards placed him squarely within networks relevant to help his claim for legitimacy.[35] Cases like de la Peña's are indicative of how identity was shaped by multiple factors beyond ancestry in the sixteenth century.[36] If mestizo status was not something determined by birth, it was clearly something that, for a select few, could be cemented through upbringing. Thus, some Spanish fathers stepped in to claim children.

Claiming Mestizos from their Mothers

Within a short time of Spanish arrival in Peru, as Alonso de Mesa's 1542 will shows, a practice emerged to move children. Spanish men carried these plans out through their legal prerogative of *patria potestad*. They notarized documents to orchestrate their children's moves. They enlisted the help of other Spanish men, perhaps their relatives, their friends, and their underlings. And in the language of these notarized documents, they emphasized the best interest of the child.

The widespread nature of this practice is evident in the legal power-of-attorney documents assigned in the city of Lima between the 1540s and 1560s. With these powers in hand, third parties claimed their mestizo children from all the places visited by Spanish adventurers: Mexico, Central America, and, finally, parts of the Andes. Don Diego de Pastrana had a child named Catalina with the indigenous Leonor, a native of the province of Guatemala, around 1540. Eight years later, Pastrana sought to reclaim the child. He issued legal power to Francisco de Cantillana to take the young girl from Pero García de Portillo or from the house of Francisco Flores.[37] Pastrana did not outline his ultimate plans for his daughter; it is likely that Catalina never lived with her father, but went to a Spanish household in Lima. It was accepted practice for colonial fathers to appoint legal guardians in order to fulfill their roles. Joan de Ortega, residing in Lima in 1560, sent Cristóbal Pérez, of Guanuco, to Panama to return with his seven-year-old son, Atanasio.[38] Ortega had left the boy in the care of Catalina de Ribera and decided to have him come to Peru. In 1597 doctor Marcos Muñoz Ternero, a lawyer with the Real Audiencia in Lima, alleged that Isabel de Jesús, *mulata*, took his daughter from Lima to Mexico without his permission.[39] Muñoz Ternero authorized legal power to Diego de Cimancas, who was embarking on a trip to Mexico, to track down the twelve- or thirteen-year-old María and return her to Callao. Muñoz Ternero agreed to pay all costs associated with the trip. He did not specify the relationship of Isabel de Jesús; she could well have been María's mother. Nor did Muñoz Ternero remark on how much time had passed since María had gone missing. Unknown details aside, the cases show that Spanish men worked to track natural children whether from Guatemala, Panama, or Mexico, in order to exercise legal and physical control over them.[40] However, locating and moving these children did not signify that the men would thereafter be present to raise them.

Spanish fathers probably claimed and took mestizo children from indigenous women more often than the record reveals because if men traveled to retrieve their own children they need not leave a documentary record of those transactions. The pattern of legal powers placed the task of locating and retrieving children in the hands of a third party. Simply put, if the men could not locate their own children, they assigned the task to others. Motivations for this could be varied; for instance, the legal power might be practical or an a priori mode to avert tension over removal of the child. Juan de Gallegos had a son, Juan, with indigenous Luisa from Nicaragua. When the boy was thirteen years old, Gallegos authorized Gaspar Tello to locate him.[41] Gallego's case was not unique in this regard; merchant Alonso Lobo wanted his six-year-old son Juan to be taken from his mother, the indigenous Francisca, of Mexico City. Lobo charged Melchior de Sangines, another merchant, with the job.[42] In both of these cases the boys were beyond the age where a child physically needs its mother. In the event of a struggle with a mother who did not want to lose her child, or another Spaniard who was benefiting from the labor of the child, these third parties had the law on their side. By giving others a legal power, fathers did not need to be present physically to claim a child, as a notarized document gave another person the authority to move the child.

Even if men did not plan to live with their children, their language reflects how they viewed their action as fulfilling their paternal roles. Antonio de Medina claimed his daughter María because "in her mother's power she cannot be well schooled and raised with polish and good breeding like I, as her father, would want to raise her and marry her off."[43] He promised a 1,000-peso dowry to María, along with the extraction of a promise from the girl's mother that she would allow him to raise her.[44] Medina made the legal transaction in June 1577. Medina never married María's mother, Isabel Yanaguar. Yanaguar was born in Cuzco, worked for Medina in the region of Charcas, and later lived on the *repartimiento* (labor levy) of Miguel Sánchez. It was from this *repartimiento* that Medina sought to remove María. He acknowledged her and claimed he loved her. In the same document, Isabel declared that eight years prior in Charcas she had been working for Antonio de Medina, had physical relations with him, became pregnant, and gave birth to his child, María. This testimony by an indigenous mother is unusual:

I declare that being in los Charcas [region of what is today Bolivia] eight years ago and in the service of the said Antonio de Medina

I had carnal knowledge [*cuenta carnal*] with the said Medina and became pregnant to him and gave birth to the said María and I have raised her until now and it is true that the said girl is the daughter of Antonio de Medina.[45]

Isabel then agreed (though she had little legal say in the matter) to give her daughter to Medina. Medina reiterated his plea for the girl, claiming that she would be better raised in the power of her father and her Spanish relatives than among Indians and with her mother. Here, as in many cases, Spanish fathers in Peru used their legal power to gain control of their sons and daughters.

The words of Spanish father Mateo Veneciano clarified why taking the mestizo boys and girls from indigenous mothers was an imperative. According to Veneciano, a Spaniard needed to "raise and indoctrinate and impress good habits upon" the children. In Lima in February 1552, Veneciano's son Alexandro was fifteen months old and living with his mother Isabel in the house of a priest in Huarochirí, a town where Veneciano had lived until only recently. Yet he did not wish to return to Huarochirí and instead empowered his uncle Pedro Tomás Griego to wrest Alexandro from the control of the priest and bring him, with his mother, to Lima.[46] The role of a mother was critical while she was nursing. [see figure 2.1] However, Veneciano's statement that a Spaniard must raise the boy implied that Isabel's role in his life would diminish as the boy grew. The idea of moving the child from a mother's care to another household was not completely new, however, as apprenticeships in early modern Spain had the same end. Moreover, the movement of peoples within the Inca empire was common, and children were known to be used to fulfill important roles for the Inca state. That said, the power dynamics of the colonial context—pitting Veneciano against the indigenous mother—were quite different. Moreover, Veneciano's claim to the child solidified his paternal legal rights and made the child his legal heir.

The fathers who sought these children were part of a generation of men whose mobility shaped their roles as fathers but did not sever that role. It was "because of the obligation that fathers have for our children" that ship pilot Pedro Rolón authorized a legal power for fellow ship pilot Álvaro Muñoz to seek his daughter. Rolón had been in the Port of Huatulco, Mexico, in 1545. He acknowledged sexual intercourse ("*conocimiento*") with an indigenous girl (*moca*) named Catalina, who was the servant of Maestro Joan Calafate.[47] Catalina moved to the service of another

FIGURE 2.1 This nineteenth-century color image depicts an indigenous woman nursing her child

Source: Courtesy of Art & Architecture Collection, Miriam and Ira D. Wallach Division of Art, Prints and Photographs, New York Public Library, Astor, Lenox, and Tilden Foundations.

Spaniard; Rolón moved his base to Lima. Yet word reached him, over two decades later, that Catalina had given birth to his child. He asked Muñoz to look in the book of baptisms for the church where Catalina's child was baptized and see if the entry confirmed his paternity. If so, he ordered Muñoz to take possession of any of his "daughter's" belongings, including the estate of her mother Catalina, now deceased. If Muñoz returned to Lima, Rolón asked that his "daughter" travel in the company of Muñoz's wife or some other trusted party. If Muñoz did not return, he asked that the girl be placed in the house of a married and honorable man. Rolón's orders showed a desire to locate and claim his heir, interest in any money she might have, and a keen cultural understanding that as her father he was bound to protect her honor through a trusted traveling companion or lodging in the household of a family. He entrusted members of his personal networks to guard her and raise her.

Non-Spanish men likewise used legal proxies to recover children. The free *negro* Francisco, who worked on board the ship *The San Juan*, gave power to Bartolomé de Ahedo to find his son Esteban and take him from whoever held him.[48] These men made the agreement in the port of Callao. The proximity of both to seafaring—Francisco as a sailor and Bartolomé through his travels—would have allowed them to sail into other Pacific ports and search for the boy.

Spanish men rarely sought out their children with African women in the same way as they sought out children with indigenous women. In contrast to tens of examples of men seeking mestizo children, this sample revealed only one case of a Spaniard seeking a child born to a woman identified as *morena* (dark-skinned women usually free), and none to women identified as *negra* (black woman usually enslaved).[49] The comparison is complex because the vast majority of African women who gave birth to the children of Spaniards in sixteenth-century Peru were enslaved and, thus, their children were the property of their mother's owner. Fathers may have been owners, and therefore did not have to seek the children. Yet two examples offer suggestive information about how racial distinctions between mestizos and *mulatos* were understood within the framework of paternal obligations. First, while mestizo children of Spaniards were frequently sent to Spain, children born of Spaniards and African women were not. The difference in the treatment of children based on the race of their birth mother is highlighted in the will of Domingo de Destre. He had two children, a mestiza girl and a *mulato* boy. He bequeathed the girl two Lima properties that he ordered to be sold to pay for her to go to live in Spain. For Andrés, the son, he left a *chacara* (farm) near Lima with no instructions to sell it and move to Spain. Both the children were young, the girl two-and-a-half and the boy three years of age. No convents existed in Peru at the time, and it is possible that Destre saw no choice other than to have the daughter sent home, whereas the boy might have a better chance at prospering in 1540s Lima. While other wills in this sample include mestizo and *mulato* children, the parents in those cases did not send any of their offspring to Spain. The early date of Destre's experiences in Peru may have influenced his acknowledgment of both children, and either gender or the mother's identity (indigenous or *negra*) may explain the different treatment.

When Cristóbal Gómez left instructions for his *mulato* son Diego in 1551, he made a distinct reference to the boy practicing a trade in the future, an indication of the class status he expected him to attain. Although his son was only three at the time Gómez wrote his will, he assigned him a guardian and asked that he be given a Christian education, learn to read and write, and taught "a trade from which he can earn his food."[50] Gómez did not envision an elite life for his son in part because his own had been modest. His specification that the boy learn a trade rather than say, study, is remarkable because no fathers of mestizo sons did likewise in my sample.

Mestizos replicated patterns of their Spanish fathers. Pedro de Çaera, a mestizo born to a Spanish captain and an indigenous mother from Nicaragua, himself had a child out of wedlock with an indigenous woman.[51] Çaera lived in Lima with his wife, the Spaniard Damiana de Bibero. In 1554, however, he had a baby boy with Leonor, an indigenous woman from Cuzco. Fearing his death at that moment, Çaera made provisions for the two-month-old boy. Çaera relied upon his paternal aunt, Ursula Çaera, to care for the boy. While Peruvian-born Çaera did not have the option to send his child to Spain, he did act in accordance with Spanish conquistador fathers of his generation.

Moving House, Changing Households

For their choice of where to place a child to be raised many men sought links to trusted kin, relatives, and networks drawn from place of origin in Spain. A standard practice for these young boys and girls was their placement within a Spanish-run household, preferably with an adult woman who was married or widowed. When Loreynte Ponce de Cabrera had his mestiza daughter in the house of Diego de Porras, he charged Ana de Sandoval, Porras's wife, with raising his daughter "with good instruction and upbringing."[52] The situation of these children within the household reflects much about how blood relatives and surrogate family operated in colonial Peru. Ponce de Cabrera followed the example of many of his counterparts when he entrusted Sandoval with the cultural education of his daughter. How did Sandoval view the relationship? Many households incorporated mestizos in a way that combined elements of surrogacy and apprenticeship, blending ties of affection with expectations for labor or payment. The Iberian precedent that biological ties are not necessary to emphasize nuture is confirmed in the Siete Partidas laws.[53] Many children, however, sat on the opposite side of a porous border wherein service was demanded for nuture, against the spirit of those same laws.

Mencia de Ayala, a mestiza *hija natural*, lived in Lima with a Spanish couple, Juan López de Aguilar and Inés de Valencia, even though her father, Pedro Caxas, and her mother, the indigenous Beatriz, were both alive.[54] The conditions in these examples (age of child and shelter in another household) mimic Iberian traditions of apprenticeship.[55] Indeed, apprenticeship contracts are frequently found in the sixteenth-century Spanish Americas as well. However, the legal documents that established where Mencia de Ayala and others would live were not apprenticeship contracts per se. Spanish fathers wanted not merely to apprentice their mestizo children but also to control their upbringing and, importantly, any potential inheritance due to the children.

Moreover, living in the "service" of Spaniards was part of a system in which mestizo children were cared for while Spanish households benefited from their labor.[56] Rather than take her on his travels, the father of ten-year-old mestiza Elena de Sayas moved her into the home of Diego García de Anteguera. García de Anteguera was married, with two children, and the whole family enjoyed the services of Sayas for six years.[57] Not only girls served this role. Nine-year-old Luis first lived in Cusco in the house of Juan de Ochandiano. Then his father, Pedro de Emberes, decided to transfer him to Lima to live with Francisco de la Cruz "in his service."[58] For Emberes, the chance for Luis to live under the power of a trusted friend who would "govern" him constituted an appropriate way to fulfill his parental obligations. Fathers viewed these children's labor as a potential source for dowry money. When Pedro Rodríguez removed his mestiza daughter María from the service of Leonor de Esquivel in Cuzco he asked for gold pesos in remuneration for her services. [59]

The apprenticeship nature of these arrangements had precedent in the Iberian context. During the same era, for instance, Juan Gómez, a tailor from the Villa of Mures, placed his eleven-year-old daughter in the service of Gaspar Luis in the Santa María parish of Seville.[60] A young girl would work in domestic service rather than receive direct training in a trade. These arrangements in Spain had further parallels to the Peru cases because in some instances parents placed their child in the long-term

power of others with a care and service component and, upon termina-
tion of the agreement, expected a lump sum payment to their child. In
sixteenth-century Seville, Sebastián Rodríguez and his wife Francisca de
Aroche placed their two-and-a-half-year-old daughter Gerónima "to raise
and serve" with Luis Hernández, pastry chef, and his wife Lucía Martín.
Given her age, Gerónima could not realistically serve the family. However,
the plan was a long-term one that anticipated her working for them, and
after sixteen years the couple was to pay her 10,000 maravedis for her
dowry.[61]

Some in Lima, however, expected compensation for taking in children in accordance with Iberian cultural norms.[62] Doña Isabel de Zúñiga,
a Sevillana living in Lima, was explicit in her claim that a father should
pay for the "many expenses" she incurred in raising his son.[63] The boy in
question was an eight-year-old born to Juan de Rojas, Spaniard, and the
indigenous María, a native of Collagua (a region far from Lima). In her
will, Zúñiga challenged, "If his father wants to take him, let him pay,"
suggesting that Juan has been in her household for years. Although it is
not inconceivable that some couples may have taken in mestizo children
for reasons of compassion, this particular woman emphasized the cost
and work associated with such a responsibility. Zúñiga may have sought
remuneration from Rojas in anticipation of lost labor for the boy. Hers was
likely a representative sentiment. Using these children in a servant-like
status would have helped justify adding an *hijo natural* to the household.[64]

A child transplanted from a mother's care and home to the household of an unknown Spanish family might have found the situation at
best jarring, at worst unbearable. Often, as the case of Isabel de Carrión
shows, this first move was not the only one for children of this status in
colonial society. Isabel de Carrión was the *hija natural* of Hernando de
Carrión, a Spaniard living in Lima in the 1550s.[65] Carrión never stated
Isabel's mother's identity, but given the date it is likely that she was
indigenous. Carrión left Isabel in the home of Pedro de Corço, only to
have the Spaniard Francisco Martín de Barran take her from Corço.
Carrión then aimed to retrieve her and bring her to Lima. Señor Carrión
authorized legal power for Miguel Ruíz and widow doña Francisca
Robles of San Miguel de Piura and doña María de Sandoval, vecina of
Lima, to represent him in the matter of tracking down his daughter.
Once recovered, Carrión wanted his daughter sent to the house of doña
Francisca to be "in her house and service" and from there sent to Lima
when a trustworthy person was making the journey. Was Isabel sold

from Corço's house as a servant or slave? Was Isabel abducted and taken as a lover? Did she leave his house willingly and seek out a life that was more appealing to her?

The placement of young women into households could have long-term implications. Beatriz Gutiérrez, a native of Arequipa, was the daughter of San Miguel and of Isabel *india*.[66] She was a single woman who had no children. She claimed to have worked for over twenty-five years as a servant of Ana Gutiérrez, the widow of Juan de Castro. How Beatriz came to be in the employ of Ana is unknown, but their shared last name suggests long-term association and, perhaps, weak ties to her birth kin. In Beatriz's telling, Gutiérrez had never paid her for those years of work. Beatriz clearly recognized how to seek redress in the colonial system, since she testated and made the claim for back payment. Still, her claims remind us that class affected the colonial experience of mestizos, how far they moved (geographically and socially), and how they experienced life wherever they lived.

Ultimately, Spanish fathers used *patria potestad* to have their sons and daughters raised in trusted networks by kin or family. A religious concern was intertwined here as well, since Spaniards assumed a Christian upbringing for their children. Given the interrelatedness of race and religion in the Iberian concept of blood cleanliness (*limpieza de sangre*), this was a fulfillment of a paternal obligation that simultaneously helped a father's half-indigenous children and ensured better status for his heirs.[67] More often than not, however, the placement of these children into households of kin was linked to some form of labor and serves as evidence of an emerging role for mestizos as child-servants, a role often ascribed to them by their own fathers.

Moving Mestizos to Spain

Moving children to Spain was the most certain way to position them closer to the kin networks of their fathers, especially if those men were extremely mobile in their careers. In 1554 Alonso Descobar from Medellín, Spain, was en route from Lima to his home in Spain.[68] In his company he had three young girls, all of whom had been born in Cuzco. One of these girls was six-year-old Catalina, his daughter, born to the Cuzco native Inés in 1548. Both parents made some preparations before the journey to help Catalina when it came time to marry. Inés, remarkably, gave her daughter 300 ducats to use for her eventual dowry, more than her father's 200 ducats payable in movable goods located in Spain. Descobar named his parents the guardians of the young Catalina were anything to happen to him on the trip. He did not ask his wife, Catalina Flores, mother of his two sons, and a resident of Medellín as well, to care for his mestiza daughter, though the family circle would plausibly have included all of them.

Flores was not the only wife in Spain to witness the arrival of her husband's children from Peru, and perhaps not the only one in Medellín either. On this same voyage, Descobar escorted sisters (or half-sisters), maiden daughters of his uncle Gómez Maçuelo, who had lived and died in Cuzco. Maçuelo's last will and testament named Descobar as the girls' guardian and ordered him to take them to Medellín. The girls, named doña María and doña Marina, came with 6,000 gold pesos for their sustenance. Descobar used some of the funds to buy a slave, Barbola, to be a servant for the sisters. He also spent money on clothing, items for their travel, and the cost of the passage to Spain. One might presume some of this money was meant for their dowries as well. Descobar was delivering the girls to the house of his paternal aunt, María Juárez. During the early 1550s, other fathers traveled with their mestizo children to deposit them with relatives on the Iberian peninsula where they would be raised in the absence of their mothers.[69]

Notarial records suggest that fathers made arrangements for their children when they were ill, about to travel, or about to enter into military conflict. The Crown needed to give express permission for mestizos to travel to Spain, and it was family members that forced the issue of sending mestizo children (and in some cases grandchildren) from the Indies to Spain.[70] Facing death, men looked to relatives in Spain who might raise those children in Peru. Thus, many wills specified plans for mestizos to make the longest voyage of their young lives.[71] Diego Martín Cabello, a Portuguese native of Cohimbra, hoped to have his mestizo son travel from the Indies to Iberia.[72] Martín had married Beatriz Hernández and fathered a legitimate son, Simón, and then departed for the Indies. Fourteen years after arriving he contemplated the future of his family as he set down his testament. While he named Beatriz and Simón as his legitimate heirs, he also left instructions to his executor to send his five-year-old mestizo son in Lima from Peru to Iberia.

Clergyman Hernando de San Pedro took care of business before departing on a trip. He notarized a legal power for Ruy Díaz de Sigure or Cristóbal de Arenas to care for San Pedro's one-and-a-half-year-old mestizo son born to Isabel, a Caxamarca native and teach him the "things of our holy faith."[73] After that, San Pedro imagined that Díaz or Arenas should send the boy to Spain, or wherever else his father was at that time. These men were entrusted with a paternal role for the young boy when San Pedro was forced to travel for his job.

Some fathers envisioned marriage in Spain for their mestiza daughters. Loreynte Ponse de Cabrera ordered that his daughter Juana's guardian marry her in Lima or in Spain, whichever location he found to be the better choice. Ponse de Cabrera noted that his inheritance from his parents, including houses, was based in Spain which could provide Juana with an appealing dowry.[74] One father used a donation as leverage to try to move his mestiza daughter to Spain so she would marry there. Diego Hierro declared Catalina Hierro as his *hija natural* and his universal heir if and only if she would move to his hometown of the Villa de Ampuero in Spain.[75] Catalina was a year and a half old in 1568 when Hierro made his will. Although her mother, Costança, a single woman from Cuzco, was alive at the time, Hierro offered her no role in her daughter's upbringing. He further demanded that if Catalina did not move to Spain or if she married before moving to the Villa de Ampuero she would be disinherited from his will.

The home of a Spanish relative was the typical destination for the children. Alonso Muñoz, a tailor in Lima, ordered his two mestizo children to Spain for upbringing when he made his will in 1552.[76] He chose the household of his uncle, Francisco Muñoz in Villa de Alarye, as the place they would live. Alonso also named his brother as the tutor for the children. In addition to dictating the customary expectations—that they be taught to be industrious, instructed in the Catholic faith, and learn good manners—he entrusted his brother with investing the children's bequests to turn them into future earnings. Muñoz's actions placed the social and financial aspects of his children's future in the hands of his close relatives.

In the port city of Lima, merchants and sailors arrived not just from Spain, but from Portugal and Italy as well, so men might ask for their children to be taken to various European locations. Juan María de Abarreta del Cablo, a native of Corsica, had a nine-month-old mestizo son, Juan, born in Potosí in 1580. In his will, the father named this *hijo natural* as his heir. The notary scribe squeezed a line in at the bottom of the will that suggested his executor "send the said my son to the said Island of Corsica."[77] The infant Juan was with his mother Ana, a Chiriguana, in Potosí and living in the household of Juan Corzo, the nephew of Juan

María. Given the baby's age, it was too soon to take him from his mother's care, yet his Corsican father had future plans for the baby. He left half of his estate to the boy, and the other half to his sisters in Corsica, a bequest presumably meant to ease the burden of caring for the mestizo Juan if and when he made the trip across the seas.

Kin networks were so pervasive in this context that the initiative to send a mestizo child to Spain might come from family members other than the father. Making his will in Arequipa in 1556, Martín Díaz, a Spaniard from Almarez, noted he was single and claimed no children. Díaz donated 300 pesos to his nephew Alonso, the son of his brother Francisco Díaz and the indigenous Catalina.[78] Then he specified a tutor for his nephew and demanded that the tutor use the 300 pesos to give Catalina money for food until Alonso reached the age of eight. In addition, the tutor Lázaro de la Torre was to use part of the 300 pesos to buy some cattle or merchandise and make a profit with Alonso's money. Then he added that should de la Torre wish to send the boy to Spain, he could do so. While Martín Díaz did not elaborate, it seems likely that his brother had died, at which point Martín became legally responsible for Alonso, yet Catalina still cared for the boy. He envisioned the possibility that Alonso could travel to the Villa de Almarez in Spain to live with his paternal grandparents.

Those children who made the trip to Spain typically lived with paternal relatives. Baltasar Ortiz took his daughters, María and Francisca Ortiz, from their mother's hometown of Potosí to his native village of Lepe, Spain.[79] (Note Lepe on the map in figure 2.2.) The town's proximity to Sevilla and to the coast more generally suggests many residents probably had ties to travel and trade in the Indies. Ortiz brought with him on the journey his niece, doña Juana Ortiz, also born in Potosí who was raised by her mother, the indigenous María Palla, on the same street as María and Francisca. Juana's father, Juan Ortiz, was brother to Baltasar and to doña Ana de Benaventes, who received the girls in Lepe. Doña Ana and her husband, Pedro Ramírez Cavala, became the girls' caretakers and legal guardians. In the case of María and Francisca, their father returned to the New World where he died and their mother died some twelve years after the girls left Peru. After several years in Spain, cousins Juana and Francisca took their vows and became professed nuns. As Juana would testify, this signified that Francisca renounced all her worldly belongings to Pedro Ramírez. Ramírez sponsored both girls' entry into the convent, Juana into Santo Domingo and Francisca into Santa Clara.[80] Convents

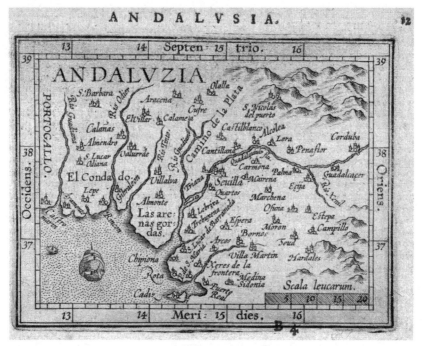

FIGURE 2.2 This sixteenth-century map of Andalucía denotes the city of Seville, the port of San Lucar de Barrameda, and the village of Lepe

Source: "Andaluzia" from Abraham Ortelius, modified by Michael Coignet, 1603, from the Lionel Pincus & Princess Firyal Map Division, New York Public Library.

were a common place to house young woman in both Spain and the New World in the care of their father.

Boys also went to Iberia for their upbringing and education. Tomás de Acosta traveled to Spain with his father Francisco Rodríguez as a boy, perhaps as young as three or four. Rodríguez was a native of the Villa of Celleorico in Portugal who ventured to the New World as a single man and never married.[81] In 1575, when Rodríguez acknowledged paternity, Tomás was seven years old. Rodríguez claimed that he had raised Tomás "from when he was small until now." What he meant by this was that he provided for the boy, since Tomás was no longer in his direct physical care. He left Tomás a bequest of 1,100 ducats to secure the boy's instruction in whatever area Rodríguez's father, brother, or brother-in-law deemed most appropriate, in addition to the basics of reading and writing. Acosta's mother may have been indigenous, given Francisco's raising of the boy and his efforts to take him to be raised among peninsular relatives.

Manuel de Herrera chose to send his daughter to Spain but keep his son with him in Peru. His family included two indigenous women and three children and eventually spanned the Atlantic.[82] His daughter Juana, born to the indigenous Catalina, sailed to Spain and lived with her father's relatives. When he died, her father left her a *solar* in Arequipa. He did not plan for her to return to Arequipa, however. He ordered the land to be auctioned, with the proceeds sent to Juana, along with five bars of silver. Herrera entrusted his nephew Gonzalo Martín to take the money and silver to Juana. All of this he hoped would be used for her dowry to enter a convent and profess as a nun. Francisco had remained in Peru his whole life. Herrera's plans for his son were not specified but since his will does not suggest the level of mobility of a merchant, bureaucrat, or ship captain, he may have wanted his son nearby as an assistant. Francisco received a decent bequest from his father to apply to his own business or trade endeavors.

The historical record in Spain provides glimpses of mestizo children from Peru who grew to adulthood in Spain. Alonso de Nava and his sisters María and Catalina went to Spain under the tutelage of their father Alonso de Nava and lived in the *colacion* or neighborhood of San Isidro in Seville. When their father passed away, the children (and their inheritances) were under the control of Juan de Rojas. Alonso de Nava, the son, admitted that Rojas cared for them and fed and dressed them and tended to him while their father was ill. His sister María died after their father did. The mother of all three children was Catalina from the village of Taquena in Arequipa. When Alonso dictated his will he did not know if his mother was still alive, but in that hope he named her as his heir.[83]

Mestizos sent to Spain might find themselves moved yet again at the behest of their fathers. The Genoese Juan Bautista Ginoves sent his mestiza daughter, Catalina, from Peru to Seville. When she approached marriageable age, he entrusted a friend from Genoa to travel to Seville to retrieve her and take her to Genoa to marry her off.[84] Catalina had been born in Peru in 1538 and was fifteen years old when Ginoves hatched this plan. Her dowry seems to have been an important motive, as he claimed to have items in his home community from which to provide a good dowry. His other motives for sending her to start married life in Genoa may have been related to other attachments to his homeland.

Economic status of a family would have mediated the experience of these mestizo children in Spain. The *hijo natural* of Captain Gerónimo Aliaga de Santomayor, who was the secretary of the Real Audiencia in La

Plata, lived in Seville as a young adult. Also named Gerónimo de Aliaga, he sought and gained legitimation, no doubt aided by the weight of his experiences in Seville. He pursued inheritance from his father's estate in the Indies in 1570.[85] Another *hijo natural*, mother unnamed but likely indigenous, sought to benefit from his "rich mother" in Peru when, as a young adult, he set up a merchant business between Seville and Spain.[86] This latter example is suggestive of how a young mestizo male's experience varied depending on his father's profession. For example, in the case of a merchant or businessman, the connections of a mestizo son could prove extremely valuable. For someone like Aliaga, his father's position with the Crown made legitimation all the more relevant for his ability to gain entrance to his father's world in order to have a successful career.

MESTIZO CHILDREN IN sixteenth-century Peru were physically moved from the homes of their mothers through the expansive legal power of their Spanish fathers. They witnessed dislocation not only from their mothers' care but also from their mothers' native Andean culture. As members of a growing colonial society in Peru, these boys and girls symbolized the social and sexual mixture resulting from conquest. Yet Spanish fathers controlled their realities to imprint a very Spanish veneer over their ancestral *mestizaje*. Typically fathers chose Spanish homes to mold them in the Spanish language, European clothes, Catholic religion, and Iberian customs. Once fathers put the children into Spanish homes they typically fulfilled a market service of some sort for the household.

In order to do right by their mestizo natural children, Spanish fathers eliminated contact with their indigenous mothers and socialized them in Spanish culture. They did this deliberately and definitively—even moving the children to Spain. Many mothers were compensated for their "services" with money, property, or goods. They were not, however, expected to remain active in their children's lives once the boys and girls survived infancy. Not all mothers ceded their roles completely or willingly. Moreover, in many instances indigenous women raised mestizos. While the historical record reveals far fewer of these cases, the children who lived among their indigenous mothers were now living under colonial control unlike the previous generation of native Andeans.

Mestizos moved conspicuously in Peru and Spain in these middle decades of the sixteenth century. The boys and girls who were shuffled from one site to another through legal powers embodied the challenges that racial mixture posed to Spain's ideas of a neatly hierarchical society.

Even as fathers made plans for mestizo sons and daughters, a parallel dialogue emerged about the establishment in Lima of Spanish households headed by a married Spanish man and Spanish woman with their biological children. Not only did children move around the empire to fulfill imperial goals, but women, specifically Spanish wives, were also targeted to be moved from Spain to Peru to support the Crown's vision of colonial society in the Andes.

3

Marriage

VIDA MARIDABLE IN A TRANSATLANTIC CONTEXT

IN 1551 MELCHIOR Ximénez wrote from Peru to Spain: "I order the said Francisca Hernández my wife to come to these said kingdoms where I am at present to carry out *vida maridable* [married life] with me as we are obligated to do."[1] Ximénez's order, in its terse notarized script, reveals important patterns and priorities about marriages in the sixteenth-century Iberian world. The issue of how to ensure *vida maridable* followed the path of conquest, from the Isles to Mexico and finally to Peru. The Crown was conscious of how imperial expansion affected marriage, and it decreed that couples with one partner in the metropole and the other in the periphery reunite. As Ximénez's order reveals, some men complied with the Crown's laws or sought the company of their wives, while others shirked marital responsibility.

This mid-century transaction tells only part of the tale, however. Petitions to the Crown from abandoned wives would reach their height in the late sixteenth century as Spanish men followed news of silver riches and ever-expanding territorial conquests. This chapter explores how the Crown attempted to control the marital unit that it saw as a cornerstone of its emerging colonial society, how couples like Ximénez and Hernández dealt with compliance, and what it meant when wives and husbands lived apart for years on end. Spanish women come to the fore in this chapter, thus revealing the interconnected pieces of family and empire. The same Spanish men who were fathers to mestizos were also husbands and fathers to families in Spain. Some men abandoned wives and children; they did not write, visit, or send money. Some fathers did not live with their children yet still fulfilled paternal roles. With husbands and wives, something similar occurred in the sense that when they lived apart a husband might still fulfill the material obligations of his role. However, the Spanish Crown attempted to regulate the relationship of these men to their wives by bringing them together in the same place.

The pact of *vida maridable* formed the heart of a 1528 Crown decree that addressed marriage in the emerging transatlantic world of the Spanish Indies. The 1528 Royal Cédula stated that married men residing in the New World had to return from the Indies to be with their wives in Spain or to make arrangements to bring the women to the New World.[2] The Spanish phrase *vida maridable*, or marital union, as used in the sixteenth century, refers to a man and woman making a home together as husband and wife, and meeting social, economic, and sexual obligations to one another. Just as obligation was a word that was used frequently to discuss marriage, unmarried men emphasized their freedom from such obligations. When Juan Luis, a Venetian, made his will in Arequipa in 1581 he clarified that "I am a free person and not obligated by marriage."[3] Diego Hernández de Talavera likewise emphasized that after his wife died he came to "this kingdom [Peru] being a single and free man."[4]

The sixteenth-century Crown considered the obligations of husband and wife to one another under God in the context of expansion in the Indies. The Crown penned its decrees precisely because many men and women, married in Spain and separated by an ocean after husbands followed conquest routes, did not live together as man and wife (*hacer vida*). One well-studied example of a transatlantic couple is Francisco Noguerol and Beatriz de Villasur.[5] Noguerol traveled to Peru to avoid having to live with his first wife. His sisters tried to trick him into returning to Spain by writing that his wife was dead, whereupon he married again. This case highlights the links between the absence of *vida maridable* and bigamy.[6] In addition to abandonment and extra-legal marriages, the historical record shows a range of responses couples had to the problem of being separated by a three-part voyage, involving two trips by sea and one by land. Multiple factors influenced decisions surrounding living together as husband and wife or resisting it, including the law, Church requirements, contemporary notions of family obligation, and sentiment.

The Crown decree from 1528 and cases of "abandoned wives" from the latter half of the sixteenth century bookend this chapter. In the 1500s, opportunities for exploration and expansion into the newly "discovered" Indies meant that many men left Spain without their wives; couples with an ocean between them had little hope of carrying out *vida maridable*, as distance challenged their ability to fulfill the physical, emotional, and financial obligations of marriage. These physical separations crippled the economic and legal status of wives who remained in Spain as well as compromised their ability to live and support their children in an honorable manner. Some women may have exaggerated their misery as a strategy to gain economic support, but for many the hardship was real.[7] Men in the New World who did not reunite with their wives frequently pursued alternate monogamous relationships and fathered additional children. Some women adapted to the challenges of being alone, if not in a legal sense, by pursuing effective strategies for earning money. Indeed some did not want to rejoin their husbands. These practices complicated family units and inheritance patterns. This chapter first discusses the legal response of the Crown to marriages separated by conquest endeavors. It then analyzes the interplay of these decrees with the marital life of men and women swept up in the wave of colonization. Ordering families to reunite was one thing; making it happen was another.

Laws serve as foundational guidelines for understanding what the Crown required of husbands and wives as well as how the Crown viewed families as part of the project of Spanish settlement. Crown decrees, especially the cédulas on *vida maridable*, reveal an emphasis on fulfilling the marriage contract in the context of transatlantic travel and empire building. The Siete Partidas, the *Recopilación*, and various royal decrees from the sixteenth century serve as guides to the legal ideals of the Crown.[8] A variety of sources yield clues on how spouses responded to travel, separation, and the formation of complex sets of partners and children. Men's actions in the wake of Crown decrees, set down by notaries in Lima and Arequipa, detail how the laws affected individual families. Letters by spouses, part of the licensing process, represent the personal perspectives of those who focused on reuniting.[9] Although not as detailed as the letters, petition requests for travel licenses to the New World show when women sought passage to Peru in order to join their husbands. While the *vida maridable* decree was written primarily to promote Crown goals in the Indies, the law opened spaces for the negotiation of wives, as well as husbands, in their personal pursuits of family structure and obligation in the sixteenth century. Wives' discourses in their pleas to the Crown typically relied on ideas about marriage and marital obligation that stemmed from Crown and canon law even as the realities of marital practice varied in Spain according to class and regional location. Women's efforts within the legal discourse were sometimes rewarded, when an abandoned wife was reunited with her husband, but relying on the Crown for support had its own price.

Male mobility over long distances is well established for this era. For men to live apart from their wives and children was acceptable within the cultural context, but the Crown, for one, established limits on the separation of married people because it aimed to colonize Peru with family units. Distance and abandonment mattered to individuals because of financial concerns, emotional ties, and the fundamental role of family networks in sixteenth-century life.

Regulating *Vida Maridable*

When Spanish exploration, conquest, and settlement of the Indies intensified, increasing numbers of men left the Iberian peninsula, especially its southern region, to follow dreams of adventure and economic success. In the earliest years of conquest, a disproportionate number of wives and children stayed behind.[10] The Crown quickly perceived potential problems raised by the long distances between husbands and those families. In a report from the early sixteenth century, Fray Bernardino de Manzanedo remarked that Spanish men in Hispaniola "are wrapped in sin and it could be that their wives here [in Spain] are in the same way."[11] Manzanedo highlighted the practices of marriage-like relationships between Spanish men and indigenous women in the New World, while also raising the valid question of how women in Spain, during their husbands' long absences, found financial or emotional comfort. Cohabitation with indigenous women, a generation of mixed-race children in the Indies, and abandoned wives on the Iberian peninsula—these shaped Crown ordinances' emphases on the institution of marriage and the obligations of husbands and fathers in the first half of the sixteenth century.

Concern about the separation of husbands and wives swelled in the decade following 1492. Members of the Audiencia (High Court) in Hispaniola pondered the issue and wrote to the Queen to take action. The separation of husbands and wives was not, of course, new to the age of discovery. The Siete Partidas, medieval Spanish legal code, included laws that made specific reference to the separation of husband and wife and attempted to fend off problems that might result. For instance, a wife might be excused from an accusation of adultery, "Where a married man leaves his country to join the army or perform a pilgrimage, or to go to some other place distant from his country, and happens to be delayed there for a long time, so that persons make his wife believe that he is dead and she marries another man."[12] Although husband and wife being separated was not novel, in the particular context of the Crown's goals for New World settlement, *vida maridable* was preferable to de facto solutions that individuals used to gain company in the absence of a legitimate spouse.

As the Crown determined what decrees to issue in the case of New World relationships, relevant legal precedent existed. The Iberian peninsula had long accepted a form of a semi-permanent concubinage known as *barraganía*.[13] King Alfonso X included *barraganía* in his thirteenth-century laws of the Siete Partidas. Men could take one woman as a concubine on the condition that this woman not be enslaved, younger than twelve years of age, a virgin, or an honorable widow. Men who kept concubines were expected not to be married and not to marry while keeping their concubine.[14] As mentioned before, however, the distinctions between written law and local tradition could be significant and while the Siete Partidas prescribed a legal ideal, the Iberian practice could vary significantly.

Moreover, at this moment of expansion into the New World, laws on marriage were about to undergo reform through the Council of Trent (1547–1563). The Council did not have an immediate impact on the regulation of marriage in Spain or the New World as it took time for those rules to be put into place. However, the spirit of reform in which the Council began points to some of the ideals about marriage as well as some practices that the Church identified as problematic. Of particular interest was the Church's intransigence on the matter of divorce and its insistence that husbands and wives cohabitate, a particular challenge in the case of husbands and wives separated for long time periods over long distances due to imperial expansion. *Vida maridable* was not simply living together under the same roof but creating a household together, raising a family, and, for men, providing for women's food and other needs.[15] Inasmuch as the Crown's early colonial decrees reflect a prioritization of *vida maridable*, they had similar goals to those that emerged decades later from the Council.

The earliest pronouncement on the separation of husbands and wives in the Indies came from King Ferdinand to Nicolas Ovando, Governor of Hispaniola, in 1505. Ferdinand ordered those Spaniards who were married in Spain to return and collect their wives. Ovando replied in 1509 that his goal was to have no man live in Hispaniola longer than three years without his wife.[16] Doctrine on the issue evolved thereafter: married men were to return to Spain or bring their wives to them in the New World.

Thus, even some twenty years before the conquest of Peru, authorities in Seville were already sending notice to don Diego Colón, Admiral of the Indies, to track down wayward husbands. In February 1511, Gaspar de Torres's wife filed a petition to ask the Crown to find her husband. Four months later, Pedro Vallejo's wife followed suit. These women complained of suffering basic needs.[17] If they missed their husbands' company we do not know; they asked for the return of their husband or that the men send an allowance for their maintenance. The financial needs of women in Spain, especially those with children, were likely considerable. Women of elevated economic status might have the chance to run their husbands' businesses in their absence, but for most women the main avenues for income were sewing, doing laundry, healing, selling food, or other petty marketing.[18] Feeding children was the main expense in early childhood; later, those children's needs grew to include, for example, dowering daughters. The chance to secure a dowry formed an important motive for women to seek out their husbands in the New World. Increasingly explicit Crown mandates assisted women with their goals.

A February 1528 Cédula was the first unequivocal order that married men residing in the New World must return to their wives in Spain or bring the women to the New World.[19] Those who did not obey could face fines, exile, or arrest and deportation to Spain. One month after its promulgation, in March 1528, Sevillana María Quixada asked the Audiencia in Hispaniola to obligate her husband Pero López de Uribe to comply.[20] This scenario would be repeated throughout the sixteenth century. Just as early conquest alliances in Peru reveal a strain on indigenous family bonds in the Andes, Iberian women's pleas for long-lost husbands to return home expose the cost of imperial development for Spanish family bonds.

By 1530, the Crown made the issue of family settlement more prominent when Carlos V prohibited husbands who were not in the company of their wives from traveling to the New World.[21] The exception of a three-year travel window was allowed for merchants. The Crown strengthened its message in 1533 with an order of exile for men in Hispaniola, New Spain, and other regions whose wives remained in Spain.[22] The 1533 decree did not apply to Peru because the conquest of the Inca empire had so recently begun. By 1536, however, notice was served to Spaniards in Peru: anyone who had been in the Indies for five years had two years to comply with *vida maridable* or face consequences.[23] In the interim period, husbands had to send money to their families for sustenance.

On October 19, 1544, the Crown issued another Royal Cédula on the issue of *vida maridable* and sent it directly to Lima. This specific Cédula gathered together the many threads of the earlier sixteenth-century decrees. It prompted a variety of responses by (for the most part) husbands in Peru and wives in Spain between approximately 1540 and 1600. Day-to-day matters of royal business in Peru were hampered, however, by the ongoing war between the Pizarro and Almagro factions, so it is possible that men in Peru were not pressured to respond to the Cédulas until the early 1550s.[24] This mandate clarified the relationship of *vida maridable* to the Crown's interest in the Americas. It lamented the fact that Spaniards in Peru did not live "with their wives and children like true *vecinos*" of their lands. The *vecino* in early Spanish Peru was someone who participated in the founding of a community or sought to become a permanent part of a community by purchasing or receiving land. To be a *vecino* was to be a citizen in a Spanish American community, which carried with it both privilege and responsibility.[25] For the Crown, those men who settled cities like Lima or held encomiendas in Cuzco attempted to enjoy the privileges of *vecino* status without settling families and fulfilling the duties of setting a good example for the indigenous population. The decree charged that these men moved around and neglected their duties "neither erecting nor planting nor breeding nor sowing nor doing other things that good settlers tend to do."[26] Instead of developing areas, they abandoned them and did not help in the growth of Spanish presence, agriculture, customs, or population. Overall, men who refused to conduct *vida maridable* with their wives caused "great obstacles to the settlement of this land."[27] From one perspective, the Crown's demand ignored the mobility necessary for the burgeoning commerce in the Andes in which many men participated. Nonetheless, the Crown did not make exception for this.

By focusing on *vecinos* in the Cédula, the Crown highlighted its expectations that elite men uphold obligations for marriage. Crown officials, court scribes, encomenderos—these men, above others, were expected to model *vida maridable* for the rest of the emerging colonial society. Indeed, most of the responses to the Cédula came from the more visible members of the social elite in colonial Lima. As a corrective measure, the Crown ordered men in Peru: "[those] who are married ... notify them that they must embark on the first navios that leave the ports of these provinces and come [to Spain] for their wives and they must not return to reside in these parts [Peru] unless they bring their wives with them or they carry substantial proof that their wives are dead."[28] If husbands did not return to Spain in person, they could grant legal power to a third party to transport their wives from Spain to Peru, provided that happened within the space of two years.[29] The decree also specified that married men who embarked on an initial voyage to the Indies be given no more than three years' license, thus keeping them in line with the requirements of the 1544 Cédula.[30] Exceptions existed to allow married men to travel to the Indies without their wives for a set period of time if they left a security deposit or if their wives had given express permission for them to travel.[31] Ecclesiastic tribunals had the responsibility to try those who refused to cooperate with the decree.[32]

In the case of Peru, in particular, single men and wealthy widows faced additional decrees on marriage, owing in large measure to a desire to stem the chaos of the 1540s Civil War in the Andes.[33] Wealthy widows were seen as "rewards" for those Spaniards who helped the Crown end the Spanish on Spanish hostilities, but the encouragement for them to marry also helped to keep encomiendas from being controlled by women.[34] In this same era, single men were ordered to marry within thirty days of a provision decreed by the Audiencia of Peru. For those who did not find a fiancée within that timeframe, the Audiencia threatened to assign a bride from among the noble indigenous women.[35] The Decree stated, "And so any odor of barraganía will disappear, moral victory will occur and the restless temperaments will be subdued; because one cleans the wheat with wind and vices with punishment."[36] How the indigenous brides were to be selected from among noble Amerindian families is unclear, but the implication is that elite native women were acceptable in locations with few single Spanish women.

This reference to indigenous women as potential brides was the only mention of indigenous people in the decree. The absence of any discussion about Andean elite families and their situation in the 1540s is telling. In Peru the Crown emphasized the establishment of family models for *vecinos* in part because their absence left a vacuum into which an already well-established native family structure could easily fit. The potential power of native families and mestizo elites undergirded much of what the Crown ordered about Peru in this moment. As we saw in chapter 2, the children of Francisco Pizarro had been ordered to Spain because of fears about the potential power of their families. Even as late as 1570, Crown officials wanted to send Beatriz Coya to live in Spain after her marriage to a Spaniard. Although she ended up in Chile, the anxieties are telling. The silence on indigenous families in the 1544 Cédula spoke loudly; Spain wanted to ensure its colonial preeminence by promoting nuclear families in households in the Andes.

"As We Are Obligated": Husbands Obeying the Cédula

Like many of the Crown's decrees, the Cédula on *vida maridable* could easily have become an example of *"obedezco pero no cumplo"* (I obey but I do not comply). Given the distance that separated Spain and Peru, the infrequency of letters, and the travel of men through various parts of the New World, the notion that men would respond to this legal requirement by the Crown might seem naïve. Even for the sixteenth century, one scholar declares that "this was in many cases [a] dead letter" and suggests that *vida maridable* decrees functioned to remove political adversaries from given regions or to extort bribes from those men who failed to comply.[37] Yet men in the province of Peru did take action in response to this Cédula as early as 1550. Specifically, since married women could not travel unaccompanied, many took advantage of the option to have a third party fetch their wives from Spain and bring them to the New World. Moreover, contemporary perceptions about family emerge in the symbolic language contained in these decrees as well as the actions undertaken by men, women, and royal officials as a result of them.

Some men who took action suggest the Crown wanted to make examples of royal officials. In 1550, Pedro Álvarez, a royal scribe in Lima, appointed Dionysio de Osorio to travel to Spain and make the return voyage with his wife, Francisca de Carvajal, and son.[38] He granted Osorio a legal power and paid him 1,025 gold pesos for his expenses as well as the needs of his wife and son. Álvarez hinted that perhaps his wife might not look favorably on the trip, pointing out that in case "she does not want to come," Osorio should offer the funds for her sustenance.[39] Álvarez used his appointment of Osorio to voice his disapproval of the Cédula. Álvarez lamented that this ruling unfairly targeted married men with a burden, financial and otherwise. In his case, in particular, having been called to serve "God's will" for the Royal Court in Lima, he complained that he had no choice in his location and separation from his wife.

Diego Medina de Alamos was another Crown appointee, as regidor of Cuzco, when he complied with the order. He gave his brother and nephew legal power to require his wife doña Costança Maldonado to accompany them to Peru.[40] One year later, he was still trying to bring his wife to Peru. One son, Diego Maldonado Altamirano, lived in Lima, but his wife and other children remained in Medina del Campo, Spain. In March 1552, Diego, the father, renewed a legal power to bring doña Costança to Lima and, in a step with greater finality, he gave her permission to sell the family's goods in Spain to pay for the trip to the Indies.[41]

Men who were not Crown officials mimicked Álvarez and Medina. Spaniards authorized legal powers to third parties in order to comply with *vida maridable* throughout the sixteenth century. These were akin to power-of-attorney arrangements. Since husbands had legal control of their wives, the women needed explicit permission to undertake the journey from Spain to the Indies and to enact any legal or economic transactions related to the journey. Husbands visited notaries to authorize permission for other men to escort their wives, thus generating records of these third-party transatlantic journeys. The biggest flurry of these transactions occurred in the immediate aftermath of the 1551 reissuance of the cédula. The aforementioned Melchior Ximénez cited the order precisely when he gave permission for Alonso Díaz and Gaspar Ximénez to accompany his wife, Francisca, from Oropesa, Spain to Lima.[42]

People took advantage of those who traveled back and forth from Lima to Spain in order to exercise their plans to bring family to the New World. Networks were critical since the job required trust with loved ones as well as, in most cases, sums of money. For instance, in 1552 Diego Maldonado, the son, was traveling back to Spain with two duties. First, his father wanted him to help sell the family goods and bring his mother, doña Costança, to Peru. Second, Alonso Hernández, a hosier, asked Diego Maldonado to bring his wife Inés López del Mançano and the couple's children to Lima from Spain.[43]

The practice of a using a third party to escort a wife and family to Peru became the norm shortly after conquest and continued into the 1560s and 1570s. Having already made the difficult journey from the Old World to the New, perhaps some could not stomach the thought of a return trip. Husbands explained why they themselves were not traveling to Spain to retrieve the women and sent their rationale via messenger. Fabian Blanco cited his "many businesses and impediments," when he asked Pedro Bermúdez to work in tandem with his sister and nephew to remove his wife from Trujillo, Spain, and bring her post-haste to Lima to live in *vida maridable* "in accordance with our holy mother church of Rome."[44] Even though Mateo de Almonazir wrote to his wife Catalina Millán de Bohórquez, "I can no longer suffer so much absence [from you]," he did not go to Spain to travel alongside the "light of my eyes" as he called his wife, but rather sent for her.[45] For men who were *vecinos* in Lima, a lengthy absence from the city could threaten their status as they would be unable to fulfill their commitments to that position.[46] Duty to occupation trumped making the return trip to Spain for many husbands, and it became far more common to appoint and pay a sort of transatlantic courier, a third party who would collect their families and see them safely from Seville to Peru.[47]

Here again men used legal powers to assist them with family matters. The numerous legal powers ordered in Lima to bring the *vida maridable* decrees to fruition show who husbands trusted to take temporary responsibility for their wives and children. The third party, usually relatives, friends, or business partners, typically received explicit instructions as well as payment for their task. Swordmaker Miguel Gerónimo called for his wife María Sánchez from Seville when a trusted friend, Jorge Dote, planned to sail from Lima to Spain.[48] When Gerónimo granted Dote legal power to chaperone his wife, he specified the route of the journey: "From the kingdoms of Spain toward Nombre de Dios to the kingdoms of Peru by sea and by land." Dote was to receive 150 pesos in payment. Further, Gerónimo ordered 50 to 60 pesos for his wife in order to purchase goods necessary for the trip and gave 200 pesos up front for expenses and promised more if necessary.[49] Relatives were particularly good candidates for the task of accompanying a loved one on the crossing.[50] In 1567 Lima resident Pedro Alonso de Paredes ordered his nephew Miguel de Burgos, a resident of Tierra Firme to bring his wife Isabel Rodríguez to comply with the *vida maridable* provision. He promised Burgos as many as 3,000 pesos in gold and silver for assistance with the task.[51]

Men used legal powers to move wives within the Indies, as well. In 1549, the wax-maker Marcos de Sosa ordered his wife María Fernández to travel from Mexico City to Lima with their family and belongings.[52] Sosa did so under duress, as Spanish authorities threatened him with the *vida maridable* ordinance. Although not as lengthy as the transatlantic journey, these trips were serious undertakings and the responsibility of entrusting one's family members to another was great. The trends emphasize both the mobile nature of life for men in the Indies as well as their attempts to fulfill obligations within that migratory lifestyle.

"I Wish Very Much to See You Here": Husbands in Peru

The development of Crown policy on marriage in the transatlantic context hides the personal concerns of husbands and wives about separation. Letters reveal both expressions of emotion and discussion of finances. In 1590 Antón Sánchez wrote a passionate plea from his residence in Cuzco, Peru, to his wife María de la Paz who lived in Seville. "You must know that I have a great desire to '*hacer vida*' with you," he wrote María. His greatest hope was for his wife to leave Seville with their children and travel to Peru:

> Sister of my life, I want to reclaim myself as I reclaim you and our children and serve God, and I cannot serve him if I do not make my life with you and have you in my company. And for this I beg you, for the love of God, that you embark on the first ship that leaves Seville and come to *hacer vida* with me, together with our children because you have gone astray and you are not serving God.[53]

Sánchez's letter emphasized the family's need to act in accordance with God's will and his commitment to marital life. Many men opted to lure their wives to Peru with promises of a better lifestyle and less work. Sánchez uniquely focused on the union of marriage and the moral obligation that bound the two.

In the 1500s, letters took months to travel from Peru to Spain. Husbands and wives, often illiterate, relied on scribes to write them. Francisco de Meza Matamores cautioned his wife, "you well know I cannot read or write." Perhaps anticipating the potential rumors about his behavior or finances or, Meza noted that: "married men run a great risk in this land, and if they do not write with a secret person, they do not know who to trust."[54] Still, he pleaded with his wife to let him know her plans and his hopes that she would travel to Peru. "I am," he said, "constantly worried that I will not see you, and I remain at your service as one who is more than obliged."[55] From the vantage point of letters, as opposed to litigation, men in the Indies appear earnest in their endeavors to bring their wives to the New World not just to comply with the *vida maridable* decree but because of affection. In addition to expressions of love, letters dealt explicitly with financial matters and with men's ability to provide for their wives, either in payment of passage to the New World or general economic support. Roberto de Burt instructed his wife Ana Franca, "I am sending you 100 ducats, so that you can prepare [to come to Peru] with the first fleet."[56]

Other men had good intentions to send financial help, but had met with little economic success in Peru.[57] For those who assumed the New World would provide material success, the reality of conquest and colonial endeavors in the Andes could be a harsh one. Men left Spain with every intention of becoming rich and returning to Spain or sending for their wives, but never earned the money to afford passage back to Spain.[58] This led to pathetic, yet earnest messages to wives: "I can't send you anything even though I very much want to," wrote Hernando González of Lima to his wife Leonor Gómez in Spain.[59] He tried to respond to her letter and her "great complaints." González defended himself as best he could by recounting how his work left him exhausted, but with little money. "I wish very much to see you here," he wrote.[60] Efforts at financial assistance for wives mark one important element of attempting to fulfill *vida maridable* across a long distance and meeting the requirements of the 1544 royal decree.

It is also clear from extant letters that many felt a great longing to be reunited with loved ones and understood they had to convince their wives to make the trip. Widespread, and not unwarranted, fear existed about travel to the New World. Even the jurist Juan Solórzano advised that if a woman feared travel on the seas she should not be made to go to her husband if he lived in the Indies.[61] At least one husband spoke to the matter directly as he tried to persuade his reluctant wife: "Don't let the ocean upset you. There is no greater joy in the world."[62]

Others focused not on the journey but on life in Peru and tried to convince their wives that they would be better off than in Spain. "If I had you in this land, there would be no man richer than I," wrote Cristóbal Páez de Becerril to his wife Agustina de Vara.[63] To convince her to travel, he emphasized the social and racial superiority of Spaniards in Peru: "If you decide to come to this land, you will be well off," he wrote. "And we will live very happily, and in the service of God. ... Because it's a very pampered life and Spanish women have everything, they don't serve or make a single thing, *negras* do everything for them."[64] Cristóbal Páez de

Becerril had nothing to send his wife Agustina de Vara, but he still tried to convince her to come to Peru.[65] He used the example of a couple known to both and reported that they were very happy living in Peru. Although he claimed to be down and out financially, he recommended a trusted man who could assist her with making the journey.

Another man, Francisco de Meza Matamoros, grew exasperated with trying to convince his wife, Gregoria de Mesa, to join him. Gregoria had not written since he journied to Peru. Ever hopeful of a reunion, Francisco sent her 500 reales with a friend who was traveling to Seville in the hopes that she would take the money and use it to visit him.[66]

The Crown decrees on *vida maridable* generally prompted two actions: women made demands from Spain or husbands in Peru made plans for wives to travel and join then. Common wisdom was that women wanted their husbands to reunite with them, but sometimes men had to pursue their wives and convince them to travel to the New World. The reasons for this are varied, to be sure. Even given all the specific elements of a husband's role in *vida maridable*, in particular, his economic support, women still might prefer to remain in Spain rather than move to the Indies. Dionysio Osorio made provisions in a legal power "in case" his wife did not want to travel to Peru from Spain. The decision to leave entailed a long and arduous journey. There was a real chance that these women would not see Spain or most of their relatives again. "I am very unhappy, and I say the Indies for whoever wants them," lamented doña María de Córdoba to her sister as she told her not to travel to Peru.[67]

Consider an apparently abandoned Spanish husband who lived out his final days in the highlands of Peru, in poor health, in ill humor, and outside the bonds of *vida maridable*. The man, one Bartolomé Saldaña, suffered in frustration as his wife Elvira Pérez, living in the village of Fuente de Cantos in Spain, refused invitations to come live with him in Cuzco, Peru. Saldaña wrote to Pérez, "It has been two years since I have received a letter from you, and I cannot stress how appalled I am with your stubbornness, when other women without husbands nor resources from their relatives come to these lands with their children in order to help them, and you having both husband and resources, have not done it."[68] The possibility that not all women viewed *vida maridable* as desirable raises another set of questions about the marital pact in the sixteenth-century world.

Although many complied with the *vida maridable* decree, Spaniards were practiced at avoiding it. Even husbands without financial excuses found ways to live apart from their wives for years on end. In 1551 Don Pedro Luis de Cabrera, encomendero in Cuzco, found himself charged by the *fiscal* for living apart from his wife. By 1552, the Audiencia in Lima ordered action on the complaint. The Crown required that encomenderos be married and living in the company of their wives. Many encomenderos tried to skirt this requirement, but Cabrera's case illustrates how the *vida maridable* decree worked in tandem with property, status, and development in the colonies.[69] The explanation centered on the necessity for "everyone to follow a good example and increase the population."[70]

Cabrera was informed that he could choose an overseer who would offer good treatment to the natives to control his encomienda while he traveled to Spain and back. Alternately, he could remain in Peru to run the encomienda and send a messenger for his wife. The Audiencia threatened Cabrera with a 2,000 ducats fee, donated to public works, for noncompliance. The court allowed that should Cabrera return to Spain to find that his wife was deceased, he could return to the Indies "as a free person, without marital obligation."[71] The use of the word obligation reinforces that spouses were obliged to one another in ways that even the growth of a transatlantic empire could not render null and void. Finally, on November 5, 1556, Cabrera made formal arrangements to have his wife brought from Spain.[72] Distance could, and did, slow compliance but the point remained, and the Crown would use royal decrees to keep spouses together. As families adapted to this age of expansion, mobility became understood as part and parcel of family experience.

"Absent in the Indies": Wives in Spain

In addition to action taken in the New World, women in Spain filed petitions to oblige their husbands to return home. Although the process was lengthy and difficult, women's desires to have their husbands fulfill marital obligations met with a sympathetic ear from the Crown. With the support of the decree on *vida maridable*, they sought to locate their husbands and make them own up to their marital obligations. In the late sixteenth century, Luisa Pendones gave her husband Manuel Hernández permission to travel from Spain to the Indies for the standard three-year timeframe. In 1591, seven years later, Hernández was still Peru. Pendones, like many women in her situation, sought *vida maridable* with her husband and petitioned the Crown in order to secure their reunion. Specifically, she asked the Crown to track down her husband and force him onto the next boat bound for Spain.[73]

Other women's petitions emphasized the economic aspects of their husband's duty to them. Not all women whose husbands left for the Indies lived in dire straits, but many found themselves in need of extra support at critical junctures, such as the impending marriage of a child. A case in point is doña Leonor de Egas who married Martín Gotria in Seville around 1552. He sailed for Peru and ended up in Potosí by 1580, when the mines were about to reach their all-time high of silver production. Egas's will suggests she made debts and intervened in a lawsuit against her nephew, exercising economic and legal power in her husband's absence. Yet unlike some "abandoned" wives, Egas anticipated the receipt of funds from her husband. She included a clause in her will stating that "the money my husband sends me with Luis Guzmán or any other person" should go to María de Nieva, maiden daughter of her nephew Pedro de Nieva. Egas cited the girl's poverty as her reason for supporting her so she could "marry in accordance with her status."[74] Egas mentioned no children of her own. But she seems to have had contact with her husband; she knew he was in Potosí and she had the name of an individual from whom she was expecting money, perhaps someone from whom she had received them in the past. Her case is illustrative; women did in fact hear from husbands and receive letters or financial support. And for many men, they understood clearly that monetary obligations to their wives and children were to be fulfilled from a distance. In fact, for some, the ability to provide financially for their families was a major incentive for the migration. Going away was, ironically, a way to fulfill a financial aspect of *vida maridable*. For many women, however, their husbands' trips to the Indies produced marked change.

Women's powers were heightened in financial and legal affairs in sixteenth-century Seville because so many of the city's men left for the Indies.[75] Doña María Dona, wife of the jurado Melchior Céquez, oversaw the sale of a slave for her husband who was in the Indies.[76] Elvira Hernández stated her husband's whereabouts not merely as "in the Indies," but "absent in the Indies" when she apprenticed the couple's ten-year-old son Esteban to a silversmith. This type of placement for a child was common in sixteenth-century Seville and not likely caused by her husband's absence, but the notation is significant. His specific location was less significant than his absence to the family by virtue of being in the Indies.[77] During this era, distance became the norm for some married couples.

When Francisca Ejos made her will in 1570 she noted that her husband Diego Gutiérrez de la Águila was in the Indies, but made no other mention of him.[78] For Seville resident Ejos, her husband's absence was interpreted within a framework of what family models might look like in an era when so many men left Seville for the Indies. The family model of the colonial era adapted to these new distances.

Many factors in Spain's new colonies could keep men on the move and away from family in Spain. Cealla Vázquez complained that her husband had been gone more than twenty years and refused to come home.[79] They had been married for three years in the city of Ávila before Rodrigo de Mançanas departed for Peru. Vázquez alleged that she and her brother wrote to Mançanas asking him to return to Spain to live in *vida marid-able* but he ignored them.[80] Compounding the problem for Vázquez was Mançanas' refusal to provide for her sustenance. After two decades of her letters going unanswered, Vázquez decided to take up the lengthy process of having the Crown track him down. She earned the sympathy of the Crown, and, in keeping with the 1544 decree, Queen Isabel issued a demand on her behalf giving Mançanas a two-year period to send for his wife or return to live with her in Spain. Mançanas had the option as well to explain why he could not live with his wife on either side of the Atlantic and to send her support.

Because these petitions could result in a royal order, the matter of establishing marriage claims for the female petitioner was a serious task. The burden fell on abandoned wives to prove their claims of marriage. In many instances this meant offering witness testimony of those who had attended the wedding or, preferably, had served as witnesses at the wedding. The *vida maridable* petitions, then, required a legal process before anyone ever went looking for a wayward husband. Because this required substantial motivation on the part of the woman, many probably waited years before beginning the process. In 1584 Francisca Manrique decided to make an official claim to find her husband. It had been ten years since her husband Gerónimo de Benavides set sail to Peru and then moved southward to the province of Chile. Manrique, at home in Valladolid, Spain, grew tired of waiting and took her concerns to the Crown. Her petition asked for a Royal Cédula to the governors and justices of Chile to lock up her husband and send him back to Spain.[81]

The Crown asked Manrique to prove her claims. She gathered several witnesses including twenty-four-year-old Luisa González, wife of Pedro de Villalobos, who said she knew the couple to be married because she had seen their wedding with her own eyes.[82] Finding an eyewitness to a wedding ceremony itself was critical in order to affirm the validity of a claim. Moreover, after the wedding González had seen them living together in a house in Valladolid. She reckoned the couple had been married about thirteen years, some three of which they spent together before Benavides left for the New World. The existence (or alleged existence) of physical evidence that the husband was in the New World was also extremely helpful in proving a case. Here González pointed to letters she had seen from Santiago de Chile. The propensity of the Crown to use resources to track down a husband was helped along by concrete proof that a man was in a particular location in the New World.

In the late 1580s, women began to include physical descriptions of their husbands in these petitions. Francisco de Olibera was a small-bodied man of forty years with a graying blonde beard. So said his wife Antonia Hernández in 1590 when she wished him home from Puebla, New Spain.[83] In 1587 Inés de Barbona described Antonio de Texada, her husband, as being forty-four years old and of medium build.[84] Texada had gone to the Indies more than twenty years before. The *morena* Catalina Martín gave more detail of her husbands' whereabouts as she spoke about him. She had suspected that Francisco Hernández' was in Zacatecas in New Spain where he had traveled in 1583. She recalled him as "a stocky man, thirty-six years old, with a thick beard and a scar on the right side below his beard."[85] All this information she gave so that he would return to Spain to take up conjugal life with her.

Women's pleas to the Crown for assistance did not necessarily diminish over time. In fact as children reached marriageable age, women's motives to petition before the Crown intensified. Ana de Sanabria, a Seville resident, said goodbye to her husband, Manuel de Utra, in 1570.[86] Utra went to New Granada where, Sanabria heard, he had become very rich through business and trade and held a large estate. Yet in thirteen years she had received no support from him. Their daughter, just a one-year-old when Utra departed for the Indies, was now fourteen and her mother was beginning to think about her dowry. Sanabria would need money from her husband to marry her daughter well or to enter her into a convent. Sanabria had no concrete evidence of his whereabouts. Seville was a city where much news passed, however, and she heard that he had intentionally changed his name in order to avoid being sent home to Spain. She urged authorities that whether he was Manuel de Utra or Manuel de Cháves, his alleged new name, his behavior was "against the ordinances."

The need to provide a dowry for daughters weighed heavily on some who had left Spain for the New World and never returned. Hernán Gómez left Lepe, Spain, for Lima and his wife Isabel Alonso and two daughters stayed behind. Beatriz, the elder daughter, married with a dowry from her parents. So, in 1562, when Gómez dictated his will, he left the younger Marina as his sole heir because she had yet to marry or receive a dowry.[87] Gómez would not assist in church when marriage banns were read for Beatriz. He would not meet her intended. He would not declare his approval of her marriage in person. Yet he would provide her dowry, one of the most keenly observed obligations of fathers to daughters. It maintained its significance, economic and cultural, during a time of massive transition. To be a good father meant to dower an honorable daughter.

This entrenched transatlantic connection between "absent" parents and children could work to a child's disadvantage as well. Parents not only kept in touch in order to offer money, but they also disciplined from afar. Grisostomos de Hontiberos, who lived in Guamanga, Peru, traveled to Lima to notarize documents that disinherited his daughter Catalina. Catalina lived in Spain and Hontiberos had not seen her in years. Yet he objected to her marrying Bernardino de Prado against his will.[88] Many fathers worked to orchestrate marriage matches and they did not appreciate meddling from other relatives or a daughter's initiative in the matter.[89]

Hontiberos's actions reminded his daughter that he had legal control of her, even from afar. Her marriage to Prado, however, suggests that distance eroded the bonds of control over time. In that sense, their family had much more in common with those whose fathers were considered "absent" in the Indies and whose wives tried to track them down. In analyzing *vida maridable* petitions by abandoned wives over the course of the sixteenth century, it is valuable to highlight the group of women who used this legal vehicle to attempt to bring their husbands home or at least to secure some financial support from them. It is safe to assume that many who had access to the legal measures to file a petition were elite, given the financial means needed to make such petitions. Noblewoman doña Isabel de Guzmán sought to track down her husband Juan López de Congones. Married for eight years to López, she only lived with him for eight months before he departed for the Indies. She wanted him to support her as he was "obliged" because, she argued, she was an "honorable person and an hija de algo (hidalgo)."[90] Her case is an important reflection of how women of elite social status in Iberia suffered economic consequences just as did their commoner counterparts when husbands sailed for the New World.

Social standing also played a role in the case of Cealla Vázquez and Rodrigo de Mançanas. Were Mançanas' order ever enforced, the decree clarified that if money and belongings were taken (forcibly) from Mançanas to send to Vázquez they should be the quantity that the Peruvian officials thought appropriate to Vázquez' social rank and in relation to the relative wealth of the New World province where Mançanas resided.[91]

Yet not all petitioners were elites of European descent. The Afro-Sevillano Madalena Hernández complained that she was poor and suffered many trials because her husband Anton Pérez left her six years earlier for Hispaniola and had not returned nor sent money.[92] Pérez and Hernández married on January 23, 1575, at Santa Catalina church in Triana with Diego Hernández and María as their *padrinos*. The problem of abandoned women and adventuresome men crossed racial lines and, in this case, resulted in a strategy identical to those of elite, white Spaniards.

Occasionally the wives' petitions worked. It is perhaps remarkable that royal servants ever tracked down husbands on the other side of the Atlantic Ocean. When they did so, the men were imprisoned, placed on ships, and sent to Seville. Gonçalo Martín arrived home to Spain in 1599. He left Peru under Crown order and was jailed upon arrival in Seville at which point he pleaded to be released to go and live with his wife.[93] One year later, Sebastián Correa traveled the same route on the galleons of don Francisco Coloma, jailed for *casado* (married).[94] The offense was not his married status per se but the fact that he was married and had not obeyed the royal order to reunite with his wife in the legally prescribed period. Coloma was sent to the Casa de la Contratación to await his punishment. His wife, Magdalena López, awaited him in their home city of Seville. In these and other cases, men who were found guilty of disobeying the Royal Cédula on *vida maridable* discovered that the fix was not as simple as returning home to one's wife. Both Martín and Correa were sentenced for the crime of not carrying out *vida maridable*. The buoyant feeling women experienced when they heard their petitions to the Crown had been successful was likely short-lived, however, as many husbands who were apprehended ended up paying money to the Crown and/or serving time in jail.

For the infraction of living in Lima without his wife, María Cabeza, Bernaldino de Castro had to swear to the Viceroy Conde de Nieva that he would go to Spain within two years and bring his wife to Peru.[95]

In addition, he had to pay a 2,000 peso fine for not having traveled to fetch her two years earlier.

Diego Fernández de Cabrera not only awaited sentencing for failure to carry out married life but also lost a good deal of silver along the way. In the early seventeenth century, Fernández de Cabrera traveled from Lima to Madrid where his wife, doña María Truchada, awaited him. Fernández de Cabrera, by his telling, left Peru with seven bars of silver, worth 4,702 pesos.[96] Silver shipments were carefully monitored at each port. Cabrera claimed to have registered his silver when the ship arrived in Panama and thus expected to receive that amount upon reaching the Casa de la Contratación on the other side of the Atlantic. Instead Crown authorities forced him to make the case for having registered the silver. The loss of mineral riches during a transatlantic crossing was nothing particularly unique; claims like Fernández de Cabrera's surfaced from time to time. His case was unique, however, because the journey was a court-ordered one. The Court of Lima found him in violation of *vida maridable* and sent him back to Spain. As if the mandatory trip home were not punishment enough, this New World adventurer stood to lose close to 5,000 pesos as well.

In April and May of 1572, a group of eight men all underwent arrest in Lima for the crime of "being married in the kingdoms of Spain."[97] This sting on married men who were not in compliance with *vida maridable* regulations is remarkable. Even in the 1540s and early 1550s, men who were seeking their wives from across the ocean did so in order to comply and were not talking to scribes from the inside of a jail cell. These arrests suggest that then viceroy Toledo wanted to make an example of men who were not elites or royal officials, like those who routinely complied (probably after official coaxing) in the earlier period. After their arrests, the men all had to post a significant sum of 500 pesos bond to gain freedom. In meeting bond requirements, both they and their guarantors agreed that they would leave Lima on the first ship to Panama and then take the first ship headed to Seville. They had to register their status on the ships as "married." During their land travel in Panama, the men had to report to the Real Audiencia of Panama and have testimony recorded as to their progress on the trip. They were given a relatively short time frame—six months—to return to Spain and reunite with their wives.

Was the arrest of these men something that came as a result of their wives beginning a process in Spain? Or did the application of the *vida maridable* decree emerge from authorities within Peru? The 1572 arrests could have stemmed from a heavy-handed attempt to inculcate order by viceroy Toledo. Notably, several of these eight men or their bondsmen were artisans, one a tailor (*jubitero*), one a shoemaker, one a mason. None of them held titles or royal positions (as had been the case with some of the men from the 1540s who, under duress, attempted to have their wives brought over to be in compliance).

The records do not follow these eight to the other side of the ocean. They may have escaped Lima and attempted to run. Or perhaps a return trip to Spain came through. But their encounter with the application of this decree emphasizes that it was not a "dead letter" law during the sixteenth century. The decree had significance for Crown policy on marriage and family, and it had an impact on the lived experiences of abandoned wives and runaway husbands. Following the *vida maridable* process through to its end is critical. It shows that the crime and the wrongdoing were never only against a wife; they were equally an affront to the Crown and its attempts to uphold marriage and use family structure to influence settlement in Peru.

Defiant Wives

These cases wherein husbands attempted to convince wives to come and live with them in Peru hint at complexities in women's lives that do not fit stereotypes about female abandonment, obedience, and victimization. Notwithstanding the difficult trials some women experienced after being abandoned by husbands, women's experiences were wide-ranging. Some wives refused *vida maridable* or abandoned their husbands to marry again (bigamy). These cases show women taking uncharacteristic stances in unique sixteenth-century Indies contexts.[98] New World exploration and settlement opened opportunities in which some women and men maneuvered for social mobility or escape from Iberian norms. When women stepped outside traditional boundaries, complex cultural contests over defining family and family obligations often ensued.

So it was that Catalina de Palma met a legal request to join her husband in Quito with a defiant "no." Married in the 1530s, Diego de Arco and Catalina de Palma spent little time together as man and wife before Arco left for Peru.[99] Catalina gave birth to a daughter, Isabel, shortly after Arco's departure and struggled to provide a decent life for the girl. Diego stayed in the New World for years, eventually settling in Quito, and allegedly fathered several children with different women. Palma's first response was to request a counter decree that would bring her husband to Spain and allow her to remain at home and forego a difficult voyage. Over the age of fifty, with a crippled hip, Palma claimed she did not have the energy to journey to the Indies. Moreover, her attorney testified that she was not "obligated" to go Peru; rather, de Arco should be arrested by officials in Quito and placed on the first ship to Spain "because this conforms to the law."[100] Sebastián de Santander, Palma's attorney, stressed not only her poor physical state but also the fact that she had to support herself through embroidery. In the attorney's words, "if she does not earn it with her needle she does not eat."[101] Sewing and embroidery were common moneymaking tasks for women in early modern Spain, but they brought a meager income. By using this example Santander stressed the fragile economic situation that Palma endured while her husband was in Peru.[102] Santander alleged that since de Arco never supported her financially she had no obligation to travel to *hacer vida maridable* with him. She argued that she needed one thousand ducats in order to make the trip, a sum that she did not have nor had her husband provided for her. In fact, Santander claimed that in his twenty-four years in the Indies Diego de Arco never sent Palma any money.

Other records in the Casa de la Contratación indicate that Catalina de Palma was granted a license to travel to Peru in 1561 with Isabel de Arcos and Diego Valer, Palma's brother.[103] Why this trip did not come to fruition is unclear. By 1565, Palma's refusal to travel to Peru in the company of her brother-in-law Francisco de Arco had landed her in the public jail of Seville. Among several points of contention for Palma was Francisco de Arco himself. He reported to authorities that he had given letters and money from Diego to Catalina; she denied their existence. Moreover, she claimed that Diego had made insufficient preparations for her to travel to the Indies with their maiden daughter Isabel. Isabel's honor was of great concern to her mother. This was legal positioning to be sure, but young women's comportment and virginity were highly valued, and assault on women aboard ships was a well-founded fear.[104]

Palma's defense heaped objection on top of objection. She claimed that because her husband had not sent sufficient money Isabel would have to travel on the ship "where he wants to put her without respect for her as if she were poor and abandoned." In addition to the conditions on the ship, her male guardian was not to Palma's liking. It was, of course, none other than Francisco de Arcos with whom Palma was engaged in the lawsuit.

How can Diego, she proposed, put Isabel on a ship to Peru "with no more protection than the said Francisco de Arcos?"[105] In Catalina's 1561 license to travel, she was listed as traveling with Isabel and her own brother Diego de Valer. The issue, then, was not the number of males accompanying the pair of women, but rather their quality. Palma insinuated that de Arcos could not adequately protect the honor of Isabel. She hastened to emphasize the care with which she had raised her daughter as well as her own status as an "honorable *hija dalgo*."[106]

While Catalina de Palma could claim that she had not received support from her husband, she had heard enough news to know that he had been supporting others. This, too, lent weight to her appeals and, from a practical standpoint, highlighted his failures to adhere to marital obligations. She knew that Diego had been "almost all this time cohabitating in those parts and has married [off] daughters of his mistress." This was a thorny issue. For twenty-odd years she had been supporting Isabel on her own while he was creating a family life with a mistress and illegitimate children whom he married off (presumably with dowries) while Isabel remained unmarried in Spain. "He married his daughters while letting himself forget the legitimate daughter and her mother," quipped the frustrated Palma.[107]

Palma's attorney secured her release from jail. But the Crown did not side with her. On March 26, 1566, the Council of Indies ruled that if Diego de Arcos provided bonds in the quantity of 1,000 gold ducats, Palma must travel on the first ship that would leave for Tierra Firme in 1566.[108] None of Palma's claims apparently swayed the Crown. The interpretation of this case strictly upheld the institution of marriage. Moreover, the sentence seemed more forgiving to Palma's husband than to the abandoned wife. Commenting on the set of decrees related to *vida maridable*, the colonial jurist Solórzano Pereira noted, "the spirit of all these provisions ... is to achieve and assure the marital life of married couples" and that "the woman who is invited by her husband to the Indies should follow him."[109] The obligation within marriage existed as long as the couple lived, no matter the distance, the double family life, or the years without support. Moreover, the need to promote family structure based on legitimate marriage in the New World provinces was fundamental.

If Palma was a wife who defiantly refused to join an unfaithful husband in the New World, other women used the New World context to become the spouse who defied marriage roles. Conquest and travel seem like the perfect routes for men to escape during the sixteenth century, but women took advantage of them as well. For instance, some women posed as men, most famously Lt. Nun Catalina de Erauso.[110] Exceptional women might also use the distance and difficulty of New World living to create new opportunities through remarriage, but the *vida maridable* decree could force them into compliance.

Doña Mencia Baltodano ran away from her first husband, traveled across the ocean, and married three times in Peru. In the eyes of her alleged first husband, Juan Vizcaino, hers was a story of bigamy and deceit from one side of the Atlantic to the other.[111] For Baltodano, it would appear that escape from a sick husband and a trip to the New World spelled opportunity. Vizcaino, a resident of Casa Rubios del Monte in Spain, married a woman known as Mencia Díaz. The two lived together for years as man and wife until Vizcaino became ill and Mencia ran away and traveled to Peru. Setting herself up in Lima she began to call herself Mencia Baltodano. She married Alvaro Martín, who soon died. Baltodano then married Alonso de Origuela whose death left her with a handsome inheritance of a *repartimiento* in Cuzco. The *repartimiento* must have seemed an attractive dowry to Hernando de Acuña, who became her fourth husband.[112]

In 1565, Acuña journeyed to Spain to make a claim on the *repartimiento*. In doing so he also testified, and had witnesses do so as well, to the death of Baltodano's first husband Juan Vizcaino. The once-ill Vizcaino had never died, and he caught wind of this news and filed a suit with the Council of Indies. He claimed that Acuña had no legal recourse to the Cuzco *repartimiento* (also known as encomienda) formerly belonging to Origuela since Acuña received the *repartimiento* through his (bigamous) marriage to Baltodano. Vizcaino asked for Peruvian authorities to send his wife, with all of her belongings, back to Spain to *hacer vida* with him.[113] This extraordinary case shows the power a spouse could wield by leaning on this decree. Through the *vida maridable* decree, Vizcaino tried to force Baltodano to uphold marital obligations, no matter how much time had passed, no matter the crimes and sins committed.

With Acuña's marriage to Baltodano made null and void, in 1565 the court arrested Hernando de Acuña and ordered the *repartimiento* to be held by a neutral third party.[114] The question of who would retain the right to the *repartimiento* rested not only on marriage but also on gender. The legal arguments in this case draw on early encomienda (or *repartimiento*) law. Women who became encomenderas in Peru typically inherited the title from a husband or father.[115] The expectation in those cases was that the woman's husband (or new husband) would run the encomienda. In 1534 Carlos I had allowed that widows could succeed their husbands to the encomienda if no legitimate heirs existed. But, he clarified, when the widow in question remarried, "the Indians were to be placed in the name of the new husband."[116] The Crown never expected women to run the encomiendas. In that vein, Carlos V had tried to revoke encomienda from women in 1546, arguing that women were "not competent or capable to have encomienda Indians."[117] Still the desire to have Spanish marriages and children in the Indies often prompted the Crown to rule in favor of women and children inheriting.[118]

These conflicting opinions on encomienda came to bear when Acuña filed countersuit in 1568.[119] Acuña, who at one time happily received access to the encomienda on the basis of marriage, indeed *vida maridable*, with Baltodano, began to craft a new argument. He cited his twenty plus years of service to the Crown in Italy, Germany, Hungary, and Peru.[120] He claimed that he "did not possess the indios only as the husband of the said doña Mencia de Baltodano as said before but I have them by virtue of a new encomienda made in my person and by contemplation of my services by virtue of which I took and attained possession of the said indios fourteen years that I have and possess by this title."[121] Upon the death of Origuela, doña Mencia received the repartimiento as Origuela's theoretically legitimate wife because no heir existed (the couple had no children together, and Origuela had no other children). But for Acuña, his service to the Crown made him more deserving of holding title to the *repartimiento* than his marriage to Mencia.

The case of doña Mencia and her many husbands might first be read as a tale of women's agency in the 1500s. Yet as the case progressed, it was the men who emerged as the primary beneficiaries of property and privileges associated both with conquest and marriage. Instead of being a lawsuit about marriage and bigamy, it gradually became a case about men, property, and power. Who would win the *repartimiento*—Acuña or Vizcaino? Who had the right to grant it? Under what circumstances would they receive the honor from the Crown? Marriage faded into the background in the final stages of this legal battle, and Acuña was granted an order from the Crown to keep the Cuzco *repartimiento*. Yet the proximity of marriage to the flight of Baltodano and the plight of both Vizcaino and Acuña serve as reminders that marital obligations always included not just a vow, but economic considerations as well. Finally, in these cases where women acted in strong contrast to legal and social norms, husbands enjoyed the support of the Crown and the courts.

THE SIXTEENTH-CENTURY *VIDA maridable* petitions filed in Spain present an overwhelming picture of abandonment of Spanish women by their Spanish husbands during the first century of New World conquest. Yet private letters, passenger lists, and lawsuits reveal a more complex picture. The motivations behind these transatlantic reunions are murky: sentiment, practicality, religion, and compliance with the Royal Cédula were all possibilities. Husbands and wives on both sides of the Atlantic responded to the royal decrees on *vida maridable* with diverse motivations in both metropole and periphery. Notarized legal powers in Peru and petitions for husbands filed in Spain show how men and women made plans to reunite and commit to *vida maridable*. These attempts involved time, money, legal processes, and the help of friends as witnesses or travel companions, as well as sheer energy and willpower.

Spanish men and women responded to new and distinct challenges to family spawned by empire-building in the provinces of Peru as the flurry of royal decrees on marriage complicated the terrain. Women could seek out enforcement for personal protection and perhaps even for punitive action against their husbands. In contrast, for some willing husbands and wives, the cédula promoted a process that sped along their licensing and passage to the provinces of Peru for the chance to renew *vida maridable*. Finally, the Crown could enforce the cédulas at will to maintain royal interests and have men locked up and shipped back to Iberia. It is hard to compare Bartolomé Saldaña's fate in Cuzco to the men who were jailed for violating the marriage decree; to him, though, his wife's refusal to cross the ocean and join him in *vida maridable* was a prison of its own. His fate is a reminder of the ever-present individual and institutional roles in the business of family. The Crown promoted the settlement of Peru by married couples, expected married women to join their husbands, and encouraged single men to marry Spanish women. Those Crown goals notwithstanding, individuals worked to promote their own family interests. For men like Saldaña who wanted their wives in the New World or women such as Pendones who could not track down their husbands, the decrees provided tools to force spouses to live up to marital obligations.

When a couple was to be reunited, a major journey stood between the two. In 1551, Alonso de León was living in Lima and about to be reunited with his wife Andrea de Campos. Not only did he ask her to journey from

Seville to Lima, he also asked her to carry out a favor for him in Tierra Firme, a stop along the route. De León requested that Andrea locate his mestiza daughter, Eugenia, born during their separation, and bring her to Lima to live in their household.[122] Bringing wives to the New World and moving mestizo children were two sets of actions that occurred in relationship to one another. Thus, a journey like Andrea de Campos's covered great lengths of territory and forced families to reckon with the events that had occurred in the context of colonial change, such as the birth of a mestizo child out of wedlock and the incorporation of such children into the family household. It is to that journey that we turn in chapter 4 to consider the relationship of family networks to the voyage itself and the impact of the increasing arrival of Spanish women like Andrea de Campos on colonial family in Peru.

4

Journey

FAMILY STRATEGIES
AND THE TRANSATLANTIC VOYAGE

IN 1561, INÉS Méndez left the city of Toledo for Seville where she boarded a ship that stopped in the Villa of San Lucar de Barrameda before departing for Peru. Méndez had a royal order to travel to Peru in order to share *vida maridable* with Pedro de la Ostia, her husband. Her brother-in-law, Juan de la Ostia, accompanied her for the transatlantic journey.[1] From the 1540s on, transatlantic travel between Peru and Spain was increasingly an activity that women and children undertook. This demographic shift highlights a particular historical moment in the development of Peru's colonial society. Moreover, the changing demographics of travel reveal family as a prime motivator in imperial migration. Indeed, family networks provided the rationale for traveling, the funds to travel, and the preparations for a safe voyage.[2] Crown rules influenced the pattern, but husbands, wives, and children moved for and with the help of family. As much as travel separated loved ones, its very undertaking was promoted and facilitated by family members.

This chapter focuses on emigration of spouses and parents from the 1540s through the end of the sixteenth century. It analyzes the bureaucratic, financial, and practical requisitioning these journeys required to argue that family connections proved key at every stage of the voyage from imagining the trip to gaining permission for the actual boarding of the ship. The chapter begins in Seville, the gateway city to the Indies, and discusses its ties to Lima, to show how interconnectedness of families in these two locations facilitated travel.[3] Family networks were critical for emotional and practical support, but the economic roles they played in this sixteenth-century transatlantic world were fundamental as well. Relatives helped people to procure licenses to travel and they shared information on how to prepare for the challenges of the voyage itself.[4] Lifestyles cultivated on a ship over weeks on end were conditioned by one's family status and its direct relationship to family honor.[5] It was commonly held that the best way to travel safely to the New World was by using family networks.[6] The network of family moved its share of the empire's weight back and forth between the Old World and the New and, as it did, the shape of the family continued its colonial transformation.

Family Connections to the Gateway City

Seville was a requisite way station for anyone crossing to the Indies or arriving from the Indies. Its role was cemented with the 1503 inauguration of the House of Trade, which regulated travel and merchandise transport between the Iberian kingdoms and the New World. With paperwork in hand from the House of Trade, ships left Seville and traveled down the Guadalquivir River to the coastal points of departure, typically San Lúcar de Barrameda. [see Seville and the river in figure 4.1] Navigating the river was complicated due to shallow areas, so large vessels did not load cargo and passengers until they reached the coast. It was faster and safer to send the heavy weight of the cargo over land between Seville and the ocean ports. Some smaller ships took on passengers along the river at Las Horcadas. All vessels passed through San Lúcar de Barrameda for final inspection before heading to sea.[7]

Given this preeminence, Seville became a constant point of reference for transatlantic economic, social, and familial relationships; it was almost an extension of the Indies in the mid-1500s. It was not just the point of departure but also an important sending location as the home of one out of every six colonists and over half of the women who traveled to the New World.[8] Large migrant contingents from outside Andalucía were often spawned because a Crown official was sent forth with a large entourage. For Andalucía, by contrast, emigration "went on year in and year out without interruption."[9] In the mid-sixteenth century, this gateway city took on greater import as a site where female residents overwhelmingly hoped to gain access to a license to the Indies, where elite officials and their entourages lodged for months on end while waiting for their ships to take sail, and families prepared for journey.

FIGURE 4.1 Seville's location by the Guadalquivir River contributed to its significance as point of departure for the New World and destination for returnees

Source: Early seventeenth-century map of Seville by Samuel de Champlain courtesy of the John Carter Brown Library at Brown University.

By the 1540s, transatlantic travel was changing fast. The earliest years of conquest promised adventure and potential riches to single men. Decades into the Iberian expansion to the New World, men and women came to Peru to live and work in cities and to reunite their families. Post-conquest, women and families increasingly traveled as colonial society became more established. The influence of family informed every part of the process. The Crown wanted women of honorable status to go to Peru. Women in Seville, for their part, were drawn first through letters, then through business transactions, and finally by voyage. Men traveled continuously during this period but their motives changed. Initially, male voyagers looked for conquest adventure: they were followed by merchants, and by the late sixteenth century most men who went to Peru were servants.[10]

Numbers reveal the importance of Seville and the Andalucía region in Lima. The House of Trade records showed 1,342 conquistadors who traveled to Peru through 1539. The opening of the new Andean viceroyalty had further impact on travel. During the 1540–1559 period 179 ships sailed to Peru in contrast to 108 to Mexico. The new viceroyalty was the most popular destination of Spaniards during this period, with a total of 3,248 emigrants to Peru.[11] As was always the case, Andalucía sent the most men and women to Peru; however, in contrast to places like Mexico, Tierra Firme, and Santo Domingo, the other sending regions such as Castilla la Vieja and Extremadura sent slightly higher percentages to Peru. Peru's population had a more varied representation of emigrants from regions such as Pais Vasco, León, Castilla Nueva, Extremadura, and Castilla Vieja, and a higher representation of foreigners than New Spain.[12] Peru lost its status as favored destination from 1560 to 1579, with about 4,000 emigrants, compared to about 7,000 for New Spain.[13] In the latter two decades of the sixteenth century, however, Peru attracted more overall emigrants (3,295), more merchants (283), and more women (954) than New Spain.[14]

Interestingly, Peru began to receive its highest numbers of emigrants at the moment when the nature of emigration to the New World shifted. Instead of a predominantly male group of arrivals, it was more common to find women, single or married, and children going to places like Veracruz or Lima. As interest shifted to the goal of settlement and stable colonial society, the Spanish artisans expected they might succeed in the New World. During the period from 1540 to 1559, in particular, passengers to Peru comprised more artisans and professionals, in addition to women and children.[15] Thus, the percentages of women increased slowly during the 1540s and 1550s and then rose considerably after 1560. In the earlier period, just over half the women who arrived were single. Over half were Andalusian, with one-third of those being from the city of Seville. The percentage of female passengers rose from 16.4% between 1540 and 1559 to 28.5% from 1560 to 1579, and then dropped off slightly to 26% from 1580 to 1600.[16] In fact between 1560 and 1579, the city of Seville launched more female than male passengers.[17] The Crown was intent on making its own contributions toward the consolidation of the nuclear family as colonial stabilizer, including passing the *vida maridable* decrees. In addition, the Crown encouraged single, marriageable Spanish women to travel to these regions so that Spanish men would have European women available as marriage partners.

Seville, as a predominant sender for the region, exemplifies the connectedness of family on the Lima—Sevilla axis. Sixteenth-century people relied on the ships coming and going in order to conduct business, relay news to friends and family, and act as couriers. The voyage kept the lines of communication open and returned loved ones to Spain. When grandmother doña Isabel de Villa left 200 ducats as an inheritance for her grandson, Antonio Parrado, she specified that the money remain with her son, Francisco Hernández, until Parrado returned from the Indies.[18] Her order was with the confidence that he would board a boat in Peru and travel homeward.

Families who communicated, traveled, and lived on the Seville—Peru axis engaged in business ventures ranging from petty trade to full-blown merchandise trade. Gabriel Moreno took merchandise worth 50 ducats to the Indies from Sevilla for Doña Beatriz de Narváez. Eventually, Moreno sent her 200 reales profit.[19] Similarly, Diego de Segura carried 40 arrobas of olive oil to the Indies to sell for his aunt, the widow Francisca Segura.[20]

Schemes to make money in the Indies involved human labor as well as goods. Inés de Cordova sent her eighteen-year-old slave Francisco to the Indies with Diego Rodríguez Llano.[21] Her goal was to have Francisco earn profits under the control of Rodriguez and then see those profits returned to her in Seville. She saw the potential for this arrangement to continue after her death as she bequeathed the slave to her nephew.

Individuals in Lima often contrived to conduct business back home through trusted friends. Beatriz de Vargas Sandoval, married to Alonso Beltrán, lived in Lima in 1555, yet still owned property in Seville.[22] In order to turn a profit from renting her houses she passed over legal power for rental to three acquaintances in Seville, Juan Beltrán (likely a relative of her husband's), Beatriz Rodríguez, and Alonso Martín. Juan de Maqueda, a constable of Arequipa, visited Seville and during that time gave legal power to Pedro de Castro to buy and sell goods for him between the two cities.[23] Here the intertwined interests of family and commercial interest, which others have confirmed for merchant families, applied in smaller scale to others as well.[24]

Fathers and sons with a history of traveling between Peru and Spain used their familiarity with the terrain to create more substantial business endeavors. In 1580 Pedro de Mollinedo and Diego de Mollinedo, his *hijo natural*, made a business agreement before a Sevillian notary that Diego would serve as the clerk for his father in Lima for selling merchandise and collecting payments. The two agreed that Diego would not leave Lima without his father's express permission. Pedro agreed to provide Diego with a house, an assistant (*moco*), and two slaves, one male and one female. The assistant would be a relative, and he could give him the usual salary. This father and son business had another family link that was announced toward the end of the agreement. Diego stated that, "because I have a rich mother in Peru and we assume and have understood that when I go there she will favor me."[25] Diego's mother was not identified, but she was likely indigenous given Diego's approximate age and birth in Peru during an era when few Spanish women resided there. The Mollinedos counted on family ties to Diego's mother even in the absence of a formal marriage between his parents. Her potential investment in their company served as extra motivation to cross the Atlantic again.

In addition to mercantile interests, women might leave Seville for marriage opportunities in Peru. Leonor Ortiz lived in Arequipa, Peru, with her second husband, Juan Díaz.[26] Ortiz's Iberian-born son, Pedro, with her first husband, Roman Ruiz, remained in Seville. The documents do not reveal Pedro's age when Ruiz died, when Ortiz remarried, or when she traveled to Peru. But the basics are instructive; as a widow, Ortiz's best bet for remarriage came with a connection to the Indies. Maybe a Spaniard in Arequipa called for a wife or perhaps she made the trip to find a new husband. Ortiz's financial situation was comfortable in the New World: she owned clothes and jewelry as well as a slave; she sought to collect over 1,000 pesos owed her by various people; and she bequeathed hundreds of pesos each to her husband, an indigenous servant, her mother, and her sister. However, when Ortiz sailed for the Indies, she left behind a son she would never see again but whom she would name as her heir. Although not as frequently as fathers, mothers, too, moved from Spain in pursuit of new opportunity during the 1500s and carried with them parental obligations to their offspring who remained in Iberia.

Wills and other bequests notarized in Lima serve as additional evidence of how family obligations crisscrossed the ocean. Juan de Fuentes moved from Lima to Seville, while his parents and siblings remained in Spain. After his father's death he came into possession of houses and goods. In November 1566 he made a legal donation to Beatriz de Fuentes, his sister (perhaps a half-sister?), of his share of houses in Seville.[27] While the donation did not specify that this was intended to help her marry, a second gift from Fuentes to Beatriz about three months later suggests this may have been the motive. In January 1567, Juan authorized his father's second wife to give Beatriz a dowry of 600 ducats.[28]

In Seville residents sought out goods left them by those who had died in the Indies. Parents received and/or sought inheritance from deceased children. When Alvaro Fernández lost two sons in the New World, one of them, Diego Fernández de Yllescas, left him two bars of silver. Fernández received them in Seville and sold them for a profit of 600 ducats.[29] Siblings also filed legal claim for inheritance lost by a brother or sister in the Indies. Juan Mosquera argued that he was the legitimate heir to the estate of his brother, Lope Mosquera, since Lope's first-named heir, their mother, Juana Hernández, was deceased.[30] News of deaths from the Indies had financial as well as emotional implications.

Ties to Seville predominated in testaments from early Lima notarial records.[31] Although Spanish women were a minority in the city, they used wills to enact family roles from across the ocean. They identified themselves in relation to the families that they had left behind, even as their presence in Lima made them symbolic actors in Spanish households in the center of the viceroyalty. Leonor Sánchez, widow of Francisco López, was a native of Seville who made her testament in 1551 in Lima. She noted that she was a grandmother so she must have been upward of forty and clearly already an adult when she sailed to the New World.[32] Catalina García, wife of Diego de Ayala, likewise emigrated early to Lima as she testated from the viceregal capital in 1554.[33] In 1553 Agueda Cornejo, who hailed from Salamanca, was married to Juan de Cuevas and maintained deep connections to Spain while living in Lima. Her father in Spain was her heir (her mother was deceased). She had debts to two people in Granada, and, in the 1550s, she assumed that a courier or representative in Spain, would pay them off for her.[34] Cosma Muñoz, a Seville native, married to Francisco Zuora, a carpenter, made her will in 1561 in Lima and left 10 pesos to her mother who lived near the Puerta del Sol in Seville as well as 100 ducats to her nephew Gaspar who lived in San Salvador.

Spaniards did not have exclusive monopoly on the significance of this transatlantic connection. Lima resident Madalena de la Paz had emigrated from Seville; her identification as *morena*, or dark-skinned, typically connotes African descent and free status. She ran a busy dry goods store (*pulpería*) and accumulated decent holdings, including two slaves. In 1566 when she made her will, de la Paz named her sister, Catalina Rodríguez, a free *mulata*, as her heir.[35] De la Paz noted that Catalina had been about forty years old when the two last saw each other in Seville. De la Paz instructed her executors that in the event of her sister's death, her children should receive the estate in equal parts. Thus, Afro-Iberians likewise maintained connections through sea voyages across the Pacific and the Atlantic oceans.

Native Andeans and mestizos also used the transatlantic routes, though more often they moved from Peru to Spain, rather than the reverse. One major difference between the voyages from the New World to Iberia and those in the opposite direction was the race of its passengers. While it has generally been thought that "few criollos . . . even fewer mestizos and no indigenous had the resources and could receive licenses to travel from the Indies to Spain,"[36] indigenous slaves formed a stream of passengers from the New World to Spain, as cases to free those slaves indicate. For example, Ana de Pero Sánchez told how she had been deceived as a young girl, brought from Cuzco to Spain, and forced to serve doña Elvira de Guzmán for twenty years.[37] Pero Sánchez was an indigenous woman who sued for her freedom, and that of her son Diego, from Guzmán after the passage of the New Laws made indigenous slavery illegal. Guzmán countered that she was only keeping her for the Captain Pero Sánchez who had brought her from Peru and had never used her as a slave. This case and others like it reveal that numerous indigenous men and women made the Peru to Seville trip.

In addition, mestizos traveled to Spain at the behest of their Spanish fathers from the 1540s though at least the 1580s. While they may not have numbered in the thousands, their presence on numerous ships, if only one or two per ship, would have been a constant reminder of the way family makeup had changed with the conquest of the New World. Spain did not encourage the practice of bringing mestizo children to Europe. The Crown ordered the most elite mestizos to travel to Spain (e.g., the Pizarros, so as to limit their power), but the Crown tried to provide for mestizos in the New World. Parents, then, rather than royal officials, secured passage for their mestizo children between Peru and Spain.[38]

Another source of information that reveals the travel of indigenous and mestizo men and women to Spain is the return requests for licenses generated from Seville when people decided to return to Peru. Some of these individuals had arrived in Spain as young children at the behest of their Spanish fathers. Indigenous men also traveled to Spain to seek favors at the royal court.[39] Although the extant sources do not always reveal how they arrived in Spain, license requests show that some of them made a round trip. Diego López, an indigenous man, crossed the ocean to return to his native Trujillo de Indias from Seville in 1557.[40] The single mestiza woman Juana de los Angeles traveled from Seville to Peru in 1557.[41] When and at whose urging did Los Angeles and López go to Spain? The merchant Manuel Martín sent his mestizo son Juan Martínez, born in Cuzco to Martín and an unnamed indigenous mother, back to Peru as his factor in 1557.[42] Martín's choice of his mestizo son as his agent is understandable given the fundamental role of family ties in merchant companies between Spain and Peru.[43]

Relative Preparations

The Indies beckoned to Spaniards as a place to earn money, while ongoing connections between Seville and Peru offered detailed information about life there. Once people imagined the trip, it took extraordinary preparation to carry it out. First, those who would travel had to make plans for relatives they would leave behind. Then, they needed to secure licenses. They also needed to gather support, money, information, and fellow travelers for their journey. For all of these preparations, family ties and support proved critical.

Transatlantic travel prompted measures to ensure well-being of family members who were not leaving on the ship for the New World. Diego Sánchez, a notary en route to the Indies, drew up a document that obliged his father to care for his wife Catalina de Morales and his daughter in his absence from their home city of Seville. He specified that his father provide food, drink, clothes, shoes, house and bed, and medical attention if they fell ill. He promised to repay his father for the expenses incurred.[44] In addition, the transatlantic trip was frequently a motivation to draw up a will. Fray Antonio de Guevara advised travelers to make their testament before embarking on the trip.[45] In 1571, Simon de Ortega, originally from la Villa de Cartaya Gibraltar, noted "at present I am in the City of the Kings, Province of Peru, en route to the Kingdoms of Spain," as rationale for making his will.[46] Sánchez and Ortega's actions reveal men getting their houses in order before travel. The Crown's blessing, however, was the only paperwork required for the voyage.

To embark for the Indies one needed a license from royal officials. The Council and the King placed the heaviest burden on those applicants who were making their first voyages to the Indies, but all potential passengers needed a valid reason for going. From the Crown's perspective, relatives in the New World provided a legitimate rationale for granting people licenses to travel.

In theory, travel was highly regulated and every person or thing on a ship was registered, but in reality plenty of people and goods traversed the Atlantic Ocean without permission. Fraud occurred, both in the form of using false documents and using legitimate documents produced for another person.[47] In addition, stowaways made their way on the *navíos* sailing from Spain to the Indies. In 1571, a ship landed in Callao and authorities found two women aboard without licenses.[48] Although they likely boarded in Tierra Firme, exactly where and how these women boarded the ship is unclear from the extant documentation. Their access to the ship may have been in exchange for domestic comforts that included sexual favors. They might have been forced aboard, although the record could have reflected such a charge by the women and it did not. In the main, though, individuals hoping to *pasar a las indias* (go to the Indies) in the early modern era needed to secure a license from the Council of the Indies, with the King's approval.[49]

In the process of obtaining a license, applicants had to specify a purpose for going to the Indies or traveling to Spain. Seventy-year-old Antonio de Ávalos, a royal treasury official from Peru, sought permission to travel to Spain in 1591. He received a license to go, but only for three years, and he would lose his salary while away from Peru.[50] Although work matters could take Spaniards to the New World, most often family connections were used to justify the travel of men and women from Spain to Peru. Letters sent from the Indies to loved ones in Spain frequently served as evidence for the onerous process of getting the license.

The interconnectedness of family and money is prominent in many petitions for licenses. In one letter presented to the Crown, a mother wrote to tell her son that she was recently widowed in Peru. Because she had no one to look after her estate lest it dwindle to nothing, she suggested he take the first ship bound for Peru. In her letter she spoke directly to the licensing process as she advised him that "for this reason those Sirs [officials] will be obliged to give you license."[51]

Another common example was the use of relatives in the New World as "sponsors" for those who wished to travel. Juan de Ayala argued that his brother Pedro de Ayala had lived in Lima with his wife and children for more than fifteen years. He wished "to go and see and visit" him and presented witnesses before a notary to prove Pedro was his brother.[52] On the same day, Juan's nephew Pedro, son of the elder Pedro, followed the same procedure, asking for a license to go and visit his parents in Lima. Witnesses attested that they had seen Pedro and Inés de Ayala treat this Pedro as their son before they left for Peru.[53] Others attested to the Ayalas' presence in Peru because they had heard his letters being read aloud in Spain. After fifteen years, Ayala's tight-knit community in Lima offered a place for his brother and son to stay and might also have offered connections for employment.

Women often sought permission to join their spouses. In 1602, Doña Bernardina de Arellano explained that her husband Ldo. Espinossa had traveled to Peru and was stationed at the high court in the Charcas region, modern-day Bolivia.[54] He sent for her, she claimed, and ordered that a man by the name of Pedro de Medina serve as her escort for the trip to the Indies. Given her elite status as the wife of a Crown official, she planned to take a sizable entourage, including her children, two male servants, and two female servants. Her request for a license to travel specified the route she hoped to take; she wanted to stop first in Lisbon because she had a debt to pay and then sail to the Indies via the Río de la Plata route, which she claimed was quicker to reach Charcas. Arellano was an educated traveler who specified her rationale for going (the Crown loved to reunite Spanish families); indicated some sophistication about the undertaking by specifying her preferred route; and, by the nature of having an escort, acknowledged the potential dangers of traveling unaccompanied by her husband.

In the case of Seville widow María Varas, family connections in Peru helped her gain a second license to travel to Peru (she said she had lost the first one).[55] Her claim may have been genuine, but the House of Trade would have hesitated; a market in selling licenses thrived in Seville. Varas had evidence to make a good case, however, based on an invitation from a son in Peru who promised to help arrange a marriage for her daughter.[56]

Varas cited the great necessities she and her daughter faced in their life in Seville. In the pleas for licenses, Lima sounded like a promised land. The council granted her a new license to travel with her daughter along with two servants.

Passengers came under different regulations, especially with regard to their marital status. A ship full of merchants left for Peru in 1557 aboard the ship "Santiago" captained by Bernardo de Andino.[57] Because married men who traveled to the Indies were given licenses that explicitly restricted the amount of time they could stay in the New World, the merchant's licenses were divided by marital status. Men like Francisco Nuñez, a *vecino* of Sevilla, and Pedro Sánchez de Aguirre, a *vecino* of Granada, had licenses to travel to Peru as single men and engage in commerce in Peru. Their married shipmates, however, had licenses limited by a three-year window during which they might benefit from commerce in Peru. Melchior de Coronado from Álcala de los Yancules, Francisco de Argumendo from Xerez de la Frontera, and Andrés Mendez from Toledo all had exact dates listed on their paperwork to mark the beginning of their three-year stints. Married passenger Rodrigo Cantos de Andrade, from Zafra, Spain, left under slightly different circumstances and received a different timeframe. In the middle of an ecclesiastical suit with his wife doña María Martel, Cantos de Andrade was allowed to travel to Peru for as long as the suit lasted.[58]

Single women also needed to go to the House of Trade to pass through the licensing process.[59] Although the Crown prioritized the travel in the direction of the colonies to those who traveled in complete family groups (wives joining husbands), it also supported licenses for single women. For most of the sixteenth century, the travel of single women to Peru was viewed as necessary in order to improve the imbalance of the sex ratio and make potential Spanish wives available for encomenderos and artisans. Thus, despite concerns about the women's travel, single women were in a good position to receive a license in the early 1500s. Under the reign of Felipe II in the latter part of the 1500s, single women were more closely scrutinized based on the possibility of unseemly behavior onboard ships.[60]

Passenger lists from this same era frequently feature men requesting licenses to join their wives and children in Peru. This would seem to belie commonplace notions about family units in the 1560s, when men traveled ahead of women and children. Yet men like Martín Ruiz de Marchena asked for permission to travel to be with wives and children in Peru.[61]

Likely a merchant who traveled frequently between the Indies and Spain, Ruiz de Marchena pled to return to wife and family in Peru, indicating the established families of Spanish descent in Peru by the 1560s.

While family connections in the New World helped one attain a license, those connections had to be ones that were linked to the proper family trees in the Old World. Men and women had to prove they were *cristianos viejos* (Old Christians), using documents or testimony from their birthplace, since the Crown prohibited men and women from passing to the Indies if they had any Jewish or Muslim ancestry. So it was that Alonso Muñoz Martínez Rengifo had to prove to royal authorities that he and his wife were Old Christians in order to receive license to travel to Peru in 1551.[62] They brought witnesses to testify on their behalf. Once this status was proven, the House of Trade would assign the applicants to a ship. From there, people journeyed to Seville to make arrangements with the ship's captain for payment and packing for the voyage. While relatives putting down roots in Peru helped provide a ready sponsor, passage was only granted if Iberian families could prove the proper lineage to the satisfaction of House of Trade officials.[63]

For individuals who did not have direct family ties to Peru, the process of obtaining a license and making the trip was more challenging as the case of the unfortunate Juana Bautista shows. A native of Seville, Bautista was charged with fraud before the House of Trade in the 1560s.[64] Bautista had tried to secure a license to travel to the Indies and in the process tried to pass off her son as a daughter so as to make a more compelling case for a license. Bautista's story encompasses many of the themes of transatlantic travel and emigration. She was a widow in Seville, with three children, who believed that a move to the Indies would bring increased economic opportunity. She did not, however, have a strong family network to help her launch her travel, and her attempt ultimately failed.

Bautista lived near the Hospital of San Gregorio with three children, a daughter named Beatriz de Villavicencio and two sons, one named Pedro and one named Antonio. Her late husband Miguel de los Reyes had made armor as his trade. She visited the House of Trade to seek a license to take one son and one daughter to the Indies.[65] Yet in the licensing documents and the visit, she presented both children as young girls, disguising three-year-old son Antonio in a girl's dress. Her alleged deception was uncovered and cost jail time, a monetary fine, and banishment from the city of Seville.

Bautista defended her actions by saying Ldo. Salazar de Villa Santa, a judge for the King's high court bound for Quito, had advised her on the matter while he boarded at Bautista's house.[66] As Bautista recounted, when she asked Salazar how she could obtain a license to travel to Tierra Firme, he responded that "as she was a widow and her daughter single they would give her a license in the House of Trade so that she could pass to the Indies and that for the boy who was so little and did not really need a license that she put him in a skirt and that he pass for a girl."[67] Bautista recalled that she questioned Salazar if this was allowed, and he responded, "it wasn't bad because it wasn't hurting anybody and these things happen."[68] If Salazar did indeed say such things he was misleading Bautista; children did need licenses to make the trip, and misrepresentations before the House of Trade were ill advised, as a judge for the high court should have known. Still, Salazar supposedly presented paperwork for Bautista at the House of Trade. Salazar's alleged advice was accurate in that women had a good chance of obtaining licenses at this moment in the sixteenth century because they were sought after as wives for single Spanish men in the New World. Bautista and her daughter might have obtained licenses even without the attempt to disguise Antonio as a girl.

In the process of reviewing her documentation for a license, the court in Seville called Bautista to appear. She went, with her daughter Beatriz in tow and, instead of Antonio, a neighbor's daughter who was four or five years old. Along with these two, several men and women appeared to testify to Juana Bautista's claims. Apparently none of the witnesses alerted the House of Trade officials that something was amiss in the story. When Bautista later was asked why witnesses would not have said anything about the child's identity she claimed that while they knew her well, they rarely entered her house and thus would not know whether she had sons or daughters. She then complicated her testimony by adding that when neighbors came by the house she had Antonio dressed as a girl. Initially, the deceit went undetected and Bautista made plans to travel to the New World.

Sometime later, however, Bautista's misrepresentation of her child's gender was prosecuted. Sadly for Bautista, her hope of traveling to the New World with her young children was dashed. Moreover, the ship they had planned to board burned while in port, with her goods already loaded.[69] Bautista lost her belongings, and then, her son, Antonio, the one at the heart of the alleged fraud, died due to illness.

Bautista's case is a most unfortunate one. But Bautista's dream of going to Peru and her actions to make it a reality illustrate how attractive a destination Peru was to residents of Seville. If the process of getting there was one that relied on family ties, it was also a destination sought after as a place to sustain family and to create new branches on the family tree. Men and women who could turn to family for support in applying for a license had a stronger rationale to receive a go-ahead from the Crown than those advised by strangers. The support of relatives would carry through from the licensing process to the trip itself.

To Journey with Honor

Families were no strangers to travel when conquest began. Pre-conquest patterns of travel on the Iberian peninsula must have had an impact on migration patterns to the New World.[70] Although the decision to leave home was not novel for men or women, the length, expense, and inherent dangers of a trip to the Indies were dramatically different than other destinations. Moreover, preserving the honor of women on this transatlantic voyage emerges as a dominant theme for this era.

As they looked ahead, passengers relied on experienced family members to provide accurate information about what it was like to cross the ocean and what to bring to make the trip bearable. They reported how much it would cost and, when possible, provided funds. They also gave plenty of advice about how to stay safe. Between Seville and Lima, people stood to lose money, honor, and even their lives. Ldo. Esteban Marañon, who served the Crown as a constable for the Real Audiencia in Lima, recounted to the Council of the Indies how he lost two of his four children in the family's journey between Spain and Lima.[71] The majority of passengers did not share Marañon's tragic fate, yet they did suffer through difficult journeys. As New World relatives prepared Old World loved ones for the crossing, they pictured their own transatlantic voyages. As one woman told her sister, "God is my witness how much I want to see you [in Peru], but the journey is so long and there are so many needs one suffers that I fear [for you]."[72] They had experience with the ocean travel, the conditions of the ships, and the behavior of passengers and crew. Husbands writing from Peru, for instance, knew well the expenses and hardships associated with the trip. So when Francisco de Ortega wrote to his wife, "I am sending 500 pesos for you to use to make good provisions [for the trip] . . . and bring with you your aunt as well as a maid who will serve you," he aimed to provide for her comfort, safety, and morals on the journey.[73] Protecting lives, goods, and honor during travel was of paramount concern to family members.

The phrase "to cross the Atlantic" implies a trip with one single direct route over the waters. In reality, the "crossing" was a series of ship voyages between one port and another, and it had distinct routes in both the parts of the ocean it covered and the ports it visited. Stopping in port cities offered crew and passengers alike a release. There they would have the chance to move about freely and seek out new social, sexual, and economic opportunities.

The system of maritime transport between Spain and the Indies developed and became regularized between 1492 and the late sixteenth century when Spain's empire in the New World reached the height of its power. The particular arrangement that became the norm was for a group of merchant ships to travel in the company of several military ships in order to secure their cargo of precious metals from Mexico and Spain. Known eventually as the Carrera de Indias, this began in the 1540s and was regularized by royal ordinances in the 1560s.[74] The discovery of silver at Potosí was a particular rationale for needing to protect the ships, as was the increase of pirate vessels intent on attacking the Spanish gains. French corsairs were the main risk between 1520 and 1559, while English and Dutch corsairs frequently attacked from 1560 through the mid-seventeenth century.[75] These marauders took some passengers to serve as crew or, in the case of women, to use as sexual slaves, but primarily sought goods from merchant ships.

Passengers to the New World all departed from the Andalusian coast. For crews on these ships, the round trip between Seville and the New World usually took nine to ten months. Their first stop was the port coast in Spain, and some ten days later they reached the Canary Islands, where they stopped for a short stay. The next leg of the journey was the Atlantic Ocean. The Tierra Firme bound ships would reach the Antilles in about one month. From there travel usually slowed and vessels took a two-week period to negotiate the waters heading south to Cartagena de Indias. They waited there until news arrived that shipments of silver were ready to leave Callao. Then, the ships set sail for Nombre de Dios in Panama. While Nombre de Dios was the original port for all Tierra Firme (Central American) voyages, over time Cartagena became an important way station due to favorable factors including a healthier climate.[76] After the travelers reached Panama, everyone journeyed overland to the southern coast of Panama, where ports received ships from Callao, Lima's port, and took on passengers and goods for the return trip.

This was the half-way point of the trip to Peru. From Panama the passage to Peru could last four months as fleets battled against headwinds. The Panama to Lima journey was divided up by stops at ports along the coast of South America such as Paita. The length of this Pacific voyage is highlighted by attempts of relatives to provide extra money for their loved ones to access in Tierra Firme. When the *ollero* Hernán González received word that his wife Ana López was en route from Spain to Peru, he empowered ship captain Alonso Rodríguez to collect 200 pesos on a debt owed him by a resident of Panama and give the money to Ana for the portion of her journey from Panama to Lima.[77] González's attempt to ensure the financial comfort of his wife during her passage was a critical part of ensuring her safety and success on the journey. Mateo de Almonazir went one step further for his wife, Catalina Millán de Bohórquez.[78] He promised 1,000 ducats would be waiting for her when she arrived at Tierra Firme. Further, Almonazir promised to meet Millán and their daughters in the port of Paita, a location on the coast of the Pacific north of Callao, which made for a somewhat shorter trip than if she were going to Lima.

The return voyage from the New World to Spain had its own route. The voyage between Callao and Panama lasted three weeks. From there ships took two or three weeks to reach Havana. After the stop in the port of Havana, captains headed for the Azores, a month-long journey. From the Azores to the Guadalquivir River, ships journeyed another month. All routes were lengthy and these voyages faced complications from weather, sea conditions, and corsairs.

Relatives took an interest in the vessels that their family members used. One brother advised his sister to be sure to come on "a good nao," suggesting that some ships may have gained a reputation for being better quality than others, perhaps for their build or their captain.[79] The two main types of ships used in the 1500s were smaller ones called caravels and the *naos* (figure 4.2). Caravels had a cargo hold big enough for 60 to 80 *toneladas* (early modern weight associated with shipping), while *naos* carried 100 *toneladas*. Royal officials and their retinue frequently traveled on galleons, larger ships with a capacity of 550 *toneladas*. The galleon was the official Armada ship that accompanied merchant ships on the crossing.[80]

FIGURE 4.2 Travelers setting sail for the New World made serious preparations as they considered their lengthy journey in vessels like these

Source: Six sailing ships from the 1545 *Carta de Navegar* by Pedro de Medina courtesy of the John Carter Brown Library at Brown University.

Most ships attempted to carry as much merchandise and as many passengers as possible to maximize profits. In a 1534 attempt to limit the weight on ships in order to make them safer, the Council of Indies mandated that no more than sixty passengers could travel for every 100 *toneladas* on board.[81] In addition to these people, a crew of fifteen to twenty would have been on board.[82]

In terms of sleeping quarters, privacy, and diet, money mattered. Ship captains aimed to maximize the use of all space on board, so those who could afford to do so rented the wooden passenger "cabins" built, in somewhat ramshackle form, on the top deck. Captains charged high rates to those who could afford to pay for the privacy afforded by these cabins. For other passengers and crew, the trunks they brought on board served as their storage, chair, and table. Many slept on mere sleeping pads rolled out on the deck. The typical passage took place in summer months during which sleeping above deck was preferable to the heat and stale air below. Descriptions from this era detail the horrid odors that worsened as the trip progressed. Rodents and bugs also thrived below deck. Most passengers became seasick on the initial leg of the trip, though it varied in its intensity. The only remedy was the passage of time to adjust one's system to life at sea.

Passengers came on board with as much as they were allowed or as much as they could afford to bring. When Alonso de Sigura traveled to the Indies his father Rodrigo de Cantillana, a *vecino* of Sevilla, gave him 130 ducats for clothing and provisions for the trip.[83] For some this included trunks full of belongings, food, and drink. Provisions varied with class status. While a ship's crew ate salted meat, chickpeas, rice, biscuits and cheese, passengers might eat a more varied diet including dried fruits, fruit preserves, honey, and capers, and they might bring animals such as chickens or pigs to kill for fresh meat during the voyage. All brought rations of water and wine for consumption on the long journey.[84] A few passengers also carried goods to fulfill requests from relatives. Diego Hurtado told his sister Juana to bring him shirts and linen as those items were more costly in Peru than in Seville.[85]

The group on board had plenty of time to pass together. While the longest stretch without a stop in a port was about one month, the entire trip from beginning to end lasted months. All sorts of pleasantries and intrigues happened en route. People entertained themselves through card games, chess, and reading, which often took the form of one person reading aloud to a group. Others on board engaged in activities such as gambling and sexual liaisons, as well as criminal activities such as theft and rape. Life on board the ship was a microcosm of all the hierarchies and power struggles of life in Iberian cities. Confinement to a limited space in fact heightened many of these tensions. Punishment on board was strict and swift.

Family members viewed the time on the ship journey as potentially more dangerous to female relatives than to males. Women risked disease, shipwreck, and pirates equally along with male passengers, but they put their reputations at risk when they traveled. Not every woman on board was of the same class status and might not have had the same intentions of behavior on the ship. Scholars have commented on this in a variety of ways, often in light-hearted fashion: "the unattached women who went to America attracted by its riches were not straitlaced ladies ... for that reason, they constituted appropriate aspirants to share a fleeting love affair with members of the crew."[86] This comment speaks to the reasonable suggestion that much sexual activity on board ships could have been consensual. Perhaps chaperones were not traveling solely to protect women from men but also to protect the women from themselves. The comment also highlights the issue of class. Female servants, many of whom traveled to the Indies during this era, did not always receive the same protections as their masters since honor was understood by many to be a purview of the elite.[87]

Relatives who ordered wives, sisters, mothers, or daughters to the Indies took their honor as great cause for concern. The scenario of a married woman traveling in the company of a trusted relative played out time and again in the second half of the sixteenth century as Spanish women went to Peru to set up house with their husbands. When Pero Nuñes, an engraver, asked his wife, Juana Çamorana, to join him in Lima for *vida maridable*, she hoped to bring her brother. Camorana would be traveling in the company of the couple's eight-year-old daughter Marina, and Sebastián Çamorana, as a brother/uncle, made a suitable companion. Juana Camorana petitioned for license for all three, and they were soon on their way.[88]

Men writing to daughters or sisters emphasized that this journey must be made honorably. Hernando del Río told his daughters to travel from Seville to Peru after the death of their mother. He sent money with a cousin who he promised would accompany the girls on the voyage. Del Río warned the girls, though, that if they could find the wife of a judge or governor they had better go in her care "because the road is so long."[89]

Men went to great lengths to offer women security for their stay in Seville while awaiting departure. Above all, women needed to be in the company of a man of the same class, preferably a married man, who could protect them. From Mexico, Juan Cabeza de Vaca wrote his sister "that the women who are honorable, honorable they leave and arrive."[90]

Precautions to protect female relatives' honor existed in part because rumors spread about the sexual violence women suffered during ship voyages to the New World. In a 1527 example, the widow Maria García sailed from Santo Domingo to Seville aboard a ship captained by Francisco García of Triana. García alleged that Captain García made unwanted advances toward her during the ship's voyage. García claimed, and witnesses attested, that the Captain entered her cabin at night. Voyagers heard her saying, "get off me."[91] Her case underscores the particular sense of vulnerability that women felt when they made seafaring journeys to the New World. The realities of the potential for rape and assault prompted the emergence of a code of behaviors around the transport of wives, daughters, and other female relatives to the New World as structured by race and class.

DESPITE POTENTIAL HARDSHIPS, the pull of a voyage across the ocean remained strong throughout the 1500s. Conquest, Crown appointments, family commitments, marriage options, and financial opportunity all drew men and women from Spain to Peru. The return voyage was made for many of the same reasons, in addition to commercial or legal business possible only in the metropole.

To make the voyage, individuals needed family support. Husbands provided a rationale for wives to travel to the New World, as did mothers for sons. Fathers provided money for children to buy provisions for the voyage. And women needed respectable males, preferably relatives, to accompany them on the multi-month journey to the Peru. Men and women also viewed their voyages as related to family goals and obligations. Women hoped for themselves or their daughters to find better marriage options across the Atlantic. Men used parents, siblings, or uncles already established in Peru to help them gain a rosier financial future than what they envisioned in Spain. An ocean crossing was necessary to work toward any of these goals. The specifics of the voyage itself—its length, physical discomfort, and potential dangers—reinforce just how great an undertaking this was even for people who went willingly. No one person could have viewed this transatlantic voyage as pure adventure. In the sixteenth century, it took courage, planning, money, and an ability to imagine a path on the other side of the ocean in order to "pasar a las Indias."

When the journey ended, relatives had to establish themselves in Peru. Emerging from the small boats that brought travelers to land were wives not glimpsed for years, children who were just babies when their fathers left, and fully grown sisters and brothers perhaps with families of their own. Moreover, the relatives who arrived from Spain often met new family members—wives met step-children, sons and daughters met half-brothers and sisters. When Francisco de Adrada traveled to Peru in 1557 on a return trip, he had with him his Spanish wife and children as well as his mestizo son fathered with the indigenous Madalena.[92] The son, Diego, probably had been taken from his mother at a young age and brought to Spain, and his voyage with the entire family suggests a role for Diego in the family. Because the voyage could keep family connected and eventually led to family reunions, it served to extend family along with empire. New contexts challenged family structures; *mestizaje* and concubinage shaped families' experiences and interactions. The overall analysis of this transatlantic journey revolves around family networks and how important they were for people to make the journey to the New World and to survive (or thrive) in doing so. The connections to a Spanish society in Iberia were embodied in the journey itself. Once in Peru, however much Iberian culture influenced daily life, there was no mistaking that Peru was not Spain and just as the landscape was different, so too were colonial families, with family members and customs that could only be found in the Andes.

5

Adaptation

CREATING THE CUSTOMS
OF THE COLONIAL FAMILY

THE VOYAGES OF the 1540s and 1550s characterize these as decades pregnant with mobility and change. Increased numbers of Spaniards arrived
in Peru, including married and single women as well as a steady stream
of men. Mestizo children traveled in the opposite direction, from Peru
to Spain. Whether or not families had a direct transatlantic experience,
the impacts of migration and *mestizaje* reverberated through Andean cities. Colonial life forged variations of family structure and family practices
that were at once tied to Spain (by ships, money and goods, relatives, and
laws) and adapted to the particulars of an emerging colonial society in
Peru. By the latter decades of the sixteenth century, mestizo children of
the first generation in Peru were adults, perhaps with children of their
own. Continued high mobility and racial and cultural mixture between
the 1560s and the 1580s shaped blended urban families and fictive kin
networks.[1]

One family in the growing colonial center of Arequipa hints at how
customary practices of family adapted to a new era. In a household along
the Río Chirí in the 1560s, indigenous husband and wife Juan and Leonor
López lived with their daughter Mariquita and perhaps occasionally with
Leonor's son, Graviel. The couple was born in Cuzco, probably during the
1520s when Huascar and Atahualpa battled for control of the Inca empire
and before the arrival of Francisco Pizarro and his soldiers to Cajamarca.
Both used titles that indicated family ties to Inca nobility. Leonor was
described as "india palla" (princess) and Juan as an "indio ynga" (Inca).
She was the daughter of don Alonso Mytima Yupanqui and a mother

with the indigenous name Cayo.² The couple married in the 1550s. Years before her marriage to Juan, Leonor bore a child with Spaniard Martín López de Carvajal for whom she likely worked. She might have known Juan from their natal Cuzco or López de Carvajal could have arranged the marriage. López had donated to her a part of a *chacra* and a house on that land. Indeed the Spaniard would not be alone in his actions if he had offered her the property as a dowry for marrying Juan. As Spanish legal code dictated, Leonor's legitimate daughter was primary heir of her estate (known in legal language as universal heir). For her son, whose out-of-wedlock birth signaled a distinct legal status, Leonor offered a different kind of inheritance; she wanted her son to have two silver *cocos* with gold trim, a valuable bequest associated with indigenous masculinity in the Andes.³

The López family illustrates important themes about the shape of family in sixteenth-century Peru, in particular how families operated in response to and within the rule of Spanish systems.⁴ These families defy categorization into "indigenous" or "Spanish." Many families had members who were mestizo, whether the household was headed by a Spaniard, an indigenous man, or an indigenous woman. Thus, Peru's sixteenth-century urban households blended mestizo, indigenous, and Spanish relatives in roles that included affection, service, and caretaking. As in the case of Leonor López, indigenous women could be awarded a dowry by a Spanish employer. When a Spaniard asked a relative to care for his mestizo child or an indigenous father consented to have his child apprenticed in a Spanish home, these actions promoted households that blended family. These examples underscore the complexities of urban colonial households that both changed the shape of families and afforded new possibilities. Blended families, with blood and fictive ties to indigenous and African peoples as well as mixed race peoples, meant that neat lines about relationships based on the *sistema de castas* or legitimacy did not exist. The notion of *mestizaje* as a process of cultural mixing proves useful as a way of thinking through how people in individual family roles and families as units adapted to colonial society in Peru. This does not mean the family was mestizo-identified, but rather that a process of *mestizaje* took place by which elements of both ancestry and culture for Iberian and native Andean engaged in the dynamic of creating and sustaining families in this era.⁵ The *mestizaje* of family emerges through individuals' experiences, material culture, legal practices, and flow of resources.

This chapter examines family units in the second half of the six-teenth century that reveal both the texture of quotidian family experi-ences and the overall patterns emergent in colonial family customs. Examples from the viceregal center of Lima and the provincial city of Arequipa offer comparison of cities hundreds of miles apart yet linked through colonial bureaucracy and economy. City life highlights the diversity of families as well as the colonial economic forces that influenced labor, dowry, and marriage. Within both locations sev-eral themes emerge. First, the chapter focuses on indigenous-headed family units, by far the most numerous demographically speaking, to show how they negotiated certain aspects of family life. It next ana-lyzes the role of dowries and dowry sponsorship in the path to mar-riage. Providing dowries for indigenous mothers, as well as young indigenous and mestizo women, was a primary concern not only of parents but also of a broader network including former sexual part-ners, employers, and kin. The chapter then turns to what might prac-tically be called "blended families" in late sixteenth-century Andean cities. Indigenous or mestizos who married Spaniards nurtured con-nections to indigenous families. Important horizontal ties (mestizo siblings or connections between half-siblings) fueled bicultural fam-ily networks. Some mestizos in the highest levels of colonial society used their half-Spanish identity to elevate their social status.[6] A more resounding characteristic of urban sixteenth-century families was that networks were based on blood connections regardless of ethnic identity and legitimacy status. In addition to the pragmatic adoption of Spanish institutions like godparenthood, wills, and dowries, indig-enous families shaped colonial society by including non-indigenous members (mestizos and Spaniards).

Urban Indigenous Families in the Colonial Era

Indigenous families' connections through marriage, birth, or parentage appear in wills and dowries and show a multitude of family arrangements during the post-1550 period. They offer an important glimpse into fami-lies whose members, like el Inca Garcilaso de la Vega or Francisca Pizarro, experienced integration with but not domination by Spanish families. Given the demographics, indigenous–indigenous marriages continued apace, and indigenous family networks were adapting to and connected to Spaniards, Spanish law, and institutions.

At a fundamental level of adaption to colonial rule, many indigenous couples married under the jurisdiction of the Catholic Church.[7] Alonso Cama was a native of Collaguas in the Colca region of Peru, near Arequipa.[8] He and Isabel Tintaguarme married and had two children, Periquito and Madalena. The couple acquired thirty sheep and llamas over the course of their marriage. Alonso's brother, Tomás Cama, kept the livestock for the couple in Coporaque. When Alonso made his will in Arequipa in 1571 he relied on a priest from San Francisco church, the same church where he hoped to be buried, to translate his Quechua into Spanish. As these indigenous men and women married and formed households, their lives become entwined with innovations of Spanish rule and with its representative agents (figure 5.1).

Yet the customs of indigenous family practices continued. One clear trend from sixteenth-century family and household units is that children frequently came before marriage and outside of it as well. Don Cristóbal Vilca Yanque, the cacique principal of Cavana, married doña Inés, also

FIGURE 5.1 Indigenous weddings and family customs adapted to the urban colonial context. This nineteenth-century painting depicts an indigenous couple being married by a priest in the company of relatives and criollo godparents. *La boda indígena. Serie Costumbres de Huaygaoc. Anonimo Cajamarquino, ca. 1860–1900*

Source: Courtesy of the Museo de Arte de Lima. Donación Nestlé del Perú.

of Cavana.[9] While the couple had no children together (at least none that survived infancy), don Cristóbal had numerous children both prior to and after his marriage to doña Inés. The church officiated their religious marriage, but other family customs were at play in their lives. Extant documents suggest it was common for indigenous men to have children prior to (in addition to outside of) their formal church marriage to their indigenous wives. This practice bears resemblance to the tradition of multiple wives among Inca elites.[10] Recall that individuals were fitting Inca family histories of multiple wives into a Spanish tradition of "legitimate" and "favorite" wives. Vilca Yanque's family shows how the pre-conquest practices continued even as linguistic shifts appeared in colonial court cases. For some indigenous observers, the actions of Spanish men in Peru who had children with indigenous lovers before marrying other women might have looked similar to their own tradition of multiple wives.

The practice of Spanish men having children with indigenous women outside of marriage signified additional instances of children being born prior to marriage.[11] Typically Spanish men later married Spanish, though sometimes indigenous, women. While this may not be surprising for men, it was also the case for many women. Specifically, when indigenous women had children with Spaniards, this did not signify they would marry the men who impregnated them, nor did it mean they would never marry. Much has been made about the importance of elite women hiding out-of-wedlock pregnancies to preserve public honor or losing their chance to marry if such a pregnancy was exposed.[12] For the indigenous Catalina Anpo giving birth to two sons, Francisco and Juan, with the Spaniard Lucas Pastor did not prevent her marriage to Tarma native Lázaro Quispe.[13] Quipse, Anpo, and her two sons lived together in Lima. Moreover, Anpo found herself the recipient of 800 pesos from Pastor when he predeceased her. Anpo's relationships suggest that colonial circumstances shaped her early life, but did not ultimately preclude her marrying an indigenous man and creating a family with him. The money she inherited from Pastor signals economic ties long after the initial relationship. Her family was like many of the era, a blended family from distinct sexual relationships of men and women, some of whom married, some of whom did not.

The ability of an indigenous mother to engage the legal system was critical for the experience of her mestizo children. Some mothers actively lobbied to influence their children's lives even when the forces of Spanish and paternal power were aligned against them. These mothers used wills to protect their natural children. Doña Francisca was a native elite who had high-ranking parents on both sides and was mother to an *hija natural*. If her claims were accurate, her father, don Pedro Alvarado Cayatopa, governor of Chachapoyas to Guanuco, had been appointed by no less than supreme Inca ruler Huayna Capac. Her mother, Catalina Chuqui Tecla, was an elite as well as the sister of the cacique of Chachapoyas.[14] In 1574 doña Francisca gave birth to a daughter, Marequita, whose father was a Spaniard named Juan García. Only four months after giving birth, doña Francisca was making her will as she lay sick in Lima at the home of Juan de Saracho. Juan García, she heard, was in Chachapoyas at the time. She thus named Saracho as the girl's curador in the absence of Juan García and named Marequita as her universal heir. She clarified her daughter's identity as a mestiza and not an *india*. Doña Francisca stated García's paternity of Marequita at three separate places in her will (this insistence was unusual). In this direct manner she used the will to force García to accept responsibility for the little girl. Because she was not married, doña Francisca had limited power with which to compel Juan García to act. Since the will made public her "secret" of illegitimate birth, she had likely used gossip to spread the word as well. Going to the notary and dictating a testament was an additional attempt to gain some measure of control over the situation.

Just as notaries and written documents might be used to wield power over child support, so too was the legal system used to control relationships between husbands and wives by indigenous families and Spaniards alike.[15] In the case of one couple, the husband Felipe Manasca, an indigenous man from Guayacondo, gave legal power to Hernando Vica Alaya to be his wife's keeper in his absence.[16] Manasca had to travel to Lima for an extended stay, and while he was away from home he wanted his wife to be under lock-and-key control of Vica Alaya. He specified that Vica Alaya was in charge of his wife, should ensure that she did not leave his presence or house, and gave him supreme power to restrain her should she attempt to leave his company. Vica Alaya chose Spanish law to impose the concept of *recogimiento* on his wife (and a Spaniard to enforce it). Some indigenous families may have relied on caciques to adjudicate such disputes through customary indigenous law without leaving a written record. Vica Alaya might have already tried to use indigenous structures, or he might have been applying two forms of law at once to control his wife.[17] If seeking to use all forms of law available to him, Vica Alaya challenged the notion of the two republics (one indigenous, one Spanish) of the colonial world.

Once indigenous couples engaged with Spanish notaries or courts they not only expanded the sphere of laws and customs that could impact their families but their choices could have unforeseen consequences. Vica Alaya used Spanish practice to limit his wife's movement and connections to her indigenous kin. Indigenous women, too, used Spanish judicial institutions to address marital situations. Inés Mormo, a native of Guanca, attempted to gain legal power to go before the ecclesiastical court and ask for a divorce and separation from Cristóbal Gutiérrez, mestizo, her husband.[18] She claimed that Gutiérrez did not fulfill *vida maridable* with her. Women denounced wandering husbands and addressed ecclesiastical courts to seek divorce.

The flip side of the potential support within colonial institutions was the power a magistrate or court could wield against colonial subjects. Especially for indigenous people with lower status, encounters with the Spanish economy and law could strike at the autonomy of the indigenous family. When indigenous husbands gave permission for wives and daughters to engage with the colonial economy this directly affected the families. The indigenous Juan allowed his wife Beatriz of Chumbevilca to be a nanny for Pablo, the young son of Juan de Quiroz.[19] Her work took her from her home to the house of a stranger and into a sphere of influence of a Spanish man. Moreover, instances arose in which Spanish authorities intervened and took power away from parents, such as the case of six-year-old Angelina and her father, indigenous Antón, from Machagua in Condesuyo.[20] The Crown's attorney for indigenous peoples, the *protector de naturales*, Francisco de Santander, represented Angelina, who was described as having no mother. Santander alleged that Angelina's interest was best served through a six-year contract to serve a Spanish couple, Diego de Torres and Lucía López. The contract required her to be fed, clothed and paid four pesos a year, terms akin to an apprentice or service contract for young boys or adult female servants. The difference, in comparison to the arrangement between Hernando and Antonio Balderrama, below, was that here the Crown took the place of the indigenous parent, as Angelina's father was stripped of his paternal authority. The attorney employed stereotypical language about indigenous men to prove that Antón was unable to fulfill the obligations of a father.[21] Antón, in Santander's representation, was a "drunken Indian" with "bad habits" who treated Angelina poorly. In contrast, Santander praised Torres and López; Diego de Torres was a "married and honorable man" and Angelina was the recipient of the couple's "charity." The document might have legalized a de facto circumstance whereby Angelina was a servant in the house of the Spanish couple. Perhaps this case reached the written record because Antón objected to his daughter's situation in the Spanish household. He might have missed her, wanted control over her, or asked to be paid for her labor. In the end, however, a Spanish couple's control of Angelina was given higher priority than the girl's indigenous father.

Indigenous couples' experiences as parents changed with urbanization and colonization. Husband and wife Hernando and María gave permission for their fifteen-year-old daughter Isabel to work for Spaniard Antonio de Balderrama. The couple lived with their family in Paucarpata, a town outside of Arequipa, and Isabel would be working inside the city for Balderrama. Her contract (*asiento*) agreed to pay her in kind but also a sum of eight pesos per year that were to be given not to Isabel but to "the mother of the said *india* for her sustenance and that of the rest of her children since they are poor."[22] This arrangement reveals multiple, interconnected points about economy, family, and colonialism. First, families living in or in close proximity to colonial cities had economic pressures to move wives/mothers and children into jobs or apprenticeships that placed them into Spanish homes. Second, from the perspective of the parents, allowing their daughter to work in a Spanish household helped Hernando and María's indigenous household in the short term (assuming her meager salary was paid). Further, the couple asserted parental power by performing the notarial ritual to allow Isabel to work in the home of a Spaniard. Still, this act confirmed an arrangement that moved Isabel into an urban sphere where her family's networks may have been weakened. In other words, parents lost a degree of control over a child. Finally, for young girls, the wages from these jobs frequently formed the basis for their dowries when they reached marriageable age. The process by which marriage was facilitated was shifting to include new actors.

Notarized dowries and incentives for marriage still originated within indigenous family networks, though extant records are scarce.[23] In Arequipa, Francisca Daqui a Chachapoya woman, used her will to provide a dowry and play a heavy-handed role in matchmaking.[24] She bequeathed an urban lot, splitting the property among a cherished servant, an old indigenous woman named Catalina, and a young girl named Isabelilla who Francisca had raised. She wanted to give her half the lot, but also arrange a marriage between the young girl and her nephew, Bauptista Chachapoya of Cuzco. She did allow that "if he does not want to come and marry her, she can marry anyone she wants." Yet Bauptista did move from

Cuzco to Arequipa and marry Isabel, thus ensuring that Isabel received her property bequest and that kin ties among the Chachapoya were linked for another generation. The keen interest in arranging partnerships highlights how the specific marriage networks being forged were as important as the institution itself.

Extending the Family Tree through the Dowry

The case of Daqui's dowry is a strong example of the continuities of indigenous matchmaking for future generations. Few extant records shed light on these arrangements, though many more must have occurred in the sixteenth century. Dowries, a widespread Spanish legal and customary obligation to daughters and other young women of marriageable age, were embedded within the making of families and the process of colonialism in the mid- to late sixteenth-century Peru. For indigenous women, it was extremely common to have former masters provide dowries. When dowries went to indigenous women from Spaniards it represented a colonial change to marriage patterns and even an intrusion of the Spanish system into the indigenous family structure. Still, this process often created or cemented additional ties between Spanish individuals and indigenous or mestizo women. Yet Spaniards, mestizos, and indigenous people collectively embraced dowries as part of the process of marriage in the second half of the sixteenth century. Just as indigenous individuals were routinely engaging in court cases to protect land interests by this time, so too did the prospect of dowry emerge as a practical way to approach the transfer of goods at marriage. Moreover, because women kept control of the property through Spanish property laws, certain objects or land could stay with an indigenous family. The mechanisms by which dowries were paid represent a process that was strong enough to become customary yet malleable enough to evolve with changes in colonial society. Its predominance in urban centers is another example of how indigenous peoples become increasingly linked to the colonial economy since they used material goods with peso value in urban markets to constitute a dowry.

In contrast to the Daqui case, in which an indigenous woman with means offered a dowry for an indigenous girl to marry, many indigenous couples who married in cities did so with a dowry provided by a Spanish male. In 1557, Diego Pérez, *indio ladino*, and Catalina, *india*, vowed to marry. Lorenco de León, a portero from Arequipa, offered as a dowry a small piece of urban property, cloth, items of clothing, and two llamas valued at 257 pesos total. Pérez, a native of Guaylas, was a tailor in Arequipa. Catalina's identity was not disclosed beyond her first name, but the sponsorship of this marriage by Lorenco de León suggests she may have had ties through domestic service to his family or his household.[25] Spanish men, including employers and former sexual partners, as well as Spanish women gave dowries to indigenous women to support their marriages.[26]

The indigenous Francisca Malla married Francisco Mostare in Lima with a modest dowry of 20 pesos that came from her master.[27] In all likelihood, Malla earned the twenty pesos that her master handed over to Mostare in her name. It can appear as a "gift," but for most non-elite women, the dowry provided by a master was accumulated payment for months or even years of hard work. The indigenous Isabel Quispe Rimache had a substantially larger dowry than Malla, with 300 pesos from her master Felipe de León when she married the swordmaker Juan Ramírez in Lima.[28] The will of a Spanish master, Gonzalo de Vega, indicates that these men did not necessarily specify who their indigenous servants were to marry. Rather they provided some form of dowry that would allow female servants to marry, an act which many viewed as their obligation. De Vega gave the indigenous Leonor 100 pesos and 100 head of cattle "so that she can marry."[29] The context in which the money changed hands, from master to servant through a notarized document mentioning dowry, emphasizes the structures of marriage and family rather than making a direct acknowledgment of labor.

Spanish men also appear in the record giving dowries for their mestiza daughters. Indeed, the dowry could be an important vehicle for a father to marry an out-of-wedlock daughter to a man of higher status. Such was the case for Francisca de Ávila, born around 1540 to hidalgo Diego Fernández, from Spain and living in Arequipa, and the indigenous Isabel Palla of Cuzco. She married a legitimate Spaniard, Joan García Jiménez from the Villa de Higuera Fregenal, with a 2,000-peso dowry in coins given by her father.[30]

Young mestiza women in the 1550s and 1560s increasingly received dowries from Spaniards who were their masters. In one exceptional case, the mestiza *hija natural* Elvira Hernández compiled funds from three different Spanish masters to form her dowry of 662 pesos for marriage to Seville native Juan de los Reyes.[31] Elvira had been a servant for one household, a nanny for another, and a wet-nurse for a third. In order to serve as a wet nurse, Elvira must also have been a mother.

For parents, especially fathers, to give dowries makes sense from the perspective of custom and of law. For others, including but not exclusively masters, to give dowries demands greater attention. Spaniards promoted dowry and marriage assiduously in the mid- to late sixteenth century with material and financial gifts that seemed to speak to something akin to parental obligation. Surrogates cared for children in Spain whose parents traveled to the New World and for mestizos whose traveling fathers wanted them raised in Spanish homes. They again stepped in around the issue of dowry with concrete support that acknowledged both nuture on their part as well as the service provided by the young women.[32] This trend emerged from a combination of labor needs, household customs, and collective social responsibility for helping young women to marry well, especially mestizas who might be viewed as innocent victims of conquest and their heritage. The role of surrogate obligations emerges alongside the story of the sixteenth-century family.

In 1564 Arequipa, merchant Antonio Hernández offered a dowry to Catalina Hernández de Olea, the daughter of Pedro de Olea and María, a native of Guanaco. Hernández's household contained three mestizo natural girls and his two daughters as well as Catalina. The dowry suggests that a single mother, María, linked all these girls. Catalina's name drew on "Olea" from her father and "Hernández" from the house where she was raised. For her marriage, he promised her a slave named Joana, a half-*solar* near the Santo Domingo monastery in Arequipa, and 125 pesos' worth of household goods and textiles for a dowry totaling 1,000 pesos. Hernández offered Catalina the dowry for "the love that I have had and have for having raised her in the company of my two natural daughters."[33] While Catalina may have labored in his house, Hernández was less explicit about that than he was about his affection for her. Still, many young mestizas who received assistance were those who worked in the houses of Spaniards (or were the children of servants). These young girls probably stemmed from the same group of children who were moved around from the houses of their mothers into the households of Spaniards.[34] The wording of a dowry was equally telling about commitment and obligation to the bride as well its economic value. When Juan Nuñez, a shoemaker and *hijo natural* of Duarte Nuñez, married Ana de Pineda, an *hija natural* who lived in Chuquiabo, they received a 400-peso dowry from Juan Velázquez de Aceveda. Velázquez made the gift for "the love he had for the said Ana de Pineda and for having had her in his house thirteen years and for the service that in this time she gave him and his wife Inés de Cavanas."[35]

In contrast to the previous example, this was more explicitly linked to labor. Moreover, the dowry contained a clause wherein groom Juan Nuñez promised that he would not ask for any more money for Ana's thirteen years of service.

While the dowry is usually associated with gifts given by fathers to daughters, or men to young women, this gender breakdown was not exclusive. Women also gave dowries to support the marriages of their daughters as well as those of young women in their care or in their service. The mestiza Madalena Hernández received a dowry from Leonor de Lorono in the sum of 477 pesos for services Hernández provided since the age of seven.[36] The sum offered in the dowry was explicitly a payment of money owed for services rendered. The two women shared the surname de Lorono, so Leonor may have been an aunt by marriage or Madalena may have adopted the name having grown up in the house. The dowry served to combine payment of services in a situation where there was no contract with the paternal/maternal role of carrying out the legal act of the dowry. Hernández was fortunate because she also received a 400-peso *arras* from her husband-to-be Luis de Monico, also mestizo.[37] Like so many of the situations created in this colonial context, however, the provision for the dowry by de Lorono blurred the line between customary family obligations and the provision for those obligations by a surrogate.

Given men's mobility in this era, it is not surprising that women or employers (as surrogate fathers) often stepped in to provide dowries. The *mulata* Catalina, daughter of the manumitted slave Inés, received a bequest of 60 pesos to use explicitly for her dowry, "and not for anything else," from Madalena de la Paz, a free *morena*.[38] De la Paz noted that she offered the dowry money because she had raised the girl. Madalena and Inés likely shared social, work, or kin ties. The extant examples of dowries for women of African descent are especially limited for the sixteenth century, but this example highlights how the Spanish community's efforts to assist mestizo daughters in marriage reverberated among other groups in the city of Lima. That a woman gave the dowry shows they understood just how important the dowry was for women's prospects.

Some young mestizos in Lima received support from relatives other than their parents and from their employers in the form of donations or bequests made in a will. Doña Elvira de Orellana lived outside Lima on a *chacara* with her husband Sebastián Ginovés.[39] The two had married in 1564 but had no children. When Orellana dictated her will, she gave small bequests to many servants who worked on her property or in her house. She offered one larger bequest—of 100 pesos—to Domingo, the two-year-old mestizo son of Guillermo Díaz. Domingo was in her household, and though she did not clarify why, Orellana wanted to ensure the toddler was given religious instruction and fed and clothed with the money from her estate. Her actions mimicked those of Spanish women in Seville during this era, when Francisca Pérez gave donations to children who were raised in her home but were not blood relations. To Francisca, who she "raised" and who "served her," she bequeathed 6,000 maravedis (small coins), a skirt and a shawl for her dowry.[40] For individuals who had no biological children, these surrogate sons and daughters served an important role, in the words of one scholar, as "artificial descendants."[41]

In some cases indigenous or mestiza women struggled to gain control of funds they viewed as rightfully theirs through labor and then promised in a dowry. In 1580, Catalina Guaco, long married, tried to claim her 300-peso dowry from Pedro de Villafuente. Guaco wanted the money to dower her own daughter Juana González. The notarized *carta de promesa* (promissory note) that Catalina Guaco presented along with her husband Juan Quispe suggests that Villafuente had stood in front of the couple and perhaps a notary to promise 300 pesos to Catalina Guaco when she married.[42] The couple's daughter had reached the critical age where the promise of a dowry was necessary for Juana González to marry Juan Daca de Olivares.

Dowries also came with strings attached that allowed the givers to promote a particular family structure in the next generation. María de Rojas had complex plans for the daughter of her longtime indigenous servant Madalena, a native of Nicaragua.[43] While Madalena received the plot of corn in the backyard garden as a gesture for her good services, Madalena's daughter María, fathered by a Spaniard from Truxillo, received 100 pesos so that she could travel to Spain. In the interim María was to live in the house of Francisca de Quiroz who was to serve as her teacher until she went to Spain. Her will does not specify any relation of Francisca de Quiroz to the daughter, so perhaps María would act as her servant while being schooled in Catholic doctrine and Spanish manners. Interestingly, Madalena was still alive and would presumably be separated from her daughter. Further, María de Rojas made assumptions about her power over the girl as if she were a slave. Although neither girl was a blood relation to her, María de Rojas used her will to send this mestiza to Spain, which was typical for Spanish fathers to have done for their mestiza daughters. María's scheme was representative of its 1554 execution date by the notary, first for the presence of the native Nicaraguan servant and, second, for the choice to send the mestizo girl to Spain.

Blended Families through Blood and Obligation

As these dowry examples illustrate, Spanish, mestizo, and indigenous men and women were deeply embedded in each other's family lives. The pre-Columbian model of Inca families marrying into "foreign" families to dominate ceased to function in the post-conquest era as it had in the pre-conquest era, yet families exhibited a weave of blood lines, culture, and material obligations that show how Spanish, mestizo, and indigenous individuals intermingled, especially in urban areas. Through horizontal and vertical ties as well as across generation, social class, and ethnic markers, the web of the colonial family was so intricate that no colonial schemes of hierarchy could fully capture it.[44]

In one primary form of connection, Spanish men and indigenous women married.[45] Because the norm was out-of-wedlock Spanish–native unions, those married couples who lived in the cities of the Andes are sometimes overlooked. The most common scenario was for Spanish men to wed indigenous women; in a few documented cases Spanish women married indigenous men. Catholic marriage was more common between elite native women and Spaniards because only marriage could ensure legal access to property. For example, in the Andes, Alonso de Mesa married the Inca noblewoman doña Catalina Huaco Ocllo in 1552. Frequently the motivation for contracting marriage across cultures in this era was not love, but rather strategic social and economic positioning. In the case of elite native women, Spanish suitors looked to the acquisition of lands and laborers tied to the woman's family.

In select cases, indigenous families may have provided attractive dowries that benefited enterprising Spanish grooms. Although the entire colonial system was established on a tribute system whereby indigenous communities supported the Spanish, within that system individual trade networks emerged. For instance, the indigenous Ana Velázquez had a dowry of clothing and a slave when she married Simón Ginovés.[46] Her husband immediately employed the clothing for a colonial trade venture. Clothing was an important part of dowries and valuable possessions for indigenous women, so this clothing represented economic value more than it did Velázquez's personal wardrobe.[47] He sent the clothing to Chile with a compatriot, Antonio Ginovés. Antonio Ginovés was married to a mestiza in Chile; whether this offered him connections for distribution of the clothing is unclear, though many indigenous women had kin connections to textile production. The larger picture that emerges from this example of a trade exchange indicates the complex cultural mixtures in colonial families in the sixteenth century. Simón Ginovés was not a singular Spanish man married to an indigenous woman who provided a connection to indigenous economy; he traded with a compatriot who married a mestiza, a woman also likely tied into indigenous family connections. Together these men suggest the groups of mixed families to be more significant than previously allowed.[48] In this instance, trade in cloth demanded connections to indigenous networks, and marriage facilitated those connections. Marriage simultaneously reinforced a union and a household in which language, dress, custom, and material culture represented the *mestizaje* of the colonial era.

Another element of family history that bears revisiting is the idea that those in the first generation of conquest had more cohabitation relationships than marriage and more illegitimate than legitimate children.[49] This would mean that if a father had an out-of-wedlock relationship with an indigenous woman, his mestizo son would be likely to do the same. The extant cases for the sixteenth century show much variation on this point and confirm the uselessness of such a dichotomy in family history. The actions of a father did not readily predict those of a son. Diego de Aguilera had several sons and daughters in Toledo, Spain where he was married. In Peru, he had a son Francisco with the indigenous Catalina of Chachapoyas, as well as a mestizo son named Cristóbal de Aguilera. Son Francisco de Aguilera became a tailor, and, through marriage, unlike his father, he legitimized his relationship with the indigenous Leonor, a native of Cuzco.[50] The couple had several children, all of whom died in infancy. As was customary in the sixteenth-century Andes, both Francisco and Leonor had children with other partners before they married. Leonor had a daughter named María with the Spaniard Luis Villareal. Aguilera had a son, Cristóbal de Aguilera, with the indigenous María of Guacrachucro, and Cristóbal lived in his father's home. María, Aguilera's daughter, was born to another Leonor, and in keeping with a well-established custom, María lived in the home of the Spanish woman doña María Castellona. Since Francisco had an indigenous mother and an indigenous wife it seems unusual that he would have kept his daughter from living in a household run by an indigenous woman; perhaps his decision to house María with Castellona was made to appease a request by his wife.

The model of integrated family that has garnered more attention is that in which a mestizo entered a Spanish family, such as the case of doña María Castellona. If indigenous families accepting Spanish men or mestizo children are considered, the emergent picture of the colonial urban family changes. Tracing property transmission through wills and dowries of mestizos or indigenous women who have married or had children with Spanish men reveals a series of flows that involve family members: individuals circulate in and out of relationships and households, property moves from one person or generation to another. In this model, the Spanish outsider often provides material benefits, but does not anchor the family.

The idea that children either lived wholly with Spanish relatives or wholly with indigenous relatives is problematic because a significant group of children experienced both. Elvira, an indigenous woman from Jauja, was a market vendor, a mother, and a wife.[51] Her belongings, including *llicllas* (native Andean dresses) and *cocos* (typical Andean drinking vessels), bespoke her indigenous identity. Elvira's daughter Lorenza was born out of wedlock to Rafael Durán, who acknowledged the girl. Her daughter's bicultural heritage dated Elvira's coming of age to a post-1532 era. Later in life she married Juan de Popayán. Elvira's will noted that she sold goods in the market. The link between economic activity and the ability of an indigenous woman to provide a dowry to a daughter born out-of-wedlock was fundamental. Even before she made a will, Elvira had already given away some of her possessions. She wanted her daughter Lorenza to inherit her *llicllas*. To her husband, Juan de Popayán, she gave two pairs of silver *cocos*.[52] Notably, Elvira named Juan Martín Durán as an executor in the will; given his last name it is conceivable that he was a brother or son of Rafael. Elvira's choice of Martín Durán as an executor suggests a trust that the blood connection to this out-of-wedlock mestiza would ensure that her daughter received what was due her from the inheritance. The continued connection of both Elvira to her daughter and of her daughter to her Spanish relatives suggests that for some children, family was not an either/or experience.

Beyond the family roles of mother or father, wife or husband, son or daughter, stepdaughter and so on, these groupings of mixed families within a household shared combined customs, food, material objects, and languages. In Arequipa, doña Elvira, *india natural* del Cuzco, lived with her Spanish husband Marcos Báez.[53] The couple married ca. 1554 and had no children. They had a store with an inventory of clothing, wine, and coca. Of the couples' personal items, the scribe listed "shirts and dresses." Interestingly, however, the will lists a *mamachumbe*, other *chumbes*, and *topos*, items doña Elvira would have used to fasten *acsus* and *llicllas*. One of the *bestidos* or dresses noted by the scribe was made of *cumbe*, the Andean cloth used to create *acsus*. The Spanish words of the scribe are complicated by the other contents of the will; in all likelihood, even as the wife of a Spaniard, doña Elvira displayed her indigenous fashions.[54] The couple represented a family united through Catholic marriage with two cultural heritages.

Every once in a while the words transcribed by notaries allow intimate glimpses of couples relating to one another and parents providing for children. They show how distinct languages, material culture, and universal sentiments formed a currency of the colonial family. In 1567 the indigenous Leonor, native Guanca, had a child with a Spanish man and later married another, Francisco Buelta, with whom she lived in Arequipa.[55] She brought a dowry to the marriage that consisted of a garden plot and part of a *solar* situated by the Rio Chirí. On one side, the land bordered a garden plot owned by Pedro Pizarro with whom she had her son, Baltasar, and on the other, it connected to a lot owned by Francisca, a fellow Guanca. The proximity of their gardens hints at the many possible ties between Leonor and Pizarro; in addition to being a partner and bearing his son, perhaps she was his servant and the garden plot was a dowry of sorts. It was with Francisco Buelta, however, that Leonor had an official Catholic marriage. The two did not have children or an economically productive marriage. Leonor's will noted that they had some financial gains, but lost them all. Still, "out of love" she bequeathed him their huts (*buhíos*) on the garden plot as well as part of the land.

Leonor's worldly goods were similar to those found in wills of other indigenous women of her era.[56] She had six *lliquillas*, five *acsus*, three *chumbes*, and one *mamachumbe*. The textiles ranged from the fine *vicuna* to top-of-the-line *cumbe*, to run-of-the-mill *pano negro*. One of the *chumbes* was specified as being a "*chumbe guanca*" or *guanca*-style weaving pattern that represented her native ethnic identity. Her other goods included leather boots, a blanket, and a silver mirror. She also had traditional dress pins, one gold *topo*, and two silver *topos*. These material objects are reminders that even in the Peruvian cities of the 1560s and 1570s, indigenous material culture was the norm and, further, that it played a role in generational ties between family members.

When Leonor enumerated what her executors, Juan Ynga and Cristóbal de Cardenas, should sell at auction, she also noted what should be kept for her son. She specified that Baltasar receive her *chumbe guanca*, one of the *lliquillas*, her silver mirror, and the *topos*. Leonor kept these objects through her relationship (however defined) to Pedro Pizarro, her move from Cuzco to Arequipa, and her marriage to Francisco. These items were both practical, as she dressed in them, and symbolic, for they held significance as identifiers of her culture and kin. As she made preparations for a Catholic burial in the main Cathedral of Arequipa, she sent objects to her son to preserve her heritage and identity in his memory.

Around the same time Leonor was remembering her mestizo son Baltasar in her will, another young man was naming his indigenous mother as his heir. Alonso de Escobar was a Cuzco native born to Beatriz, native Cañare, and Joan de Escobar soon after the Spanish arrival in Cuzco.[57] Alonso de Escobar's trails of business exchanges, debts, and credit transactions reached deep into urban Cuzco and necessitated his travels to Arequipa. He had a relationship with an indigenous woman, also named Beatriz of Asangaro, a woman he probably met en route to Arequipa, given Asangaro's location on the other side of Lake Titicaca from Cuzco. He honored this Beatriz by donating to her a plot of terraced agricultural land (*andén*). His heir was his mother, who stood to inherit her son's belongings including, importantly, "certain goods and estate" promised in the will of his father Joan de Escobar. In this case, the goods of the Spanish father were channeled to the indigenous mother through the mestizo son. Alonso's biological family unit reflects how short-term partnerships between Spanish men and indigenous women had long-term social and economic implications.

In cases where a relationship to Spanish men provided economic assistance to indigenous women, select individual family cases provide contrast with those mestizos who were moved from their natal homes. Women acquired money or material goods through relationships with Spanish men, but they also accumulated wealth through family connections (inheritance) and activities in the urban economy. Some indigenous peoples, especially women, were accused of becoming "Hispanicized Indians," or acculturated to Spanish culture in ways directly related to family networks.[58] The documents do not reveal when women might have been opportunistic with Spanish men or when their feelings were genuine, but they speak to how mestizo children created links between a Spanish man and indigenous woman that continued after a relationship ended.[59]

The family of doña Ana Palla enjoyed material benefits from their connections to her Spanish partners. Her situation offers a detailed view of life for the many women who raised their mestizo children in their own household. Never married, Palla raised three daughters: Francisca and Ana, her children with Martín López de la Serna, and María, fathered by Antón Díaz de Corrales.[60] Both fathers had died by 1586. María inherited goods from her father, including the house in which Palla lived. Securing the house cost Palla time and energy in a legal suit; keeping the house in good repair cost her, in her words, "many more gold pesos." She argued that other heirs of Antón Díaz de Corrales attempted to take the house away, but since she had spent so much money on it and on raising his daughter, she was confident in the claim that María keep the property.

After Francisca married a man named Luis de Vargas, Ana stayed at home and helped her mother. Palla noted that Ana "has always been obedient," and she honored Ana's service with the bequest of her clothing, dresses, and other goods.[61] By and large these goods were the traditional Andean female dress: *llicllas* (dresses), *anacos* (shawls), and *chumbes* (belts), along with *topos* (dress pins). She emphasized that María de Corrales should not have access to these goods, and "if necessary I will give them to her [Ana] by way of the fifth (*mejora*)."[62] Francisca had received a dowry when she married; María and Ana were named as heirs. Yet it was Ana, adult yet not married, who looms large in the will as responsible and obedient. She was named executor for her mother and tutor for María. And she was the recipient of her mother's cherished cultural identity through her indigenous clothing.

The elevated social and economic status of Palla's indigenous networks and her quasi-kin relationships with her former Spanish partners put her among a relative elite compared to many indigenous mothers of mestizos. Palla followed Spanish legal traditions as she used her will effectively to account for material obligations to her three daughters. She had dowered Francisca; she had initiated legal action to protect the inheritance from María's Spanish father; she offered recompense to Ana for her help and companionship through the years. She did not marry; she gave birth to, and raised, three girls, and she did right by them in terms of legal obligation. In a sense, giving the girls each other was important, for sibling networks proved fundamental to colonial family structures.

Sibling relationships for indigenous, mestizos, and Spaniards were conduits of support through to the next generation. If indigenous men and women recognized that Spanish structures of law and economy challenged the makeup of indigenous families, they still used some of those same mechanisms to strengthen family ties through wills. In the case of Beatriz Sisa Ocllo, she reinforced strong ties to siblings, nieces, and nephews.[63] Beatriz was born in Cuzco and lived in Arequipa after marrying Juan Ynga. Since she had been married for ten years when she dictated her will in 1571, she was probably born in Cuzco after conquest, perhaps close to 1540. Her status was considerable given that she had five indigenous servants, all women. She owned a house and a plot of land in Arequipa, while her husband Juan owned rural land. Moreover, the material objects in her will include not only clothing but also valuable pairs of silver *cocos* and silver and gold *topos*. Sisa Ocllo had no children, at least none who survived, but in her will she remembered two nephews, Topari Mache and Topayapangue, who lived in La Paz, and a niece, Tocto, who lived in Copacabana with her parents. Sisa bequeathed to each of the three a pair of silver *cocos*. These bequests of symbolic Andean objects strengthened family ties between Sisa and her siblings and moved the ritual drinking vessels to the next generation. At the same time, Sisa's will forged tight connections to her spouse and his children (born prior to their marriage) through naming her husband as her heir and leaving bequests for both of his daughters. From a legal standpoint, Sisa could have named her siblings as her heirs above her husband, but she chose not to do so. Juan Ynga's children, Juana and Isabel, were young women; Isabel had already married. In a gesture rich with tradition, emotion, and value, Sisa left them traditional clothing, all woven of the high-quality *cumbe* cloth. Like Ana Palla's gift of her indigenous clothing to her daughter, Sisa's gifts of clothing and the *cocos* serve as stark reminders that family histories were not one-way in Hispanicization. Even in the 1570s and 1580s, from which these examples date, and beyond, these objects served as part of an indigenous legacy that colonial families used to anchor themselves in a changing world.

Mestizo children often appear in discourse as a mass group or in isolation from a family tree, but in fact they were neither. Many in Peru had mestizo siblings or half-siblings, and they supported each other in making their livelihoods, creating community, and caring for children. In Lima mestizo María Beltrán married Juan de Segovia Maldonado with whom she had a son, Cristóbal, in 1565.[64] Beltrán was the daughter of

Juana *india* of Nicaragua and Cristóbal Beltrán (after whom her son likely was named). The record does not reveal if Beltrán lived with her mother, if she was born in Nicaragua and then brought to Lima, or if her mother had been brought to Lima as a servant or slave by her father during the earliest years of Spanish presence in Lima. One of her bequests reveals that Juana, her mother, had another child named Mateo. Given her mention of him in her will, María maintained some ties with this brother or half-brother. Like many other mestizos, María had a sibling connection that was outside the legal boundaries of family yet within the practice of family in sixteenth-century Lima.

Older siblings might be called on to care for younger ones. Lima's administrator of *"mulatos, mestizos y naturales"* appeared before a notary to place a seven-year-old mestiza girl Madalena in the employ of Gaspar de Herrera in exchange for food, clothing, and, eventually, a 150 peso dowry. The girl appeared to be, in effect, going to work for her dowry. A note in the document's margin, however, says that it "did not pass" and no signature from the notary appears on the page. The scribe jotted down that "a married sister of the girl appeared with fifty pesos to pledge for her dowry."[65] Whether this sister rescued her young sibling from a worse fate or acted out of self-interest (perhaps to hire her out), her ability to provide a dowry satisfied official concern for the girl and symbolized an element of control as well as security.

In the progression of lives, brothers and sisters became aunts and uncles who could care for nieces and nephews. Elvira Hernández de Herrera, a mestizo *hija natural*, was born in Potosí to Hernández Gómez de Herrera and the indigenous Isabel, but eventually moved to Lima.[66] Although married to a Spaniard, Gaspar Gutiérrez de Benavides, Elvira had a son, Geronimo Hernández, out of wedlock with Antonio de Montemayor. The major piece of property in her estate was a *chacra* in Potosí that she co-owned with her brother Diego Hernández de Herrera. Elvira entrusted her brother, not her husband, to come and claim the young Gerónimo after her death. She highlighted their blood connection as she sought a caring adult for the boy. In these seemingly mundane examples, families of mixed Iberian and Andean descent support one other to protect the family unit. For all the changes of the sixteenth century, relatives still functioned within parameters of the larger unit of family.

Family business was not only about caretaking, but about the business of enterprise. Sisters María and Juana de Carvajal conducted petty urban trade together.[67] María enjoyed numerous sustained networks with, in particular, indigenous and African women in Lima. Her sister Juana was a close companion who knew all the same people that she did and could, for instance, identify the indigenous Inés Chilca or the *negra* Catalina to whom María owed money. The shared network of friends or potential clients whom María relied on Juana to identify suggests the sisters may have conducted business together. María, the daughter of Nicolás de Alcochel and Isabel Chilca, was herself the mother of Teresa, an *hija natural* born to a Spaniard. She saved silver pesos (thirty-one of them) in a silver chest, wore Spanish-style clothes, and collected jewelry, including gold necklaces and earrings. Her will showed bequests of these items to Juana and Teresa, and in a gesture that suggests either they were living companions or that she hoped Juana would care for Teresa, she bequeathed her bed, mattresses, and white linens to the two of them.

An example with more explicit economic ties comes from Arequipa where half-brothers set up a business together in 1581. Pedro de Bozmediano, the legitimate son of Juan de Quiroz Bozmediano, received lands that he placed in the care of his half-brothers, both *hijos naturales* of Juan de Bozmediano, for a period of ten years.[68] He gave them use of the lands to cultivate in exchange for a percentage of the profit. The brothers, Luis de Quiroz and Cristóbal de Quiroz, were of age to conduct business without a representative so they were probably over twenty-five years old.[69] At any rate, the family links between these half-brothers created economic opportunities for all three children. That Pedro was owner of the lands, donated to him by his father and mother, doña Isabel de Mediano, shows the preference for legitimate children and the hierarchies that existed within families. These hierarchies were not exclusive; Luis and Cristóbal were embraced as useful and trusted members of a family business. Yet that embrace had its limit.

Three generations in the family of Juan de Rojas also illustrate that legitimate children were given preference, but again show *hijos naturales* as part of the family structure. Around 1560, Spaniard Juan de Rojas and Cuzco native Inés de Coya Cica Ocllo had a natural son, Diego.[70] The couple lived in Tucumán, but Diego Rojas eventually moved to La Plata. Rojas, then, had daughters Magdalena and Inés de Rojas with the indigenous Barvola when both were single. Barvola predeceased Diego. In 1580 he married Magdalena de Villafuera and the pair had a daughter, Francisca, and four sons, Diego, Martín, and twins Baltasar and Gaspar. Yet his involvement in the lives, and specifically the marriages, of his natural daughters Magdalena and Inés suggests they grew up in close proximity.

When Magdalena married Juan de la Puente without her father's permission, he gave her a small piece of land in Mamaota as a dowry in acknowledgment of the "service" she had shown him. This language sounded much like that an employer would use in granting a dowry to his former servant. Perhaps Magdalena lived as a servant in his home to wait on Rojas's wife and legitimate children. The treatment of Magdalena's sister undermines this interpretation, however. When Inés grew to adulthood Diego married her to Juan López de Huriosa with a dowry of 4,000 pesos because, in his words, she "married with my blessing." This substantial lump sum ranked admirably among dowries of this era.[71] Notwithstanding his own birth as an *hijo natural*, Rojas had five children within his marriage to Magdalena de Villafuera who would be his heirs.

Rojas provided for all of his children, those born both in and out of marriage in varying degrees. Further, these children may have grown up in the same household. The presence of mestizo natural children in the father's legitimate family was not unusual. At times, it was the death of a father that would prompt this blended family as men attempted to ensure their out-of-wedlock children were cared for after their death. For Diego Hernández, a native of Spain, it was crucial that his wife Isabel Cespedes care for his natural mestizo son Francisco. Not only did he ask for her to raise him, but he also specified that she "treat him as my own son and for the love of God [that she] bring him up under her hand."[72]

Relatives other than wives were drawn into the care of mestizo children. Francisca Cambero, a Spanish woman who formed part of the wave of female migration to Peru, moved from Spain to Lima around the 1540s.[73] Her son Alonso de Cea was twelve years old when she left him in her mother's house in Antequera to travel to the New World. Widowed by 1553, Cambero likely traveled to Lima with her husband Bartolomé de Cea, and left their young son behind. She had family connections in Lima through a brother Gines Cambero, who was a clergyman, and a brother-in-law Francisco Martínez de Cea in Lima. Moreover, she raised her brother's daughter, the mestiza Gerónima Cambero as part of her household. Francisca carefully considered Gerómina's long-term well-being. In preparing for her death, Cambero promised Gerónima 100 gold pesos as well as her clothing and specified the name of a trusted woman, Isabel de Quintanilla, who could keep the girl "until her father Gines Cambero comes to get her."[74] As her heir, she named her son Alonso in Spain. She continued to acknowledge her maternal obligations to the boy and sent him support from across the ocean. Moreover, developments in her family in Peru turned her into a custodian for her niece, born to a native Cuzco woman in the early post-conquest era.

The family obligations to these children extended to Spanish step-mothers or half-siblings if a father died. In 1558, Hernando del Salto asked his legitimate daughter María del Salto to care for his eight-year-old mestiza daughter Inés Sica del Salto.[75] He also asked that his mestizo son, Juan del Salto, fall under the legal power of María and her husband Antón de Rodríguez. He asked the couple to teach the boy to write, read, and count; for Inés he left a dowry of cows and their calves. Salto made no mention of either child's mother in his will and shifted the responsibility for these two children to their half-sister.

One dying father asked his wife and children in Spain to care for his unborn out-of-wedlock child. Alvaro de Solano and Ursula Hernández married in Spain and had two children, Francisco Solano and Inés Gutiérrez. Solano left Spain for the New World where he became involved in a relationship with Juana de Alfaro, a single woman. Solano bequeathed 150 pesos to Alfaro in his will because Alfaro was pregnant, allegedly with his child. Solano asked his heirs, Francisco and Inés, to "favor, raise, and feed" the baby as if it were his son or daughter.[76] Solano ordered his son Francisco to travel to Lima to collect his estate and then return to Spain and divide it with his sister Inés. Solano's confession in his will and his donation to Alfaro "to unburden my conscience" were common practice for men with families in both the Old and New Worlds.[77] How closely Francisco and Inés heeded their father's plea is unknown, but theirs was not the only family legacy to include siblings half a world away. These examples highlight how a family of primarily Spanish makeup in either Peru or Spain shifted with colonial expansion and how these shifts might be felt most keenly at key moments, such as a father's death.

ADAPTATIONS OF FAMILIES such as these have often been overlooked in an attempt to follow either exclusively Spanish or exclusively indigenous families, when, in fact, blended families were mainstream in cities such as Lima and Arequipa. By the 1580s and the 1590s, families were two and three generations removed from conquest. Indigenous communities witnessed a loss of members due to migration. People moved to cities to find work and in the process they witnessed changes in marriage patterns and marriage sponsors. Indigenous families, especially those in urban areas, increasingly created ties to Spanish families and households. When Spanish masters provided dowries for young indigenous and mestiza women, they played a role in family networks that blended labor and affection. Sibling ties were an important form of connection for indigenous families as well as mestizos. Half-brothers joined together in business networks. Half-sisters became guardians and members of the same household. Women traveling from Spain to Peru were asked to raise the children of indigenous women. In mid- to late sixteenth-century Peru, families identified in historical scholarship as "Spanish families" often included children born outside of marriage who were claimed by Spanish fathers and not sent to Iberia. Family structure allowed for some flexibility with regard to these relationships, as in the case of Francisca Cambero and her mestiza niece Gerónima. Much has been made of how these blended families were not really families and mestizos were incorporated as servants. While mestizos were not always treated with the same respect and affection as their legitimate siblings, neither were they ignored. Their physical presence and integration into economic and social networks show they inhabited a space within the boundaries of the colonial family in sixteenth-century Peru.

These family networks reveal how families connected through blood and/or marriage were engaged in a continuous flow of goods, services, and emotions. Parents and children; spouses and unmarried couples who shared parenting; brothers and sisters—all of their actions belie the dichotomies of legitimate–illegitimate and married–cohabitating because colonial Andeans had adapted the meaning of the institution of family to their changing universe through a process of *mestizaje*.

6

Legacy

RECOGNITION, INHERITANCE, AND LAW
ON THE COLONIAL FAMILY TREE

BESIDES HIS TWO illegitimate sons in Arequipa, Diego Hernández de
Talavera had a daughter in Spain and a granddaughter in Arequipa, both
named María. The two Marías shared a name and a family, but were
separated by a generation, by an ocean, by birth status, and by racial
identity. Hernández's legal obligation to his legitimate daughter, María
Cornejo, who was a lifelong resident of Spain, was to name her as his universal heir. In the division of his estate, Hernández acknowledged that
María was his legitimate daughter. However, he cautioned that should
she attempt to take all of his estate on the grounds that sons, Nicolás
and Diego, were *hijos naturales*, he would authorize a legal donation to
the sons as their part of the inheritance.[1] His attempt to create an equal
partition among natural and legitimate children (not permissible within
the Spanish legal system) suggests a deep sense of obligation to his sons
owing to their long-term proximity. In challenging family legal codes,
Hernández was not alone in creating a last will and testament to fit the
complexities of his family life. In fact, his will exemplifies how the colonial family often stretched across the Atlantic with children on two con-
tinents and mothers from two cultures, and had to grapple with the legal
issue of how fathers should or could care for their families legally as well
as culturally.

Although Diego Hernández was legally obliged to his daughter in
Spain, this did not diminish the obligations he felt to his sons and granddaughter in Peru. This complex tale of transatlantic family began some
forty years earlier, during the same year that Pizarro moved his troops

into the Andes to conquer the Inca empire, when Diego Hernández married Teresa Cornejo in Spain. Teresa died eleven months into the marriage, while María was a newborn. Afterwards, Hernández, like many Spanish men of his generation, voyaged to Peru, where he worked as a shoemaker in Arequipa.[2] Hernández left his daughter María in the care of her paternal aunt, Catalina Sánchez, in the Villa of Talavera. Teresa Cornejo's estate went toward the costs of raising María. Sometime around 1565, Hernández furnished an 800-peso dowry and sent it across the Atlantic so his daughter could enter a convent.

During the intervening decades, Hernández's family grew as he fathered Diego and Nicolás, with the indigenous Luisa, a native of Nicaragua. Luisa, Hernández was careful to note, was a "free woman with whom I could marry," though he never did.[3] She received indigenous clothing and land from Hernández in his will. He claimed to have donated the lot to her years earlier, but used the occasion of his will to ratify it, presumably to ensure that Luisa would enjoy ownership of the property without legal challenges. Her ownership was limited by the restriction that it would pass to their sons after her death; his provisions thus gave her the means to support herself during her lifetime but the gift was not one of movable property.

Hernández acknowledged the boys as his sons and actively participated in their lives. When Nicolás found himself in a legal bind after wounding a man by the name of Montalvan his father helped him pay legal costs.[4] And, after Nicolás fathered María, Hernández gave his only grandchild four grown mares and fifty goats from his ranch.[5] For Hernández, who gave these gifts to his granddaughter María "for the love that I have for her," these animals provided a good dowry for the girl's eventual marriage. Hernández appointed Diego an executor of his will; he did not make Nicolás, the seemingly more adventurous son, a co-executor. Diego and Nicolás came of age in an era when the Crown eyed mestizos with suspicion; in Hernández's will, however, these men were not rebellious youth, but sons and the Andean roots of Hernández's family tree.[6] The more expected examples of Spanish fathers caring for mestizo children involve their provisions for daughters; Hernández's family shows his abiding attachments to both male and female descendants.[7] This chapter focuses explicitly on choices about inheritance made in accordance with and in tension with the law. Fathers like Hernández crafted their own scenarios for the future of their family trees through donations, bequests, and requests within notarized documents. Significantly, their actions along with the language they used merged custom and law as they shaped the colonial family.

Parents showed a range of responses to their legal and cultural obligations as well as their intentions for the future generation. Here the focus is on concepts of fatherhood as demonstrated by the language parents used in notarial documents. Next, an analysis of wills reveals patterns about how and when natural children became heirs. Having established the general patterns, the chapter then looks at individual cases of parents who provided for children when they had two families, such as men with children on both sides of the Atlantic or a family of legitimate children in conjunction with a family of children born out of wedlock. Extant information favors those of Spanish ancestry as well as fathers, who more frequently used legal means available to dictate children's destinies than did mothers. The few examples that do exist of indigenous parents and Spanish mothers reveal important shared norms of gifting by parents for their children. Finally, the chapter illuminates the "willful unlawfulness" of some parents who ignored or challenged legal codes to protect their gifts to out-of-wedlock children. These individuals tried to figure out how to creatively accommodate the law to their particular familial situation.[8]

A Father's Recognition

Because Diego Hernández recognized his paternity of María, Diego, and Nicolás, there was no question about who their father was. In the absence of such a claim, the sixteenth century offered no scientific means to prove paternity. Fatherhood was understood in terms of a set of culturally and legally determined characteristics.[9] A woman might claim that a particular man was the father of her child, as did Isabel who acknowledged *cuenta carnal* with Antonio de Medina.[10] On rare occasions, men, too, acknowledged paternity by specifically referring to the physical act of sex, as Pedro Rolón did when he noted his *conocimiento* of the indigenous Catalina.[11] Often proof lay in the suggestion of physical resemblance. In addition to the undeniably important physical component of fathering a child, men became known as fathers by family, kin, and peers by reproducing a commonly held set of behaviors: caring for a child during one's life, leaving a bequest to care for the child in the future, naming a child as a universal heir, or expressing love. A legal recognition of paternity by the father notwithstanding, any and all of the above might be considered proof.

A significant legal case from the sixteenth century highlights how colonial society made the case for paternity by connecting a man's behavior while alive and provisions after death in tandem with physical recognition. Juan Pizarro dictated a will in 1536 wherein he acknowledged the "services" of an unnamed indigenous woman who had a daughter, Francisca.[12] Pizarro did not claim this child as his daughter, but should she reach marriageable age he ordered that she receive a dowry of 2,000 ducats.[13] Pizarro died in the Manco Capac rebellion of 1536 so, even if he wanted to, he was never able to set the record straight on the issue of paternity. If he had survived into the 1540s, he might well have done what many of his contemporaries did in their old age: acknowledge her and provide a donation. Without clarity, a legal case emerged by the 1570s to prove the paternity of the adult Francisca.

The interrogatory for the case contained leading questions to prove resemblance as well as Pizarro's fulfillment of a paternal obligation. Pizarro's attorney asked witnesses if "the said doña Francisca Pizarro looks much like her father Juan Pizarro in the physiognomy of her face."[14] Further, witnesses attested to a physical resemblance, specifically a "large mole and other secrets," that proved her descent from Juan Pizarro.[15] Álonso Davila, a member of the conquest cohort of Juan Pizarro, stated that he "saw that when she was a girl . . . her father said many times with her in front of many people 'yes this is my daughter and she looks a lot like me and she has the markings that I have.'"[16] A different witness made reference to the large mole on her neck as a sign that she was the daughter of Juan Pizarro.[17] Testified one witness, "No person who had seen the said doña Francisca upon looking at her face and the shape of her face would say she wasn't the daughter of the said Joan Pizarro for she looks so much like him."[18] These men assured the court that a girl who had been two years old when her father passed away looked exactly like him, despite not having seen him in thirty years.

While physical resemblance was tantamount to blood ties, it was not enough; witness testimony from the 1500s centered on how a father should act. Those pursuing the case attempted to show that Pizarro was indeed her father by certain actions: "he recognized her as his daughter and named and fed and clothed her and the necessary and said to many people that she was his daughter."[19] In this single line the verbs enumerate the multiple elements of being a father. To the issue of the young Juana being fed and clothed, the witness recounted that Juana was raised in a Spanish household at the cost of her deceased father's estate (as befitting the daughter of a conquistador). The most compelling evidence, however, was the handsome dowry he left her in his 1536 will. This act fulfilled a fundamental paternal obligation.

The Pizarro case was lengthy because he never recognized his daughter with paper and pen in front of a notary, despite all else he allegedly did. Indeed, the legal implications of a child's birth status for her ability to inherit from her father were of paramount significance as Spanish legal code reached across the Atlantic. Within legitimate family, sons and daughters inherited equally and thus one could assume the obligations and hopes of fathers to their children for the next generation would be fulfilled through the last will and testament.[20] Laws had also developed to address inheritance for children born out of wedlock. In general, Spanish law required that legitimate children inherit an estate, unless they had committed some unforgivable act. If a testator had no legitimate children, his or her parents were the next in line to inherit an estate. If a man or woman had children born outside of wedlock, these children could inherit the estate, but certain conditions had to be in place. First, the child had to have been born when both parents were unmarried. Second, the parent had to publicly acknowledge the natural child in order to name him or her as an heir.[21] If a child had been born while his father was married to another person, they were considered a bastard and could not be named as an heir. The child could, however, still receive a bequest (or the *mejora* or fifth of the estate) from their father. In the sixteenth century, Spanish conquistadors and settlers named parents and siblings as heirs over natural children. Frequently, however, wills of Spanish men in the 1540s and 1550s declared their natural children as their sole heirs.

While demographics favored out-of-wedlock births in Peru, the practices of being a father to an *hijo natural* were not entirely new to the colonial setting. In 1564, Diego de Herrera died in Peru and his uncle, his executor, confessed that "my nephew has a son in the kingdoms of Spain that he had in a certain woman . . . and he communicated to me that I send him [the son] 1000 silver pesos."[22] Similarly, Jaime de Salazar, who traveled to Peru in the 1500s, left behind a "bastard" daughter in the town of Cayora in the kingdom of Valencia.[23] He explored the Andes, buying mines in Guanuco, and settling for a time in Arequipa. In his will, he asked that if the Guanuco mines had any proceeds the sum of 150 ducados be sent to the daughter, Catalina, whom he had left in the care of his brother Miguel de Salazar.[24] He also specified that 50 coronas de oro, which he had left with Miguel, should be given to Catalina. Both the potential 150 ducados, as well as the 50 coronas, constituted a dowry for Catalina. Salazar never named Catalina's mother, though he did say that if his daughter had died, those 50 coronas de oro should go to her mother. Salazar's use of the word *bastarda* is notable because its usage is rare in the sixteenth-century legal record compared to *hijo natural*. The term connotes a child born out of wedlock to at least one married party; Salazar was not married, but perhaps Catalina's mother was. Father to Catalina though he was, her status as a bastard meant he could not name her as his heir. He appointed his parents, Joan Adrián de Chinchilla and Catalina Adrián, instead.

Thus, unmarried parents and families with children born in as well as outside of marriage combined law and custom to figure out provisions. Married men, Spanish and indigenous, often left bequests to or named as heirs children born out of wedlock or an unborn child.[25] The legal rules surrounding bequests were a distinct issue to naming heirs; bequests could be left to any person regardless of relationship to the testator.

For a child born out of wedlock to be an heir, however, a father's recognition was required. Indeed, claiming paternity was an exercise in extending kinship and creating legacy. The blacksmith Diego de Ojeda made a legal donation to his daughter Francisca wherein he noted, "As my natural daughter I have had you and recognized you."[26] The word signified that society and family, including Ojeda's Spanish wife Luisa de Sepulveda, knew of Ojeda's child with the indigenous Beatriz of Pampacolca. Once a man had "recognized" a child, all of society would "know" the child as part of a family line. Recognition was not the same as legitimatization (a process that took applicants before the Crown) and did not bestow all honors of legitimacy on a child. Still, recognition was an admission of obligation on the part of the father and necessary for a child to be an heir.

Part of the process of recognition was naming a child, both selecting a Christian first name and granting use of one's surname. One man dictated the names for his unborn child in his will. Domingo de Otre left provisions for the child to be born to Francisca, a native of Cuzco. Whether boy or girl, the baby was to receive 500 pesos. He hoped to name the child, even if posthumously, and asked that if Francisca gave birth to a boy, he be named Martín and if a girl, Catalina.[27]

When men declared themselves fathers in documents, one common clerical change was the after-the-fact addition of the word *natural* behind the word *hijo* or *hija*. Thus, when Domingo de Destre, a native of Aragón who lived in Lima, acknowledged his mestiza daughter María, the scribe returned to the document and wrote in *"natural"* above the line.[28] Was this an afterthought, Destre's answer to a question of the notary scribe, or a clarification sought by Destre himself? The document records both an original uncertainty and an ultimate need to specify. Given the early date of this testament, 1542—a decade after Spanish arrival—it is possible that Destre did not feel the need to clarify. The significant word for him was child; he had claimed his daughter.

The recognition of a child was prompted in part by an understanding of paternal obligation. In some instances, this obligation was a transaction since provisions were made for goods or pesos to change hands. For many fathers, however, the obligation could be imbued with strong emotional attachment. Documents scripted by template and multiple agencies are the best extant source about the emotions and obligations fathers felt for children in sixteenth-century Peru. The language of paternal (and sometimes maternal) obligation is often business-like, steeped in notions of responsibility. Yet occasional flourishes of emotion hint at a larger spectrum of paternal responses. In some instances, words and phrases in conjunction with legal orders/actions reveal evidence of deep affection.[29] But the emotions expressed never strayed far from a critical set of issues about family structure and notions of familial obligations.

Fathers left clues about their perceived role as providers, as well as their actions as such, in sixteenth-century Peru. The scribe who penned Nicolás del Benino's donation to his daughter summed up his role as father succinctly: "I have the obligation as your father to reform you and marry you honorably."[30] The scribe may have used this phrase repeatedly in such instances; it demands attention because it reflects what colonial society expected of a father, and in this case of a father who was making a legal donation from his estate to an out-of-wedlock mixed race daughter. Fathers had an obligation to dower their daughters; further, if they had the means to do so, they needed to provide their daughters with a dowry generous enough to attract a man of the highest possible social status. It was not merely enough to marry a daughter; she should ideally be placed in an honorable marriage. In addition, his note that he needed to reform his daughter was an explicit reference to the need to remedy her situation as a mixed-race and out-of-wedlock child. Through his gifts to her, this condition would be partially modified. The use of these words and phrases in numerous notarial documents suggests a script that was connected to the social reality from which it emerged. Some fathers may have tried to do the right thing with as little money or affection as possible, simply to keep up appearances. Others understood obligations to their offspring in more expansive terms. To the notary's script, they added the particulars: names of children and mothers; marital status at the time of birth; how much of their estate they transferred to a child and in what form; an expression of love. When fathers recognized natural children, the law offered them different possibilities to fulfill obligations to those children. A minority of these children were named as universal heirs, but most received a single bequest in a last will and testament or received a legal donation during their parents' lifetimes. In this case, the daughter, 23-year-old María del Benino, received shares in the Potosí mines as her dowry, a donation that gave her much to work with as she contracted marriage in 1570s Arequipa. Benino's dedication to his paternal obligation offered her a marriage partner of a higher status.

Indeed, discourses of obligation and affection are woven throughout the documents of legal donation. One father made his gift, he claimed, "because of the obligation that fathers have to their daughters."[31] The cleric Felipe de León made a donation of a mine share in Potosí to his natural son Gomez Felipe for the "love and voluntad" he had for the boy as well as "the good deeds I received from you and you have given me and you are obedient in all."[32] Pedro García de la Cuerda's notarized document went further stressing the God-given duty of fathers: "now considering the natural obligation that fathers owe [deven] to their children to raise them and teach them good and praiseworthy habits and endeavor [to ensure] their honor and growth."[33] In what he termed a "natural" obligation, he gave 1,000 pesos to María, his daughter with Juana Palla, india.

Women employed a similar language of obligation in their entreaties to have fathers provide support. María Alonso implored of her children's father, "I beg and plead that their father watch them and have them in mind as he is obligated."[34] Alonso was a long way from her birthplace of Truxillo, Spain, when she ran a small clothing store in Lima in 1554. She was one of only a few hundred native women of Spain who lived in the city at the time. When Alonso made a will one month after the birth of her twin daughters, she noted that she was healthy. However, she needed the will to protect the twins, who were her natural daughters, with merchant Alonso Sanmartin. Alonso's will employed language to make Sanmartin care for the girls, calling it his obligation. She also named Sanmartin as the guardian of her daughters Juana and Ana because, she repeated, "I am confident in him as he is obligated to look out for and provide for the said my daughters." Her poignant words speak to her deep concern for the girls and play on commonly held notions about family roles and responsibilities. They are also a reminder of how much hinged on a man's decision to recognize his out-of-wedlock children and assume his paternal role.

Occasionally, a child would receive a sum of money from a Spanish man who was at pains to fully acknowledge paternity. Some men did not feel confident, either in their paternity or in their obligation, and would thus make a gesture that was halfway toward recognition but had no sure-footed legal standing. For instance, the young mestizo Diego received 200 pesos from the ill Martín de Aguirre, a Viscaino who offered a less than forthright acknowledgment as he referred to the boy: "Diego, who says that he is my natural son and son of Barbosa."[35] The bequest was to remain in the control of his Spanish wife Beatriz González until Diego reached 25, the age of majority. Aguirre's strings on the bequest ensured not just adult, but Spanish, control over the money.

Notaries might influence the divulgence of paternity as well. Pedro de Castillo, the mestizo son of Diego de Castilla and indigenous Madalena of La Paz, gave donations to several children. His will specified 150 pesos for "a young mestiza girl who is named Beatriz daughter of a so-called María who is in this city [Arequipa] to help her marry or enter the convent." In the margins of the will, however, the notary penned "who he suspects is his daughter."[36] Not placing too much weight on the chance Beatriz was his daughter, Castillo specified three additional donations of 100 pesos to mestizas. His heir was not the mestiza Beatriz but his mother, the indigenous Madalena, who lived in the city of La Paz. Why Pedro de Castillo hedged his bets on the paternity is unknown, but some men might have had legitimate questions about whether they had fathered a child, based on timing or rumors. Yet the writing in the margins suggests that he mused to the notary his suspicions, never suspecting that someone might actually put them in writing after his signature had dried on the page.

The moment when a recognition or legal donation became part of the written record yields insights about life stages and the motivations that prompted fathers; big life events such as travels, illness, and marriage. Impending death was a powerful motivator, and some natural children came to light between a will and a codicil. For instance, five-year-old Alonso and one-year-old Baltasar Alexos received handsome bequests of 3,000 gold pesos each. Yet their father, González Gallego, a tailor in Lima, did not mention them in his will. Ill and fearing death in April of 1554 Gallego returned to the notary to dictate a codicil in which he acknowledged the boys, both born to the indigenous Isabel of Chaquichaguana, and offered each a substantial sum.[37] Waiting until the very last minute to make a written recognition of the boys as his sons suggests Gallego's discomfort with the confession of paternity. Many men no doubt felt as Gallego did but never made it to the notary to dictate a codicil.

Marriage was another life-changing event that presented an opportunity to square away property donations to an out-of-wedlock child. Arequipa *vecino* Francisco Ramírez fathered a son, Juan Rafael Ramírez, with the indigenous Ana.[38] Later, at the time of his marriage to the Spaniard Ana de Saldíbar, Ramírez made a legal donation of 400 pesos to Juan. Juan's indigenous mother received a bequest of land, from which Juan might have benefited. Thus, Ramírez acted in accordance with informal custom by donating a respectable sum to his natural son and making a gift to the boy's mother. Importantly, years later when he wrote his will, Ramírez left another 1,000 pesos to Juan. His legal heirs in the last will and testament were the legitimate children he conceived with Ana de Saldíbar in their ten years of marriage.

If children were born prior to their fathers' marriages, perhaps they received more of the estate. The mestizo *hijo natural*, Juan, was not an heir; he received a sum total of 1,400 pesos from his father, likely much less than the other children stood to receive. Still, 1,400 pesos is a substantial amount compared to other financial bequests for mestizos in sixteenth-century Lima. The fact that Juan was born before Ramírez's marriage to Saldíbar might have made it easier to give him a high sum, as opposed to men who had children in Spain prior to traveling to the Indies. Juan's case suggests the timing of the birth of a mestizo child was a strong factor in how he was compensated in a will. This was not always the case, however, because some natural children lost their status as heirs upon the marriage of his fathers.[39]

Illegitimacy and Universal Heirs

Bequests to natural children were important, but being named as an heir by a father was a far more significant act in legal, social, and economic terms. It was standard practice for Spaniards and indigenous peoples in Peru to appoint a universal heir when they dictated their wills. The written law allowed that even when fathers had no legitimate children, they might choose others as heirs over their natural children. For instance, Diego de Hojeda privileged his role as a brother; he designated his sisters, back in Spain, as heirs to his estate. He did not name his mestiza *hija natural* as his heir, nor did he name his wife, despite explicitly asking her to care for the daughter.[40] In contrast, the indigenous Juan Garabito favored his daughter Francisca, technically a "bastard," as his universal heir, while giving his wife a dress that had been her dowry and 30 pesos for her services and his love for her.[41] These contrasting examples raise questions about how many fathers (and some mothers) tried to provide for their children in the next generation.

A sixteenth-century sample demonstrates that many men and women acknowledged natural children and, further, that their overall tendency was to name those children as heirs when they could legally do so (table 6.1).[42] By focusing exclusively on the sixteenth century, this sample allows for more specific understanding of how birth status affected parents' mandates and wishes for the next generation.[43] The results are remarkable indicators of how family members adapted inheritance practices to the situation on the ground in colonial Peru.

Out of 416 wills in notary records in Lima, 226 of the testators had at least one living child when they dictated their wills. The majority of the children acknowledged in the wills were legitimate children. A slightly lower number were acknowledged as exclusively *hijos naturales*. By way of reminder, the legitimate children were entitled, by law, to receive equal

Table 6.1 Children Acknowledged in Wills in Peru in the Sixteenth Century

	Lima (416 wills total)	Arequipa (114 wills total)
Acknowledge living child/ children	226	64
Acknowledge only legitimate children	107	22
Acknowledge only *hijos naturales*[a]	85	33
Acknowledge both legitimate and natural children	18	3
Acknowledge children, but did not specify legal status	16	6

[a] In both the Lima and Arequipa samples, three testaments specified bastard children as opposed to natural children.

shares of their parents' estates. The parents had the option to set aside one-fifth of their estates to give to anyone of their choosing (to favor one child or to give to another relative or even to charity). Table 6.2 shows who parents chose to name as their heirs. In Peru, a majority of the testators named their natural children as their heirs when they did not have legitimate children.

Other fathers recognized their natural children but did not name them as heirs. In these cases, parents acknowledged natural children and made a (usually small) bequest to them while naming someone else as their universal heir. In six cases the choice of the other heir was not complicated; those fathers named their legitimate children as their heirs. In other cases, however, individuals chose their wives (Spanish and indigenous), their parents, or a sibling. In some cases people wanted to split the inheritance among legitimate and natural children. One testator named the *Hospital de Españoles* as his heir, while another asked for all of his estate to be used for masses for his soul.

Table 6.1 is instructive in the case of the 114 Arequipeño wills. Of this number, sixty-four testators had children.[44] Twenty-two of the testators who were parents had children within marriage. Thus, thirty-one Arequipeños had natural children, a higher percentage of *naturales* acknowledged than in Lima; moreover, the actual number of *naturales* is higher than the number of legitimate children. In Lima, however, a higher percentage of testators acknowledged both legitimate and natural children in the will.

Table 6.2 Wills Naming Natural Children as Heirs in Peru in
the Sixteenth Century

	Lima Wills (100)[a]	Arequipa Wills (35)[a]
Named natural children as their heirs	65	20
Named legitimate children	6	2
Named wives	6	2
Named siblings	5	3
Named parents	9	6
Named their soul	2	1
Split among above categories	7	1

[a] Number in sample that recognized natural children.

Of the thirty-five testators who acknowledged natural children, twenty named their natural children as heirs. As with the people in Lima, a number named their parents, several named siblings, two named a wife, two named legitimate heirs, and one named his soul. These numbers help to sketch a broad outline of family relationships in the 1500s. For many sons or daughters, their illegitimate birth signified that they would not be universal heirs and instead received some other bequest from their fathers. If fathers did not have legitimate children, though, they typically chose their natural children as their heirs.

The high number of bequests for *hijos naturales* compared to the low number of heir appointments makes clear that Spaniards who fathered children out of wedlock with indigenous women complied with a standard that offered some form of material compensation to those children. Specific family trees help to make sense of these statistics. The following examples are a group of fathers who did the expected: they did not name illegitimate children as heirs but did make some provisions for them. Merchant Lázaro Cabeça, a native of the Villa of Penafiel, in Spain, fathered five children, two outside of marriage.[45] In 1554 when he wrote his will he named his three children with his wife, Pedro Cabeça, Madalena Ribera, and Isabel Ribera, as his legitimate heirs. He sent his executors to find out if Bernardino, his son with the indigenous Ana, was alive and, if so, authorized them to give him 100 gold pesos. Cabeça's other child was a ten-month-old son of the indigenous Inés to whom he bequeathed 100 pesos. Pedro, Madalena, and Isabel enjoyed privileged status as legitimate children and Cabeça was fully within the law to make this division of his estate as he did.

Even in the absence of a legitimate child, men did not have to name their *hijos naturales* as their heirs. In 1552 Sebastián Bernal ordered bequests to his sisters, his nieces, his brothers, and the usual religious causes, and to Angelina, the mother of his daughter, Juana Bernal.[46] Even though Bernal had no wife and no legitimate children, he named his soul and not Juana as his universal heir.[47] Juana received five mares, his bed and bed clothing (mattress, canopy, blanket, two *mantas*, and two pillows, six sheets). Bernal also appointed Diego de Ribera as Juana's tutor and ordered that Ribera augment her property of the five mares. The hope with agricultural bequests was that animals would propagate and their value would increase over time. If Ribera did his job, Juana's inheritance could grow in time to provide her with a timely dowry when she came of age to marry. The material objects constituted not only a complete bedroom set for Juana to use, but a potential part of the dowry as well because each of those items carried a peso value as movable property.

The gift of the mares to Juana was atypical for Lima, but reflective of many bequests to children from Arequipeño fathers who worked closely with rural endeavors. Thus their bequests acknowledged their paternity and attempted to give their children goods to earn for a future in Arequipa. Trujillo native Martín López de Carvajal made a living in agriculture and his gifts to his three mestizo natural sons reveal the nature of his work and his estate. He bequeathed to García, Francisco, and Nuno de Carvajal an equal share of his sheep and ordered Francisco de Grado to serve as the tutor to the boys. [48] In theory, Grado would ensure that the boys' inheritance was properly administered until they came of age.

Widower Francisco de Quiros became a resident of Arequipa after moving to Peru from Toledo, Spain.[49] His only children, Beatriz and Catalina, were born to the indigenous Isabel, a native of Arequipa. Quiros made no specific mention of the girls' day-to-day relationship with Isabel, nor did he state where he expected them to live after his death. But he recognized the girls as his *hijas naturales* and appointed a tutor to care for them. A man named Diego, enslaved to Quiros, was obliged to serve the girls for four years, and then he would gain his freedom. Exactly how Diego would work for the girls was not specified, but his labor may have been tied to their father's bequest to them. Quiros held wealth in farm animals, specifically hundreds of cows, goats, and pigs, some of which went to Beatriz and Catalina. A share in this agricultural property would serve as a desirable dowry when it came time to marry.

In addition to making bequests to his two daughters and his servants, Quiros gave 15,000 maravedis to Antonio and Juan Niebla, his stepsons, who lived in Spain. Quiros's parents were still living in Toledo in 1556, and he named his father as his universal heir. Legitimacy, not race or gender, was the major factor in this decision. Had Quiros married Isabel, the girls would have been automatic universal heirs. In the overall picture, then, Quiros's father and his stepsons received far more than his daughters or the mother of his daughters. Quiros showed no interest in sending his daughters to Spain to be raised. It is possible that the girls continued to live with Beatriz. Quiros himself may have continued a relationship with her. Unlike some other fathers, he kept his daughters in Peru and gave the girls the means to marry and settle in Arequipa. Spaniards with agricultural holdings saw animals in both productive and reproductive terms as a valuable bequest to their natural children.[50]

Native Andean fathers, like Spaniards or others, distinguished between legitimate and out-of-wedlock heirs and passed on their status to the next generation. Andean traditions long distinguished between a man's off-spring among different mothers to determine who would inherit the status of *kuraka*, or chieftain. In the colonial period, this continued, though native elites took care to emphasize legitimate lines so as to protect claims to chieftaincies and limit litigation over that inheritance.[51] They employed strategies of extending lineage and fulfilling obligation, as did don Juan Guaca Condori who had a son prior to marriage and another during marriage.[52] In his 1586 will, Condori acknowledged twelve-year-old Miguel Oscam as his natural son with the deceased Isabel Ammra. Condori's relationship with Isabel was distinct from many Spanish–indigenous ones because they made a house together, and Isabel had not been his servant. Condori gave ten llamas, a *chacara* to Miguel, a "small house that I made with his mother Isabel Ammra that is next to the others I have," and 6 pesos. While the land, house, and money would help sustain the boy, Condori also passed on sentimental items: two shawls (*mantas*) and a men's shirt; two books; two large *keros* (that he or the notary specified were "what the Indians drink with").[53] Miguel Oscam would not inherit his father's status as cacique because after fathering Miguel, don Juan Guaca Condori married Madalena Ava.[54] He left their home in Collaguas only to receive notice that Madalena Ava had given birth to a son. Much like a Spanish father of an *hijo natural* and a legitimate child would have done, don Guaca Condori gave a modest, but important, inheritance to his *hijo natural* Miguel and made his legitimate son his universal heir. Guaca Condori was a native elite in Collaguas, and his son with Ava would have been direct heir to that level of native political power. Naming that son in the will allowed him to pass on his status in his native community and the recognition that son could gain in the Spanish system. Guaca Condori used a similar division of status that a Spaniard might have in terms of a title passing to his legitimate child and goods passing to his natural son. Guaca Condori's gifts of clothing and *keros*, as well as land and animals, show his desire to provide both objects of cultural identity and affection, in addition to future earnings for the natural son.

If no legitimate children existed, indigenous fathers might look more favorably on their natural children. Cuzco native Don Juan Rimache was married to Catalina Nusta, a Porco native, and the couple had no children.[55] Rimache did have an *hijo natural*, Diego, who received a modest bequest in the will and was appointed its executor. Rimache named his wife Catalina as his universal heir but specified that the property he was giving to her be passed down to Diego upon her death. In a practice seen elsewhere, Rimache provided for Catalina during her life but ensured that legal control of his estate was preserved for his son to carry into the next generation. While Diego did not immediately gain access to his father's estate, he would ultimately inherit it.

The numbers, such as they are, reveal with clarity that the majority of natural children were not named as heirs above other relatives. The exceptional cases, then, deserve analysis for they highlight conscious attempts of families to interrupt colonial hierarchies in a transgenerational way. Here is a set of cases from the mid- to late sixteenth century, where Spanish men named their *hijos naturales* as heirs to their estates deliberately in the absence of legitimate children, but over a spouse, living parent, or sibling. Examples culled from the 1550s, the 1570s, and the 1590s reveal that fathers made this exceptional choice with continuity. In the 1550s, Alonso Hernández de Valderrama acknowledged his two natural sons, Juan Graviel and Alonso, and named them as his heirs.[56] Juan Graviel was born to doña Luisa Palla of Cuzco and his brother Alonso was born to Catalina of Collao. Alonso wanted his estate to go toward the boys' board, religious instruction, and schooling (in grammar and science, specifically). In the same decade Diego Maldonado, native of Salamanca, left his goods and property to his natural daughter Ana because, in his words, his parents were deceased and he had no other children.[57] For some this is a Spanish re-creation of a ruling class because they have no legitimate Spanish child. For instance, Maldonado left a Spanish male as a tutor for Ana. But the complexity of family structures like this one complicates the contention that a replication of a colonial class could occur. In the case of Ana, her mother, a native of the valley of Lima, was raising her. As his heir, Ana stood to gain the property necessary to marry well and ascend the colonial social hierarchy; because she lived with her indigenous mother, however, her socialization was not a refashioning, and not a repetition, of the colonizing class.

Similar to the case of Ana, Pedro Bernal de Cantalapiedra named his mestizo natural son Luis as his heir in 1571 even though he seemed to allow for the boy's indigenous mother to raise him.[58] Cantalapiedra himself was born out of wedlock to the Bachillera Miguel Ruiz de Cantalapiedra and an unnamed mother. As Bernal de Cantalapiedra lay sick in the hospital, nine-month-old Luis was living with his mother Ana. Bernal de Cantalapiedra did not appoint a tutor and guardian for his son. He left his estate, including a *chacara*, to the boy; Luis's mother Ana received a horse and saddle as well as goats. The absence of concrete plans for the boy in the will might indicate nothing more than the haste with which it was dictated from a hospital. However, it is worth pondering that Pedro, mother unnamed, *hijo natural* himself, may have had strong kin connections in Arequipa to help raise Luis. In such instances, indigenous mothers perhaps maintained stronger control of their children.

Cristóbal de Quiros was himself an *hijo natural*, born to a Spanish father and indigenous mother.[59] He lived in the city of Arequipa, where he was involved in a local *cofradía*. Over time Quiros amassed belongings in the city as well as rural property and animals. He engaged in business dealings with a cacique and had eight law books in his possession. Quiros never married, but he was the father of Isabel and Juana, and he expected to become a father again when he made his 1591 will. Assuming María Guayro successfully gave birth to his child, Quiros asked that his estate be split among the three children. He ordered a modest 40-peso donation to María Guayro. Like most parents in this era, Quiros appointed a tutor to care for the children in his absence. Quiros asked Lucas Martínez Vegaso to keep the three children in his home and educate them with good manners. Remarkably, nearing the end of the sixteenth century, sixty years after the arrival of the Spanish to the Andes, and decades removed from the trend of putting mestizo children on ships to Spain, Quiroz modeled a life for his mixed-race children that fit the pattern of Spanish fathers of mestizos from the 1540s and 1550s.

Another late sixteenth-century example shows the integration of inheritance and Hispanicization into plans for a daughter.[60] Born in the Villa of Moguer in Spain, Bartolomé de Carmona made his way to Potosí, where he ran a local mercantile store with an impressive inventory. During the 1580s, Luisa Tocta worked for him and bore his daughter, María de Carmona. In 1591, when María was approximately five years old Bartolomé Carmona wed a peninsular widow named Catalina de Losa.

Carmona remained connected to his family in Spain. Although he had no children there, his will left monetary gifts to two sisters, with the widow Juana Carmona receiving 1,000 pesos and the married Beatriz Carmona a sum of 500 pesos *ensayados*. His higher gift to the widow acknowledged the difficult economic situation widows often faced. In contrast to these sizable gifts to his sisters, Carmona dictated that a sum of 100 pesos *corrientes* be given to Luisa Tocta for "the service she has given me." This clause clearly recognized Tocta as the mother of his daughter

María, but his recognition of her was minimal, given that that phrase was commonly used in wills for indigenous servants and slaves, and the amount of money he provided was a mere one-fifth of what he sent to Spain for his sisters.

Although Carmona was more generous to María, he gave uncommonly specific orders for María's future. One suspects he took the girl from Tocto and had her under his guidance in Potosí. Notably, Carmona did not focus on María's racial identity by referring to her as *mestiza*, even though he consistently referred to Tocto as *india*. Instead, he called María only his *hija natural*. His worldview of race, class, and power informed how he wrote his will and planned for his only child's future. In case anyone might contest María being named his universal heir, Carmona clarified that the girl had been born to Tocto when both were single and could have married legitimately without any dispensation. Carmona never clarified why they did not marry, and it was probably never in his plans. Yet the single status of both father and mother was critical to ensuring that María was not a bastard and could, in fact, serve as his heir.

The rest of Carmona's desires with regard to María aimed to remove her from any indigenous influence. Catalina de Losa, rather than Luisa Tocto, was named María's tutor. Moreover, Carmona ordered his eight-year-old daughter to marry his stepson, Gaspar de Losa, as soon as she came of age. This act would keep his inheritance tied to his wife's family. It was also an attractive marriage arrangement because María, a mestiza, would marry Gaspar, who was presumably a Spaniard. The inheritance of Carmona, then, served as a dowry for María to make her a desirable bride. Instead of following the example of many fathers from the 1550s through the 1570s who had shipped their young mestiza daughters back to Spain, Carmona would rely on cultural training from his Spanish wife and ensure cultural and economic continuity in the family by having her wed his stepson.

As the sixteenth century progressed, yet another set of parental decisions emerged: those who made decisions about inheritance while facing choices between potential heirs within Peru though not necessarily across the ocean. Eugenio de Gudiel was born in the silver-rich city of Potosí to the indigenous Jauja native, Luisa, and the Spaniard Juan Sánchez.[61] As an adult he came to live in Lima, where he fathered a son, Gerónimo, with Juliana, a mulata slave of Inés Nuñez. In a last testament Gudiel left his entire estate to Gerónimo because Sánchez had died and he had no word from his mother. However, when news came from Potosí that Luisa Jauja was living, Gudiel returned to the notary. He dictated a codicil naming his indigenous mother as his heir and leaving his Afro-indigenous-Spanish son one-third of the fifth of his estate. Technically as long as Gerónimo was not legitimate, Gudiel was bound to transfer the estate to his mother over from his child. In the event of Luisa's death, however, two-year-old Gerónimo was to receive everything.[62] Like fathers of first-generation mestizos, Gudiel left his estate to his mother, an ascending heir, instead of his natural son. The similarity of the act should not overshadow what was quite different about this case; here both potential heirs were non-Spanish. Gudiel's mother was indigenous and living in Potosí, thus likely integrated into urban culture.[63] His son, Gerónimo, was of Spanish, indigenous, and African descent, and born to an enslaved mother. The family network literally embodied the changes in sixteenth-century urban Andean society.

Unlawful Wills

The testament was a final opportunity to influence children's status in society, to leave a legacy, and to provide for the future generation. Some used wills to exclude someone from inheritance or to privilege one child over another. The printed legal code looked black and white, but some parents and their notaries nonetheless sought the gray area where they might shape the application of the law to favor beloved sons and daughters who were illegitimate.[64] This might seem insignificant if applied only to one family; but given the considerations of how inheritances and property could be linked to colonial labor, land, or tribute, the stakes for inheritance could be quite high in the colonial context.[65]

One father tried to argue his case within the legal, discursive space of a document written and signed by the notary. Nicolás de Almacan was husband to Olalla de Merlo, father to several legitimate children and to Luisa de Almacan, his bastard daughter with the indigenous Catalina.[66] Almacan made his New World home in Arequipa, where he had been awarded an encomienda. Merlo and all of Almacan's children, including Luisa, lived in Spain. He had the financial means to care for all his children, but he feared that conventions in Spain might prevent Luisa from being looked after. In 1568 he decided to donate 8,000 pesos to Luisa. As did other fathers, Almacan made stipulations for Luisa's future. If she were to marry against his will while he was alive, she would not receive the money. Should she decide to take her vows and remain in the monastery, she would receive substantially less money—only 1,000 pesos, 500 for a dowry and 500 for habits.[67] Still, Luisa stood to have an 8,000-peso dowry with which to marry. In order to maximize her chances to receive that large sum, Almacan argued his obligations as her father. He hoped the dowry would give her "what I in my life should have and was obligated to give [her] in food and clothing and other good customs."[68] Further, he acknowledged her precarious situation in Spain: "I brought her from this kingdom to that of Spain where she is alone and with little remedy."[69] Despite her many years in Spain, he was not confident that she was accepted by his first family or, perhaps, the broader community because of being mestizo and illegitimate.

Even though the rationale for the donation fit within cultural understandings of a father's duties to his daughter, Almacan worried that this large donation would be objectionable to his legitimate family. In order to ensure that this donation would not be contested, he communicated to both his wife and his eldest son, Fabian de León, the news of this donation and his wish that Luisa receive the money. Fabian, who stood to succeed his father in his encomienda, was the child with the most power to withhold money from Luisa. With consent of his wife and eldest son, Almacan made the donation to Luisa "for stated reasons and others that move me and for the love owed to my said daughter."[70] Almacan further argued his action on a humanitarian level that all children regardless of issue, deserved protection: "Because even though similar children [illegitimate] are excluded from inheritance, according to divine law and the laws of these Kingdoms she cannot be denied food and sustenance."[71]

Almacan understood that parents with both natural and legitimate children had to be as clear as possible in their wills about what they left to whom. In doing so, individuals sometimes dictated wills, as he did, that either ignored inheritance law or reshaped it to fit their needs. Limeño Jorge Palomino's instructions for his children's inheritance provide another such example of willful unlawfulness. Palomino, a free *moreno* in Lima, married three times, to *morena* Leonor Díaz, to Costanca, and to the indigenous María Fernández. He had one legitimate son, Juan Bo, with María Fernández, as well as an *hija natural*, Barbara, born to an unnamed indigenous mother who was never his wife. He left his modest estate to both of these children without distinguishing how they would inherit.[72] Palomino ignored common legal practice; Juan Bo should have been his heir and it would have been within Palomino's legal right to award Barbara the fifth of his estate. The notary did not correct Palomino's intentions, perhaps out of disinterest due to the small estate or a careless error by an assistant. What stands for the record, then, is how a father wished his estate to be left to his children regardless of its ability to stand up in court.

Many men had children on both sides of the Atlantic. While distance was not a factor for law, it weighed into parents calculations for their wills. For Diego Hernández, whose family opened this chapter, proximity to his Peruvian-born sons seems to have swayed him to favor them. Francisco Martínez offers yet another example of someone with children on both sides of the Atlantic.[73] His legal actions toward the children in his testament are unique and highlight the primacy of race identity over legitimacy. In the 1530s, prior to traveling to the New World, Martínez had a daughter with Isabel de Mora. This girl, María Martínez, grew up in the house of his brother in Zamora. In Peru, Martínez fathered two children, Domingo and Francisca, both with indigenous mothers. In his will, Martínez gave María 200 pesos for her dowry and named the mestizo children as his heirs. Technically the three children should have inherited legally. Domingo, age five, and Francisca, one and a half, were much younger than María; perhaps he thought they were in greater need of the estate. Notably the mestizo children received more than the Iberian-born María. The rationale behind Martínez' testament lies somewhere between his own will and his dialogues with Simón de Alzate, his notary. Proximity to Domingo and Francisca and distance from María might explain his favoring the small children. Moreover, having relied on family networks in Spain to raise María Martínez, Francisco might have expected resources to be given to her from his brother or other family members. Had she earned a dowry of sorts from her uncle's family for domestic service over many years (as was customary with mestiza and indigenous servants in Peru)? Even if the rationale remains murky, the intent of the will is remarkable because Martínez did not behave as did most of his counterparts and favor Iberian children; though anecdotal, this is precisely the kind of act that complicated colonial visions of family and society.

Some men made provisions for suspected children without acknowledging them, and in the course of their estates being settled, their donation became more significant than they might have initially presumed. In the city of Arequipa in 1585 Domingo Carvallo from the Villa of Citubar in the kingdom of Portugal promised his three legitimate daughters equal shares of his estate as his universal heirs.[74] The girls, Violante, and Inés, had not followed their father, Carvallo, to the New World where he owned a store selling wine and foodstuffs. His will specified that once his debts had been paid, the remainder of his estate was to be taken quickly to the Kingdoms of Spain by Tomo Hernández, confidant of Carvallo, to be enjoyed by his heirs. Caravallo's will did not make an outright declaration of any children born to him in the New World. Yet he singled out "a young daughter of an indigenous woman" named Barbola to receive a monetary donation. Given the pattern that exists in other wills, it is possible that Barbola was the mestiza child of Carvallo. Carvallo ordered a modest 20 pesos to be given to the girl, who lived with her mother in the house of the Arequipan notary Alonso de Luque. Carvallo assured the notary that his executor, Antonio Hernández, knew the girl. Barbola might have been his daughter or she might have been his one-time servant. Ultimately when the estates' debts were paid, the *alcalde* overseeing the transaction ordered the 20 pesos be paid to Barbola. After much time, the remainder of Carvallo's estate, 131 pesos 6 reales, returned to the villa of Citubar. Divided among the three daughters, each received about 44 pesos each. Barbola's sum of 20 pesos was less than half of their inheritance but the two sums were closer than one would expect between legitimate heirs and a mestiza *hija natural*. Carvallo probably did not anticipate this; he may have overestimated his financial worth and underestimated his debts. In this case, none of the three young women was set up with a handsome dowry for marriage. Among the working poor, the economic benefit received between legitimate Spanish versus out-of-wedlock mestiza children was not as different as it was with wealthier Spanish fathers.[75]

The consequence of writing a will that did not conform to legal code was the chance that the will would be contested. The judicial cases that resulted from someone challenging a will, known as *bienes de difuntos*, reveal that sometimes sons or daughters in Spain were not content with the provisions their fathers had made for *hijos naturales*, those half-brothers and sisters they had never met.[76] In other words, the legitimate children's view of family obligations did not always match those of the parent. Juan de Renera, a man from Fuente el Encina in the kingdom of Toledo, made his way to the city of La Plata in los Charcas, Peru.[77] Renera was married to Juana Larrecuenca and had two children, a son named Agustín and a daughter named Juana López de Larrecuenca. Both his wife Juana and Agustín passed away. During his time in Peru, Juana, the daughter, married the son of Pedro Sánchez Salmeron. Renera never traveled back to Spain to see any of his first family.

Although Renera would name Agustín and Juana as his children and state, "I had no other children," his codicil told a different story. Several days after making the original testament, Renera called a scribe to dictate a codicil wherein he made a new and significant declaration. He had a young mestiza daughter named Magdalena. Magdalena's mother was an indigenous woman named Elvira who, at the time Renera dictated the will, was married to Lorenco Piruru, a *yanacona* (a non-tribute-paying indigenous servant) of Gabriel del Encias. Renera attempted to provide for the girl, calling on a powerful Spaniard in La Plata to assist him. He directed his plea to don Gabriel Panyagua de Loaysa, Knight of the Order of Calatrava, to give Magdalena some part of his inheritance so that she could marry well. He claimed that he was not "informed of what he can give her" and "if I can, I order the sixth part of my estate."[78] His will was challenged in Spain and resulted in a legal case. Such *bienes de difuntos* challenges would be brought by legitimate heirs and typically when an estate was sizable, as people generally did not spend the time or money on a case for little material gain.

Other types of challenges occurred for *hijos naturales* who received bequests from their fathers but had difficulty obtaining them. Six-year-old mestizo Diego, born to Catalina and Juan Hidalgo, received a bequest when his father died in Chile. Diego lived under the tutelage of Graviel Rodríguez in Lima and Rodríguez found he had to make a legal case to wrest control of those goods from the estate administrator.[79]

The evidence for this chapter focuses overwhelmingly on fathers and their role as it was legally and socially constructed during the era. Cases for mothers appear less frequently in the record, as they typically had fewer resources to leave behind. Moreover, for a woman, the legal case was slightly different: a mother's natural child was automatically considered an heir if named in the will.[80] Otherwise, the mothers have much in common with the testating fathers. The extant cases for this period where mothers made arrangements for children reveal that economic and material provisions by women were understood to be an important part of being a mother. Further, women used legal documents to oblige men to carry out their roles as fathers.

Mothers, like fathers, used wills to recognize their children and to name their children's fathers. Beatriz Hernández, a resident and property owner in Lima, declared her two natural daughters in her 1562 will.

One daughter, Isabel de Carmona, was living in Seville in the house of Cristóbal de Molina. Beatriz's other daughter, Leonor de Castro, lived in Lima. Beatriz left both women as her heirs and stated, "I declare them for my natural daughters, declared so that there is clarity."[81] Hernández was short on details of paternity or the girls' birthplaces. Her frank discussion of their birth status, however, was meant to fend off any legal claims against their ability to inherit from her.

Mothers used wills in order to protect children with uncertain birth status. Leonor Martín was married to Andres Martín and living in Lima in 1553.[82] In 1550, prior to her marriage, she had given birth to a daughter named Juana. When Martín made up her will she specified that the two-and-a-half-year-old Juana be her heir and that she had no other heirs. The widowed Beatriz de Vives, a native of Seville, enjoyed a comfortable life in the upper echelons of limeño society.[83] She had a son, Gerónimo, by her first husband and, as a widow about to remarry, a daughter by her intended. When she dictated her will in 1577 she took care to describe the status of both her children. Her first husband, Andrés de Biedma Salazar, had received 1,100 pesos yearly from the *repartimiento* (royal land grant) headed by doña Paula of Cuzco, a benefit she was trying to pass on to her son. She alleged the Marques de Cañete had given her husband two *vidas* (literally two lives, but meaning the chance to pass the *repartimiento* down to the next generation) on the *repartimiento* and asked her executors to use the decrees and award it to Gerónimo, her legitimate son by Biedma Salazar. She also declared a legitimate daughter, doña Catalina de Guzman, three years old, born "under promise of marriage," whose father died before the banns could be published. The young girl's status was precarious compared to her brother's, and Vives used her will to protect the girl.

Although the more typical situation was for fathers to be away from home, Spanish mothers also wrestled solo with transatlantic parenting. Born in the Villa of Garrovillas, Spain, Catalina Rodríguez made her way to the New World as an adult. Rodríguez ran a store in Potosí and claimed many business dealings in her will, including debts with Limeño residents and property holdings (slaves) in Lima.[84] Rodríguez acknowledged three legitimate children in her will, one daughter and two sons, though she made no mention of a husband or father. In 1577, at the moment of writing her will, her daughter, María, was eleven years and living with her grandmother in Spain. Her two sons, Juan and Sebastián, were ten and six, respectively, and living in Potosí. Rodríguez divided her estate equally among the children. She sent her daughter's portion on the next ship bound for Spain for her guardians to hold until she was old enough to marry.[85] María's share came to a total of 342 pesos. After Catalina Rodríguez' passing, the two boys were cared for in Peru by Francisco Moreno. Despite Rodríguez' acts to care for her children in both the metropole and colony, all three members of the next generation died within three years of their mother.

Women, like men, also dictated wills that did not follow the letter of the law. Francisca Rodríguez, a free *morena*, had a legitimate daughter, Juana Bermeo, but she attempted, to leave as her sole heir Diego Díaz, her *hijo natural*. Legally, she was not entitled to favor Diego as an heir and disinherit Juana without reason. She did offer Juana 30 pesos "for responsibility I have," but the absence of any offense that would merited disinheritance is notable. Juana was a legitimate child, thus Francisca had a legal obligation to name her. It was Diego who should have received at most the fifth of her estate. Juana was married by 1565; had Francisca paid a dowry to Juana, and assumed she need not endow her further through the will?[86] Was Diego born before her marriage to Pedro or after Pedro died? Francisca left a small bequest of 12 pesos to Diego's wife, Costança Goméz, for her to buy a *saya* that suggests that Francisca was close to her son. Like other members of colonial society, mothers and fathers were interested parties in a legal process and saw their wills as the beginning of a test as to how something might play out in the judicial system in the hope that their wishes for their family could be realized even if they did not follow the letter of the law.

FAMILIES SERVED AS sources of support as well as conflict in the colonial era. Inheritance plans set forth by a parent constitute a place for potential conflict. To give order to this conflict, inheritance laws established strict parameters for who could and must give money to whom. Yet customary law, an important factor in the colonial context, did not always concur with laws on the books and traditional Iberian inheritance norms were tested by *mestizaje*, illegitimacy, and distance. Custom, being molded by cultural mixing, new economic trends, and mobility, attended to the moral obligations of the New World parent, especially fathers. Custom played a role, too, in how parents chose heirs.

Understanding the legal and customary obligation of a father serves as a critical basis for underlying inheritance issues. The rich language of obligation and affection used by parents and notaries crafts a compelling view of the sixteenth-century father. Fulfilling obligations did not always mean naming heirs. Bequests were commonly acknowledged for natural and illegitimate children in modest amounts, at around 100 pesos. In these instances, sons and daughters received equal bequests, as Spanish laws prescribed. A religious component existed alongside parental obligations as the motivation for many material gifts. One's salvation was linked to good acts; making bequests to *hijos naturales* and their mothers constituted good acts. Evidence of people doing good for these boys and girls is clear in the wills of parents as well as a larger sector of the colonial urban population that drew on their labor.

Being named an heir was less common for natural children and indicates that while parents supported illegitimate children, they routinely did so in a manner less committed than for legitimate children. The examples of the Condori case and Francisca Rodríguez show that native Andeans and women could share this tendency to favor legitimate heirs with the mainly Spanish male testators viewed in the sources. Still, what is perhaps more remarkable is that more fathers in this era did name their natural children as heirs than in the later colonial period.[87] In this sample, it was common to name natural children as heirs when no legitimate children existed. The demographics of the sixteenth century lent themselves to this outcome, a fluidity by which legitimacy and racially mixed heritage were not factors that disqualified someone from being an heir. Rather than evidence of the colonial class reproducing itself, this shows how the 1500s do not simply precede the patterns that emerge in the 1600s. Patterns in these early colonial years indicate the shapes of families and the mixed cultural, linguistic, and racial heritage that they embraced.

This is nowhere more evident than in the legal challenges to inheritance law. These challenges point to the customary instincts in the colonial family. For individuals and families, the will was a threshold document that marked a move from customary practices of family in daily life to the law on the books. But the will was also a *précis* of sorts, looking ahead and attempting to provide order and instructions so as to avoid a legal process. For some parents, including those cited here, this stage prompted a challenge by asking: What is right and just for me to give to my children? How does their birth status affect what is just? If legal processes are part of a conversation, these fathers (and, to a lesser extent, mothers) writing wills engaged the colonial state in a conversation about what constituted family.[88]

Leaving some form of material legacy to children was not only a legal but also a customary obligation of parenthood. Conquest and colonial expansion created new challenges to that legacy, but parents adapted their responses to the law and the new, often transatlantic and interracial families they created as the moved around the empire. As a result, individual legacies emerged at the same time this era bequeathed to Peru a collective legacy in the shape of colonial family structure.

Conclusion

ONE COULD ARGUE that the epilogue to this book has already been written in studies on the seventeenth- and eighteenth-century Latin American family.[1] It is true that many historians have addressed the family through practices deemed non-normative such as illegitimacy, bigamy, or marital conflict, wherein the family as projected by discourses of colonial hierarchy existed in tension with the lived experience of peoples who were connected in a web of family. In such works, the opening chapter might address the 1500s. The sixteenth-century focus in *Transatlantic Obligations* therefore puts analysis of the backstory front and center. In general, family history in sixteenth-century Peru was framed in dichotomous fashion where families were either legitimate or illegitimate, Hispanic or indigenous.[2] Those scholars who moved away from this dichotomy focused their research on a later period.[3] With the overwhelming concentration on work from the period seventy years or more after Spanish arrival, the dynamic family structure of an emerging colonial society remained unexamined. This study offers fine-grained analysis of family structures in this earlier era and in so doing provides a two-pronged contribution to colonial scholarship. The first is a social history that foregrounds the diversity of family experiences in the sixteenth century and adds a range of historical actors to a topic for which elites and Spaniards had been more familiar subjects. This social history creates a foundation to explore the "tense and tender ties" of colonialism in sixteenth-century Andean families.

The second, related, contribution is revealed by a deliberate attempt to track family networks and definitions through actions, fully integrating family roles and structures into our understanding of colonialism. The subject of family is often viewed as fundamental to genealogy, women's history or elite biography, yet tangential to topics such as colonial politics or economics. *Transatlantic Obligations* exposes the composition and actions of the family as both central to and in tension with the colonial project.

Families drove transatlantic voyages as much as external factors that prompted people to flock to the New World. In houses and around tables, through letters or through couriers, family connections moved along lines of colonial expansion. Promises came from Peru for jobs, a higher standard of living, access to labor of indigenous servants and African slaves, and potential marriage matches for young women. The Crown's discourse on family worked explicitly and implicitly to support colonial expansion. During this period of dramatic change, individuals used the legal system to define and cement family connections. The Crown and the law helped to legitimize and reinforce familial bonds. Women like Luisa Pendones sought the Crown's assistance when they petitioned for their husbands' return to Spain. So desirable were Spanish families as role models in the settling of Lima that the Crown required husbands to bring their wives to the New World. Simultaneously, the makeup of families and their lifestyles in Peru presented an outright challenge to the social and racial hierarchies of colonial rule. A Spanish wife arriving to meet her husband in Lima in accordance with Royal Decrees might also greet a mestizo stepson. At an institutional level, the Crown saw married Spanish women as an "honorable" solution to raising the natural children of Spanish fathers. Yet the presence and role of these children in the family, not to mention their eventual role as adults in the colony, was a primary marker of cultural transformation.

By force of the historical moment, then, family relationships responded to the colonial context with a process that reflects a *mestizaje* of the family. Iberian practices were transplanted and native Andean customs adapted to a new imperial regime. Families incorporated members across boundaries of race and legitimacy. Few "Spaniards" were of pure Iberian descent.[4] Few families were "pure" either. Practices initiated in 1532 (and earlier for other parts of the Indies) shaped the way individuals created families. The mixed cultures represented within those families, such as material culture, language, inheritance, or dowry practices, reveal more than transculturation; indeed, a *mestizaje* of the family had occurred. Legal and customary guidelines from Iberia and the pre-Columbian Andes could not function exactly as before; those guidelines constitute the warp to the weave of colonial change. In the intersection of the two lay the order of colonial family.

This book's conclusion about the *mestizaje* of the family shows the clear advantage of narrowing the chronological analysis to the 1500s at the same time it points to a methodological argument. Whereas religious and prescriptive writings indicate types of families and hopes for behaviors, they are less helpful with tracking the working of families over time, especially in a newly settled colony which few of the most influential authors or priests had visited. Instead, studying families through notaries and court cases reveals spaces of family formation that both add to and are distinct from religious spaces. Thanks to this approach, the chapters of this work pull apart "types" by highlighting individual cases as well as studying patterns to show where accepted wisdom does not apply. Types such as conquistador fathers, victimized indigenous mothers, mestizo children, abandoned wives, or new world emigrants, are studied as members of family units and in roles they themselves claimed and pursued. And so, the book argues, these family members understood obligations of behavior as they related to Iberian and indigenous custom as well as the changing circumstances of the emerging colonial society.

Some types emerge more fully than others. The book argues for a more nuanced understanding of Spanish men in Peru in their roles as fathers during the sixteenth century. The customs of being a father that influenced Iberian tradition in Spain traveled the ocean to Peru, and Spanish fathers tried to implement them, for better or for worse. The underlying message of learning more about these men's actions is not to sanctify the Spanish father of the mestizo child. Rather, it isolates patterns of behavior practiced commonly in Lima and Arequipa and shows how Iberian traditions responded to situations in the Andes. Spanish fathers present a complex set of behaviors that included domination over indigenous families and, in particular, indigenous women as well as rejection of indigenous culture for Spanish culture. Simultaneously, many actively carried out obligations to their children, regardless of birth status or race, and others evoked touching affection and sentiment.

Since many of these Spanish men were fathers of mestizo children, it follows that indigenous women emerge as another important locus of study and analysis in this book. Their roles as family members, as mothers, wives, companions, daughters, or siblings, are a thread that runs from chapter 1 to chapter 6. In its opening, this work complicates elite indigenous women's agency in the 1532 era when they were participants in or offspring of political marriages of conquest. In time, however, the political elites fade to the background in subsequent chapters to focus on non-elite or lesser elite indigenous women.[5] The book reveals indigenous mothers prevented from raising their children as well as those who spent their days in a household with their sons and daughters. These indigenous mothers used legal means, if necessary, to fulfill their maternal obligations. They also frequently provided important bequests to their children, whether or not they had physically raised them. For some these bequests were financial, but for others they were important objects that held increased cultural significance for family traditions in a colonial society. In contrast to allowing for moments of tenderness in the figure of the Spanish father, in this study the figure of the indigenous mother gains complexity through illustration of the extraordinary scope of actions these mothers had with their children and on behalf of their children.

Transatlantic Obligations moves beyond individual figures of mothers and fathers to investigate the groupings of colonial family that emerged in Andean cities from 1550 forward. It argues that what was happening in the sixteenth-century families did not lead to a straightforward reproduction of a colonial ruling class. Thanks to the growth of cities such as Lima and Arequipa, and the mechanisms of the colonial economy, indigenous and Spanish men and women interacted frequently. In some instances, meaningful and lasting family connections were made both in and outside of marriage and across racial lines. Francisco Mexia de Yabes and Isabel Coca, both single, had a daughter named Mariana.[6] When Mariana turned six years old, Mexia decided to make her a legal donation. Mexia gave his daughter property in the city of La Plata to use for her dowry and marriage citing his "fatherly love" as rationale for the donation. He highlighted his feelings for Mariana's mother, Isabel, as a reason for giving Mariana the property. Isabel had provided many good services, in particular, "with her earnings and skills she helped me to buy the houses."[7] Mexia's detail was unusual for a letter of obligation. He acknowledged his debt to a native woman, their economic partnership, and their shared responsibilities as parents of Mariana. Born in 1601, Mariana's family experience bears some resemblance to those of the 1540s with regard to fathering children out of wedlock, assuming some obligation to provide, and blending indigenous and Spanish elements in a lasting way.

In studying urban families, the answer to an important question emerges. We know that the structures of indigenous family were pummeled in the sixteenth century due not only to the presence of Spanish colonials but also to demographic changes resulting from the violence associated with colonial rule and migration. What, then, happens to the indigenous family during this era? This study contributes a partial answer by showing that indigenous families were busy with labor, love, and cultural formation in cities. Their makeup, however, did not always look exactly like we expect them to as their households and kin networks might also have included mestizo children or time spent in conjugal relationships with Spaniards.

The urban indigenous families of the 1570s or 1580s are linked to changes that began when family units underwent a *mestizaje* in the 1530s. This process occurred in both legal and domestic settings. Recall that in Spanish court Francisco Ampuero declared that his wife Quispe Sisa was "a legitimate daughter according to the *custom of the country*."[8] He meant that her parents, Huayna Capac and Contarhuacho had what amounted to a legitimate marriage in the eyes of the Inca system, which should have been good enough for the Spanish court to consider her legitimate. Ampuero's argument took advantage of the Crown's recognition of indigenous pre-Columbian family structures within a new colonial framework. At the same historical moment that Ampuero made this argument, similar reframings of family relationships were occurring across the Andes, and to a lesser extent in Spain, as people tried to make sense of the changes wrought by Spanish expansion into the Indies. The Crown spoke of "mestizos lost among the Indians" and priests worried about abandoned wives "wrapped in sin" in Iberia while their husbands lived in Peru. During these same decades, individuals unwittingly prompted a new "custom of the country" through a *mestizaje* of the family that conformed to their daily realities.

These new family arrangements and customs would eventually work their way into notary offices and the ritual by which people wrote wills wherein they determined their provisions for their children. The ability of a parent to use their will to shape the future was governed by Spanish inheritance laws. Yet, as explored here, individuals dictated provisions that questioned or challenged that law when their family's need put them in a position of having to willfully create an unlawful bequest for a child, especially one born out of wedlock.

Demographic realities in the 1530s and 1540s occasioned many relationships between indigenous women and Spanish men. Emerging soon after was the question of what to do with the children of these relationships in the 1540s through the 1560s. Fathers of natural children wanted them in Spanish households or in Spain. Alonso Muñoz, a Limeño tailor, sent Francisca, daughter of the Chincha native Leonor, and Francisco, son of the Nicaragua native Juana, to Spain in 1552.[9] As legal powers and wills overwhelmingly show, Spanish fathers enacted plans to ensure their natural sons and daughters had an Iberian, Christian upbringing and a chance for a comfortable, if not elite, socioeconomic status as adults.

Yet not all mestizo children lived in Spanish households, and the blended families that became more common from the 1560s on reveal how indigenous Andean culture informed family experience even when such a family might include important ties to a Spanish man. Along with the obligation to assist children economically, indigenous families prioritized material culture as a vehicle for transmission of custom and history. While laws guided what parents must do with regard to inheritance shares, some practices were not specified by law. The objects given as bequests by fathers and mothers as glimpsed in a will or another notarial document brought memories associated with their context. What did it mean to have objects of native significance (*llicllas, chumbes, topos,* or *cocos*) in an urban household in the 1570s and 1580s? Imagine who wore the finely crafted *vicuña* shawls or which men gathered to drink *chicha* together from the pair of silver drinking vessels. From the pages filed in a notary's office, to the houses and streets of Lima or Arequipa, people's families and the memory of family came alive through these objects. While an inheritance of money helped a child in the future, mothers and fathers understood that bequeathing a material object could preserve the past for years to come.

All the family artifacts and pesos notwithstanding, families of indigenous or mixed-race descent suffered continual discrimination in the colonial period because of policies that privileged Spaniards. Even so, their actions frequently complicated Crown or Church views of a colonial reality. From 1532 to the late sixteenth century, this study offers a step-by-step view of individuals and family units as they adjusted to new norms decade after decade. They carried with them (whether Spaniard or indigenous) the customs that they knew, and their patterns of upholding obligations, especially as parents, led to acknowledging family units comprised of legitimate and illegitimate kin. All the while, weighty links between labor and family connected former masters and servants who were also parents or half-siblings who shared business interests. Illegitimacy, migration, and removal of children (or child circulation) are themes that continue to dominate the legal and cultural constructions of family throughout Latin American history. This study invites comparison from other regions in the sixteenth century to cast more light on how families, urban or rural, shifted in the first seventy years after Spanish arrival. On its own, however, *Transatlantic Obligations* hints that previous interpretations have emphasized the tense ties of family in exclusion of the more tender ties that persisted and sometimes challenged dominant colonial discourses.

With dowries and bequests, fathers and mothers met obligations and not infrequently showed love and affection. Extant sources limit a present-day view into the emotions of long-ago moments. This study shows, though, that those moments offered in the sources must be analyzed as rigorously as one might analyze property values. "Son of my heart," wrote doña Francisca Maldonado to her son Jerónimo Leandro Maldonado. "I received a letter of yours. It is now some fifteen years after I left you [in Spain] with so much heartache. . . . What consoles me is the understanding that neither my absence nor that of your father has done you harm."[10] Although her letter does not elaborate on how she knew that Jerónimo had been fine in her absence, it suggests a long-standing unease on her part that her migration to the New World could have signified a bad outcome for her son coupled with extraordinary relief that had not been the case. The sentiment also reveals her understanding of an obligation for caring for Jerónimo who stayed with surrogate parents when she traveled to the New World. Francisca expressed optimism that she would return to Spain to see him again, but it was more of a wish than a plan as she simultaneously confessed that she was nearing the end of her life, in her words "old and toothless."

The webs of family that make up the bulk of the research for this book show that families separated by an ocean, like Maldonado and her son or Isabel Tocto and her daughters, did not cease to be families in the face of distance, illegitimacy, or race mixture. Nor did families within Peru's cities function less like families if they did not fit the norms prescribed in terms of marriage or legitimacy, such as the family of Juan and Leonor López. Family entities contained within them hierarchies and borders, albeit porous ones, that were drawn by legal provisions with regard to marriage, legitimacy, and culture as well as life in Spain or Peru. Yet overwhelmingly, people responded to the notion of obligation inherent in whatever family role they occupied, and family units adapted and improvised to meet those obligations. The term "obligation" surfaces time and again in sixteenth-century sources and its usage reveals to us that as much as obligation could be a burden, it might also be seen as something of value. Across Iberia and the Andes, to be a part of family demanded obligations, but to be without family was to be impoverished in multiple ways.[11] When Cristóbal Páez de Becerril told his wife that when she traveled to Peru, "there would be no man richer than I," his words spoke not only to his love for her but to the larger sixteenth-century understanding of family as network for the present, tie to the pre-colonial past, and legacy for the colonial future.

Notes

INTRODUCTION

1. Archivo General de Indias (hereinafter AGI), Contratación 242, N.1, R.15, Herederos de Isabel Tocto yndia sobre cobro de bienes, 1579, fols. 23r–24r.
2. Nara Milanich argued that attention to the particularities of family in Latin America, especially hierarchies of caste and class, can help Latin America histories of family speak to historians of family elsewhere. See Nara Milanich, "Whither Family History? A Road Map from Latin America," *American Historical Review* 112, no. 2 (April 2007): 439–458.
3. See the lively study by Alexandra Parma Cook and Noble David Cook, *Good Faith and Truthful Ignorance: A Case of Transatlantic Bigamy* (Durham, NC: Duke University Press, 1991). The most comprehensive study on bigamy in colonial Mexico is Richard Boyer, *Lives of the Bigamists: Marriage, Family and Community in Colonial Mexico* (Albuquerque: University of New Mexico Press, 1995).
4. Ida Altman's pioneering work exposed the tight-knit world of migration networks between Spain and Mexico in *Transatlantic Ties in the Spanish Empire: Brihuega, Spain, and Puebla, Mexico, 1560–1620* (Stanford, CA: Stanford University Press, 2000). Carlos González Sánchez analyzes the family ties of non-elite Spaniards between Spain and Peru in *Dineros de ventura, la varia fortuna de la emigración a Indias (siglos XVI–XVII)* (Seville: Universidad de Sevilla, 1995).
5. Yuen-Gen Liang offers a vigorous reworking of ideas about power and elite family in empire with a case study of late fifteenth to the mid-sixteenth century Iberia and northern Africa. See *Family and Empire: The Fernández de Córdoba and the Spanish Realm* (Philadelphia: University of Pennsylvania Press, 2011).
6. The reference is to Ann Laura Stoler, "Tense and Tender Ties: The Politics of Comparison in North American History and (Post) Colonial Studies," *Journal of American History* 88 (2001): 829–865.

7. With this argument I want to move beyond a dichotomous indigenous–Spanish notion of family structure that dominated society as suggested by, for example, James Lockhart, who claimed of Peru "even in the first generation Hispanic society in Peru had enough Spanish women to preclude the simple loss of any important cultural elements." *Spanish Peru, 1532–1560: A Social History*, 2nd ed. (Madison: University of Wisconsin Press, 1994), 169.

8. For work with an emphasis on Spanish bloodlines, see Pilar Gonzalbo, *Familias novohispanas, siglos XVI al XIX* (México, DF: El Colegio de México, Centro de Estudios Históricos, 1991). A more recent paradigm for understanding family is Bianca Premo, "Familiares: Thinking beyond Lineage and across Race in Spanish Atlantic Family History," *William and Mary Quarterly* 70, no.2 (April 2013): 295–316. Colonial family history for Mexico owes a debt to the influential school of family history begun by the work of Lawrence Stone, *The Family, Sex and Marriage in England, 1500–1800* (New York: Harper & Row, 1977).

9. For a work that brilliantly places illegitimacy in the forefront as the norm in colonial Lima, see María Emma Mannarelli, *Pecados publicos: La ilegitimidad en Lima, siglo XVII* (Lima: Ediciones Flora Tristán, 1993). In contrast to Mannarelli, historians who have studied family in transatlantic context have focused primarily on legitimate family structures and nobility (pecheros vs. nobles), such as Altman, *Transatlantic Ties in the Spanish Empire*.

10. Nancy van Deusen, "The Intimacies of Bondage, Female Indigenous Servants and Slaves and Their Spanish Masters, 1492–1555," *Journal of Women's History* 24, no. 1 (2012): 13–43.

11. On the influence of the pre-Columbian into the colonial era, see Pedro Carrasco, "Indian–Spanish Marriages in the First Century of the Colony," in *Indian Women of Early Mexico*, ed. Susan Schroeder, Stephanie Wood, and Robert Haskett (Norman: University of Oklahoma Press, 1997), 87–103.

12. On eighteenth-century Latin America, see Ann Twinam's study of paternal behavior, "Honor, paternidad e ilegitimidad: Los padres solteros en América Latina durante la Colonia," *Estudios Sociales* 3 (September 1988): 9–32, as well as Bianca Premo, "An Old Father in a New Tragedy: Fatherhood in the Legal Theater of the Spanish Atlantic, 1770–1820," *Clio* 40, no. 1 (2010): 109–130, on the changing dynamic of paternal authority in the Age of Revolution.

13. The seminal Latin American work on children and fathers or other figures of paternal authority is Bianca Premo, *Children of the Father King: Youth, Authority, and Legal Minority in Colonial Lima* (Chapel Hill, NC: University of North Carolina Press, 2005). For Spanish law on family matters, see Robert I. Burns, S.J., ed. *Las Siete Partidas*, Vol. 4, trans. Samuel Parsons Scott (Philadelphia: University of Pennsylvania Press, 2001). The influence of the Siete Partidas in sixteenth-century Iberian approaches to family is fundamental, even taking into account the nature of law to evolve over time.

14. R. Jovita Baber explores this balance of custom and law in colonial Mexico. See R. Jovita Baber, "Categories, Self-Representation and the Construction of the *Indios*," *Journal of Spanish Cultural Studies* 10, no. 1 (March 2009): 31–32. This prominent interplay between law and custom in colonial contexts prompts Lauren Benton to argue that colonial cultures were in fact critical to shaping legal pluralism. See Lauren Benton, *Law and Colonial Cultures: Legal Regimes in World History, 1400–1900* (Cambridge: Cambridge University Press, 2002).

15. For a useful definition of fatherhood within sixteenth-century patriarchy, see Daviken Studnicki-Gizbert, *A Nation upon the Ocean Sea: Portugal's Atlantic Diaspora and the Crisis of the Spanish Empire, 1492–1640* (New York: Oxford University Press, 2007), 80–81.

16. Karen Viera Powers, *Women in the Crucible of Conquest: The Gendered Genesis of Spanish American Society, 1500–1600* (Albuquerque: University of New Mexico Press, 2005).

17. AGI, Indiferente 737, N. 66, F. 2, 1551.

18. On the importance of surrogacy in the early modern era, see Sandra Cavallo, "Family Relationships," in *A Cultural History of Childhood and Family in the Early Modern Age* (Oxford: Berg, 2010), 29–32. On attempts to protect poor children in colonial Quito, see Cynthia Milton, *The Many Meanings of Poverty: Colonialism, Social Compacts, and Assistance in Eighteenth-Century Ecuador* (Stanford, CA: Stanford University Press, 2007), 125–151. Being raised outside one's birth home is also referred to in the Latin American literature as "child circulation." See Laura Shelton, "Like a Servant or Like a Son? Circulating Children in Northwestern Mexico (1790–1850)," in *Raising an Empire: Children in Early Modern Iberia and Colonial Latin America*, ed. Ondina E. González and Bianca Premo (Albuquerque: University of New Mexico, 2007), as well as Nara Milanich, *Children of Fate: Childhood, Class, and State in Chile, 1850–1930* (Durham, NC: Duke University Press, 2009), esp. 103–127, 157–182.

19. See, e.g., Steve J. Stern, *Peru's Indian Peoples and the Challenge of Spanish Conquest, Huamanga to 1640* (Madison: University of Wisconsin Press, 1982), 154, 70–171. On colonial Lima, see Paul Charney, *Indian Society in the Valley of Lima, Peru, 1532–1824* (Lanham, MD: University Press of America, 2001).

20. Karen Graubart, *With our Labor and Sweat: Indigenous Women and the Formation of Colonial Society in Peru, 1550–1700* (Stanford, CA: Stanford University Press, 2007).

21. See the argument by van Deusen, "The Intimacies of Bondage," 34. Van Deusen's findings on indigenous women for this early chronological era have served as a beacon in an otherwise murky historiographical terrain.

22. Harold Livermore, "Introduction," *Royal Commentaries of the Incas and General History of Peru* (Austin: University of Texas Press, 1966), quoting Bivero, p. xxvii.

23. For a deconstruction of the label "Spanish," see Elizabeth Kuznesof, "Ethnic and Gender Influences on 'Spanish' Creole Society in Colonial Spanish America," *Colonial Latin American Review* 4, no. 1 (1995): 153–176, as well as the response by Stuart Schwartz, "Colonial Identities and the Sociedad de castas," *Colonial Latin American Review* 4, no. 1 (1995): 185–201. Stuart Schwartz and Frank Salomon offer a masterful analysis of mixed-race identities in South America in "New Peoples and New Kinds of People: Adaptation, Readjustment, and Ethnogenesis in South American Indigenous Societies (Colonial Era)," in *The Cambridge History of the Native Peoples of the Americas*, ed. Frank Salomon and Stuart B. Schwartz, vol. 3, *South America*, part 2 (Cambridge: Cambridge University Press, 1999), 443–501. On the complexities of the category of indio, see David Cahill, "Colour by Numbers: Racial and Ethnic Categories in the Viceroyalty of Peru, 1532–1824," *Journal of Latin American Studies* 26, no. 2 (1994): 325–346.

24. Felipe Guaman Poma de Ayala, *The First New Chronicle and Good Government*, trans. and annot. David Frye (Indianapolis: Hackett Publishing Company, Inc., 2006), 76. See also this reference in the complete Spanish edition, Felipe Guaman Poma de Ayala, *Nueva Coronica y Buen Gobierno*, trans., prólogo, notas y cronología Franklin Pease (Caracas: Biblioteca Ayacucho, 1980), Vol. 1, p. 149.

25. F. E. Ruan, "Andean Activism and the Reformulation of Mestizo Agency and Identity in Early Colonial Peru," *Colonial Latin American Review* 21, no. 2 (2012): 211–212.

26. My emphasis here responds to Kathryn Burns's calls for further historicizing the use of racial categories in historical writing. See Kathryn Burns, "Unfixing Race," in *Rereading the Black Legend: The Discourses of Religious and Racial Different in the Renaissance Empires*, ed. Margaret R. Greer, Maureen Quilligan, and Walter D. Mignolo (Chicago: University of Chicago Press, 2008), esp. 191–199.

27. Joanne Rappaport, *The Disappearing Mestizo: Configuring Difference in the Colonial New Kingdom of Granada* (Durham, NC: Duke University Press, 2014), esp. 95–132.

28. Kathryn Burns, *Colonial Habits, Convents and the Spiritual Economy of Cuzco, Peru* (Durham, NC: Duke University Press, 1999), 36.

29. For references to this practice in sixteenth-century Lima, see Lockhart, *Spanish Peru*, 188, and in seventeenth-century Ecuador, see Karen Powers, "The Battle for Bodies and Souls in the Colonial North Andes," *Hispanic American Historical Review* 75, no. 1 (February 1995): 42.

30. James Lockhart concluded that Spaniards showed serious interest in their mestizo children. See Lockhart, *Spanish Peru*, 190. For the case of sixteenth-century Arequipa, Keith Davies noted the concern of encomenderos to marry well their mestiza daughters. Keith Davies, *Landowners in Colonial Peru* (Austin: University of Texas Press, 1984), 75.

31. See Verena Stolcke and Alexandre Coello, eds., *Identidades ambivalentes en America Latina (siglos XVI–XXI)* (Barcelona: Ediciones Bellaterra, 2008).

32. Kuznesof asks what the category of "Spanish" really meant. See Elizabeth Kuznesof, "Ethnic and Gender Influences on 'Spanish' Creole Society in Colonial Spanish America," *Colonial Latin American Review* 4, no. 1 (1995): 153–176.

33. Baber, "Categories, Self-Representation and the Construction of the *Indios*," 27–28.

34. Baber, "Categories, Self-Representation and the Construction of the *Indios*," 34.

35. See the pathbreaking study of María Elena Martínez, *Genealogical Fictions: Limpieza de Sangre, Religion, and Gender in Colonial Mexico* (Stanford, CA: Stanford University Press, 2008).

36. Jane E. Mangan, "A Marketplace of Identities: Women, Trade, and Ethnic Labels in Colonial Potosí," in *Imperial Subjects: Race and Identity in Colonial Latin America*, ed. Andrew B. Fisher and Matthew D. O'Hara (Durham, NC: Duke University Press, 2009).

37. Quoting Ann Laura Stoler, *Carnal Knowledge and Imperial Power: Race and the Intimate in Colonial Rule* (Berkeley and Los Angeles: University of California Press, 2002).

38. When conceptualizing the role of empire in family, I find Stoler helpful. She argues that race mixture "called into question the distinctions of difference that maintained the neat boundaries of colonial rule," see Stoler, *Carnal Knowledge*, 79.

39. My familiarity with Andean history and archives prompted me to situate this study in Peru. Historians who have approached this issue for Mexico, albeit in more narrowly defined conceptual frameworks, include Camila Townsend, *Malintzin's Choices, an Indian Woman in the Conquest of Mexico* (Albuquerque: University of New Mexico Press, 2006) and Donald Chipman, *Moctezuma's Children: Aztec Royalty under Spanish rule, 1520–1700* (Austin: University of Texas Press, 2005).

40. Nancy van Deusen calls for a rethinking of the periodization of sixteenth-century historiography to acknowledge that violence did not end at 1550 and accommodation did not begin only at that point. See van Deusen, "The Intimacies of Bondage," 14–15.

41. On these circuits of commerce, see Lockhart, *Spanish Peru*, 6, 102–103.

42. Drawings by Felipe Guaman Poma de Ayala are one example of a visual record of people of mixed-race descent in this era. These are available in digital format at http://www.kb.dk/permalink/2006/poma/info/en/frontpage.htm.

43. Other historians of the early modern family have noted this contrast between family relationships as presented in prescriptive sources and judicial records. See Cavallo, *Family Relationships*, 16.

44. Extant ecclesiastical archives are limited for the sixteenth century though baptismal records have been ably researched by Nancy van Deusen for the 1530s–1550s, analysis which appears in "Diasporas, Bondage, and Intimacy in Lima, 1535 to 1555," *Colonial Latin American Review* 19, no. 2 (2010): 247–277.

45. Alejandro de la Fuente, *Havana and the Atlantic in the Sixteenth Century* (Chapel Hill, NC: University of North Carolina Press, 2011), 7.

46. See the revealing analysis of these notarial practices and how they formed a "composite agency" in the production of written documents in Kathryn Burns, *Into the Archive: Writing and Power in Colonial Peru* (Durham, NC: Duke University Press, 2010).

47. Archivo General de la Nación–Peru (hereinafter AGNP), Protocolos 42, Gascon, fols. 339–340, Testamento de Luis de Tapia, 1552.

48. The classic study of Africans in colonial Peru is Frederick Bowser, *The African Slave in Colonial Peru, 1524–1650* (Stanford, CA: Stanford University Press, 1974). People of African descent in the Trujillo region are a major focus of Rachel Sarah O'Toole, *Bound Lives: Africans, Indians, and the Making of Race in Colonial Peru* (Pittsburgh, PA: University of Pittsburgh Press, 2012).

49. Nancy van Deusen, *Between the Sacred and the Worldly: The Institutional and Cultural Practice of Recogimiento in Colonial Lima* (Stanford, CA: Stanford University Press, 2001), 37–58.

50. Historian María Rostworowski argues that the "memory of the vast majority of anonymous mestizas is lost to oblivion." See her book *Doña Francisca Pizarro, una ilustre mestiza* (Lima: Instituto de Estudios Peruanos, 1989), 78.

51. Kathryn Burns, "Gender and the Politics of Mestizaje: The Convent of Santa Clara in Cuzco, Peru," *Hispanic American Historical Review* 78, no. 1 (February 1998): 5–44.

52. AGI, Charcas 415, Libro I, fol. 232v.

53. See Rebecca Earle, "Letters and Love in Colonial Spanish America," *The Americas* 62, no. 1 (July 2005): 17–46.

CHAPTER 1

1. Peter Gose, *Invaders as Ancestors: On the Intercultural Making and Unmaking of Spanish Colonialism in the Andes* (Toronto: University of Toronto, 2008), 6. Gose recognizes potential critiques of his approach, see pp. 4–5. In contrast to Gose, Silvia Rivera Cusicanqui offers a representation of conquest and colonial domination as "open genocide." See Silvia Rivera Cusicanqui, "La raíz: colonizadores y colonizados," in *Violencias Encubiertas en Bolivia*, coord. Xavier Albó and Rául Barrios Morón (La Paz: CIPCA, 1993), 22.

2. Of the millions of people who lived in the territory of the Inca empire, some 40,000 had Inca identity. See Arnold Bauer, *Goods, Power, History: Latin America's Material Culture* (Cambridge: Cambridge University Press, 2001), 33.

In this chapter, I use the term "Inca" to refer to individuals who were part of the Inca kin structure and to their specific imperial practices, and I use the term "Andean" to refer to others of indigenous descent in the region who were not ethnic Inca.

3. See the innovative work by Gonzalo Lamana, *Domination without Dominance: Inca-Spanish Encounters in Early Colonial Peru* (Durham, NC: Duke University Press, 2008), which studies the *probanzas* in order to analyze the native side of sixteenth-century conquest history.

4. Lamana, *Domination without Dominance*, 164.

5. See, for instance, Ward Stavig, *The World of Tupac Amaru: Conflict, Community, and Identity in Colonial Peru* (Lincoln: University of Nebraska Press, 1999), 38.

6. Spanish observers characterized the role of the *aclla* according to their narrow Iberian worldview, see Karen Graubart, "Indecent Living: Indigenous Women and the Politics of Representation in Early Colonial Peru," *Colonial Latin American Review* 9, no. 2 (2000): 213–235.

7. Peter Gose, "The State as a Chosen Woman: Brideservice and the Feeding of Tributaries in the Inka Empire," *American Anthropologist* 102, no. 1 (March 2000): 85.

8. See the full discussion in Gose, "The State as a Chosen Woman," 84–97.

9. The practice of multiple wives among native elite continued well after the Spanish arrival. See the Royal Cédula on caciques in Peru keeping more than one wife, Richard Konetzke, ed., *Colección de documentos para la historia de la formacón social de Hispanoamérica, 1493–1910* (Madrid: Consejo Superior de Investigaciones Científicas, 1953), 1:295.

10. Catherine Julien, *Reading Inca History* (Iowa City: University of Iowa Press, 2002), 34.

11. Tom Cummins, "Forms of Andean Colonial Towns, Free Will, and Marriage," *The Archeology of Colonialism*, ed. Claire Lyons and John Papadopoulos (Los Angeles: Getty Press, 2002): 228.

12. Julien, *Reading Inca History*, 33.

13. Rivera Cusicanqui, "La raíz: colonizadores y colonizados," 21.

14. Rivera Cusicanqui, "La raíz: colonizadores y colonizados," 214.

15. Lamana, *Domination without Dominance*, 150.

16. Lamana, *Domination without Dominance*, 109.

17. Kerstin Nowack, "Aquellas señoras del linaje real de los incas, vida y super-vivencia de las mujeres de la nobleza inca el en Perú en los primeros años de la Colonia," in *Elites indígenas en los andes, nobles, caciques y cabildantes bajo el yugo colonial*, eds. David Cahill and Blanca Tovías (Quito: Ediciones Abya-Yala, 2003), 23. See also Sabine MacCormack, "History, Historical Record, and Ceremonial Action: Incas and Spaniards in Cuzco," *Comparative Studies of Society and History* 43, no. 2 (2001): 342.

18. Nowack, "Aquellas señoras del linaje real," 22, citing Titu Cusi Yupanqui.

19. Nowack, "Aquellas señoras del linaje real," 19.

20. Catherine Julien, "Francisca Pizarro, la cuzqueña, y su madre, la *coya* Ynguill," *Revista del Archivo Regional del Cuzco* 15 (June 2000): 53–74. Julien's article provides an insightful reading of the primary sources on this mother–daughter pair and determines that evidence exists to confirm Juan Pizarro as Francisca's father. This chapter is indebted to Julien's research and analysis, and places her findings within the larger context of my research on families for the sixteenth-century Andes.

21. Julien, "Francisca Pizarro, la cuzqueña," 59.

22. Julien, "Francisca Pizarro, la cuzqueña," 53–54, citing the will of Juan Pizarro.

23. On the heels of the discussion of Quispe Sisa and Ynguill, the work of Camila Townsend on Malintzin bears mention. The experience of Inca nobles' families in the first generation after conquest certainly bore resemblance to what had transpired some ten years earlier in Mexico. Townsend's work expands our understanding of Malintzin, and the experiences of her children. One contrast, though, is that while Quispe Sisa and Ynguill were elite women accustomed to relative luxury, the Mexican woman created her own position of leverage through her role as translator and ally to Cortés, not by the fact of her birth. See Townsend, *Malintzin's Choices: An Indian Woman in the Conquest of Mexico* (Albuquerque: University of New Mexico Press, 2006).

24. Catherine Julien, "Introduction," in Titu Cusi Yupanqui, *History of How the Spaniards Arrived in Peru*, trans. with an intro. by Catherine Julien (Cambridge, MA: Hackett, 2006), p. xi.

25. AGI, Lima 472, No. 2, fol. 12r.

26. AGI, Lima 472, No. 2, fol. 2v, Capitulations with Titu Cusi Yupanqui.

27. John Hemming, *The Conquest of the Incas* (New York: Harcourt, Brace, Jovanovich, 1970), 314–315, 459.

28. AGI, Lima 472, No. 2, fol. 9r.

29. AGI, Lima 472, No. 2, fol. 9v.

30. AGI, Justicia 657, No. 1, R. 2, fol. 327r. "Cristoval de Bostinzo en nombre de Pedro de Bostinzo su hermano tutor y curado de doña Beatriz de Mendoza, hija del Ynga, y el Fiscal: contra Arias y Cristoval Maldonado hermanos, en cuya casa estava depositada la dha dona Beatriz, menor de siete anos, casamiento clandestino con el expresado Cristobal Maldonado, 1566." See also Cusi Yupanqui, *History of How the Spaniards Arrived in Peru*, p. xii.

31. AGI, Justicia 657, No. 1, R. 2, fol. 332r.

32. María Rostworowski de Diez Canseco, *Doña Francisca Pizarro, una ilustre mestiza, 1534–1598* (Lima: Instituto de Estudios Peruanos, 1989), citing a letter for the King from Toledo, 81–82.

33. R. Jovita Baber, "Categories, Self-Representation and the Construction of the *Indios*," *Journal of Spanish Cultural Studies* 10, no. 1 (March 2009): 33.

34. See the discussion of claims about Manco Inca as heir in Julien, Introduction, p. xxv, and in Titu Cusi Yupanqui, *An Account of the Conquest of Peru*, trans., intro., and annot. by Ralph Bauer (Boulder: University of Colorado Press, 2005), 31–32.

35. María Elena Martínez, *Geneaological Fictions: Limpieza de Sangre, Religion and Gender in Colonial Mexico* (Stanford, CA: Stanford University Press, 2008), 61–87.

36. Rostworowski de Diez Canseco, *Doña Francisca Pizarro*, 16. Huayna Capac is also spelled as Guayna Capac, especially in Spanish documents. I have used Huayna throughout.

37. Sara Guengerich, "Capac Women and the Politics of Marriage in Early Colonial Peru," *Colonial Latin American Review* 24, no. 2 (2015): 147–167.

38. Rostworowski de Diez Canseco, *Doña Francisca Pizarro*, 18.

39. AGI, Justicia 1088, Autos Fiscales Lima, No. 4, R. 1, fol. 1r.

40. Anthony Anghie, *Imperialism, Sovereignty, and the Making of International Law* (New York: Cambridge University Press, 2004), 26.

41. Rafael Varón Gabai, *Francisco Pizarro and his Brothers: The Illusion of Power in Sixteenth-Century Peru*, trans. Javier Flores Espinoza (Norman: University of Oklahoma Press, 1997), 142–144.

42. AGI, Justicia 1088, Autos Fiscales Lima, No. 4, R. 1, fol. 10v.

43. AGI, Justicia 1088, Autos Fiscales Lima, No. 4, R. 1, fol. 11r.

44. AGI, Justicia 1088, Autos Fiscales Lima, No. 4, R. 1, fol. 11r–11v.

45. AGI, Justicia 1088, Autos Fiscales Lima, No. 4, R. 1, fol. 12r, Testimony of Nicolas de Ribera el Viejo.

46. AGI, Justicia 1088, Autos Fiscales Lima, No. 4, R. 1, fol. 18r–18v, Testimony of Gomez Caravantes de Macuelas.

47. AGI, Justicia 1088, Autos Fiscales Lima, No. 4, R. 1, fol. 21v, Testimony of Antonyo Poma.

48. One witness claims he does not know if the two are married, though he responds to most of the interrogatory that he does not know. AGI, Justicia 1088, Autos Fiscales Lima, No. 4, R. 1, fols. 13–14.

49. AGI, Justicia 1088, Autos Fiscales Lima, No. 4, R. 1, fol. 18r.

50. AGI, Justicia 451. See discussion of this in Guengerich, "Capac Women and the Politics of Marriage in Early Colonial Peru."

51. For the significance of indigenous caciques' litigation in the Royal Court, including don Melchor, see José Carlos de la Puente Luna, "A costa de Su Majestad: Indios viajeros y dilemas imperiales en la corte de los Habsburgo," *Allpanchis: Historia y Sociedad* 39, no. 72 (2008): 11–60. His name was spelled in historical documents as both Melchor and Melchior.

52. AGI, Lima 472, No. 6, fol. 140v. Valladolid, 4 noviembre 1603.

53. AGI, Lima 472, No. 6, fol. 136v. Pretensión de don Melchior Carlos Inga, 11 agosto 1604.

54. AGI, Lima 472, No. 6, fol. 136v. Pretensión de don Melchior Carlos Inga, 11 agosto 1604.

55. AGI, Lima 472, No. 6, fol. 140v.

56. AGI, Lima 472, No. 6, fol. 140v. Valladolid, 4 noviembre 1603.

57. Gose, *Invaders as Ancestors*, 6–7.

58. For an early mention of these women's experiences, see Lockhart, *Spanish Peru, 1532–1560, A Social History*, 2nd ed. (Madison: University of Wisconsin Press, 1994), 244–245.

59. AGNP, Protocolos 109, Martel, fols. 609v–611r, Testamento de Juan Flores, 15 octubre 1557.

60. María Emma Mannarelli, *Private Passions and Public Sins: Men and Women in Seventeenth-Century Lima*, trans. Sidney Evans and Meredith D. Dodge (Albuquerque: University of New Mexico Press, 2007), 17.

61. Karen Powers, *Women in the Crucible of Conquest: The Gendered Genesis of Spanish American Society, 1500–1600* (Albuquerque: University of New Mexico Press, 2005), 71.

62. Nancy van Deusen, "The Intimacies of Bondage: Female Indigenous Servants and Slaves and Their Spanish Masters, 1492–1555," *Journal of Women's History* 24, no. 1 (2012): 16, 22–23.

63. Karen Powers argues that Pizarro arranged the marriage. See Powers, *Women in the Crucible of Conquest*, 75.

64. Mannarelli, *Private Passions and Public Sins*, 8.

65. Townsend, *Malintzin's Choices*, 157.

66. See the arrangements for Leonor *india* as detailed in AGNP, Protocolos 29, Alonso de la Cueva, fols. 125r–128r, Testamento de Francisco de Aguilera, 6 diciembre 1580, and AGNP, Protocolos 29, Alonso de la Cueva, fols. 234–235r, Testamento de Leonor yndia natural del Cuzco, 5 julio 1579.

67. See AGNP, Protocolos 33, Esquivel Franco, fols. 158–159v, Testamento de Alonso Benito, 17 marco 1571; the indigenous mother of Benito's son Francisco, Catalina, married an indigenous man some years after the birth of Francisco. For a sixteenth-century example of this practice, see Karen Graubart, "The Creolization of the New World: Local Forms of Identification in Urban Colonial Peru, 1560–1640," *Hispanic American Historical Review* 89, no. 3 (2009): 485.

68. Allyson Poska, "When Love Goes Wrong: Getting Out of Marriage in Seventeenth-Century Spain," *Journal of Social History* 29, no. 4 (Summer 1996): 874–876. This is also related to practices of financial or material gifts to women who were *barraganas* in medieval Spain as discussed by Heath Dillard, *Daughters of the Reconquest: Women in Castilian Town Society, 1100–1300* (New York: Cambridge University Press, 1984), 128–134.

69. AGNP, Protocolos 160, Sebastián Vázquez, fols. 864v–865, 6 marco 1553.

70. AGNP, Protocolos 9, Simón de Alzate, fol. 1114–1114v, Testamento de Juan Flores, 10 marco 1554.

71. AGNP, Protocolos 127, Estevan Pérez, fols. 1r–3r, Testamento de Gonçalo Gutiérrez Nombre de Pila, 18 abril 1560.

72. AGNP, Protocolos 127, Estevan Pérez, fol. 2r, Testamento de Gonçalo Gutiérrez Nombre de Pila, 18 abril 1560. See also AGI, Contratación 256A, N. 1, R. 4, where Bartolomé Carmona gave a sum of 100 pesos to his natural daughter's indigenous mother Luisa Tocta.

73. Archivo Regional de Arequipa (hereinafter ARA), Protocolos 99, Juan de Vera, Testamento de Francisco Ramírez, F. cvi (vuelta), 30 mayo 1568.

74. AGI, Contratación 476, N. 1, R. 1, Bienes de Manuel de Herrera [date]. For a similar bequest of a *solar* and textiles in Arequipa, see ARA, Protocolos 1, Diego de Aguilar, R. 10, fols. 323v–328r, Testamento de Diego Hernández de Talavera, 8 noviembre 1577.

75. AGNP, Protocolos 160, Sebastián Vázquez, fols. 258–263, Testamento de Sebastián Bernal, 11 febrero 1552. See also AGNP, Protocolos 9, Simón de Alzate, fols. 1009–1011, Testamento de Alonso Hernández de [no date—around noviembre 1553].

76. ARA, Protocolos 33, Gaspar Hernández, Testamento de Francisco de Quiros, fol. lxxx (vuelta)—fol. lxxxiii (recto), 2 marco 1556. See also AGNP, Protocolos 9, Simón de Alzate, fols. 994–995v, Testamento de Francisco Martínez, 26 agosto 1553.

77. Archivo Histórico Protocolos de Sevilla (hereinafter AHPS), Signatura 19716, Oficio 12, Andres de Herrera, Will of Diego Alonso de Sotomayor, 17 abril 1570, fol. 311, "una yndia difunta que le soy a cargo."

78. Rostworowski de Diez Canseco, *Doña Francisca Pizarro*, 36.

79. Rostworowski de Diez Canseco, *Doña Francisca Pizarro*, 30.

80. Rostworowski de Diez Canseco, *Doña Francisca Pizarro*, 40–41.

81. Rostworowski de Diez Canseco, *Doña Francisca Pizarro*, 45, "mal recaudo."

82. Rostworowski de Diez Canseco, *Doña Francisca Pizarro*, 45.

83. Rostworowski de Diez Canseco, *Doña Francisca Pizarro*, 65.

84. Rostworowski de Diez Canseco, *Doña Francisca Pizarro*, 68–69.

85. Julien, "Francisca Pizarro, la cuzqueña," 53–54, citing the will of Juan Pizarro.

86. Julien, "Francisca Pizarro, la cuzqueña," 55, notes that one document states a lump sum for to a woman who had "raised and dressed" doña Francisca.

87. Julien, "Francisca Pizarro, la cuzqueña," 55.

88. Townsend, *Malintzin's Choices*, 170.

89. Townsend, *Malintzin's Choices*, 163, 177.

90. Harold V. Livermore, "Introduction," in El Inca Garcilaso de la Vega, *Royal Commentaries of the Incas and General History of Peru*, trans. Harold V. Livermore (Austin: University of Texas Press, 1989), xx.

91. Julien, *History of How the Spaniards Arrived in Peru*, p. xxvi.

92. Garcilaso, 594

93. Garcilaso, 506–507.

94. Garcilaso, 40–41.
95. Margarita Zamora, *Language, Authority, and Indigenous History in the Comentarios reales de los Incas* (New York: Cambridge University Press, 1988).

CHAPTER 2

1. AGNP, Protocolos 153, Salinas, fols. 812–816v, Testamento de Alonso de Mesa, 12 septiembre 1542.. See discussion of Mesa, and fathers of mestizos more generally, in James Lockhart, *Spanish Peru, 1532–1560: A Social History*, 2nd ed. (Madison: University of Wisconsin Press, 1994), 244.

2. On Spaniards who raised these children in Lima, see Teresa Vergara, "Growing Up Indian: Migration, Labor, and Life in Lima (1570–1640)," in *Raising an Empire: Children in Early Modern Iberia and Colonial Latin America*, ed. Ondina E. González and Bianca Premo (Albuquerque: University of New Mexico, 2007), 76, 79–81. On mestizos living among indigenous communities, see for sixteenth-century Lima, Lockhart, *Spanish Peru*, 188, and for seventeenth-century Ecuador, see Karen Powers, "The Battle for Bodies and Souls in the Colonial North Andes," *Hispanic American Historical Review* 75, no. 1 (February 1995): 42.

3. Lockhart, *Spanish Peru*, 186–191, and Karen B. Graubart, *With Our Labor and Sweat: Indigenous Women and the Formation of Colonial Society in Peru, 1550–1700* (Stanford, CA: Stanford University Press, 2007), 107.

4. This trend may be in contrast to the experience of illegitimate children in Spain who would not be taken from their mothers for the same cultural motivations. Altman's work is important on this front as it provides some comparison with the Spanish experience before conquest. Still, the movement of children from family homes for financial motives, apprenticeships, and religious or social training was commonplace in the sixteenth century. See Sandra Cavallo, "Family Relationships," in *A Cultural History of Childhood and Family in the Early Modern Age*, ed. Sandra Cavallo and Silvia Evangelisti (Oxford: Berg, 2010), 29–32.

5. See, for instance, the insightful analysis in Karen Powers, *Women in the Crucible of Conquest: The Gendered Genesis of Spanish American Society, 1500–1600* (Albuquerque: University of New Mexico Press, 2005), ch. 3.

6. Graubart, *With Our Labor and Sweat*, 106. Joanne Rappaport analyzes mestizo identity in colonial New Granada with the goal of furthering our understanding of mestizo as a category of "exclusion" and not inclusion, see *The Disappearing Mestizo: Configuring Difference in the Colonial New Kingdom of Granada* (Durham, NC: Duke University Press, 2014), 7–15.

7. This is another way to look at the issue of identity in this era. For Lockhart, "Spanish women" included some mestizos (*Spanish Peru*, 170–171). Elizabeth Kuznesof, "Ethnic and Gender Influences on 'Spanish' Creole Society

in Colonial Spanish America," *Colonial Latin American Review* 4, no. 1 (1995): 153–176, argues the same as well. The construction of identities was forged by Spanish fathers and by the complex colonial context in which these children lived.

8. Cavallo, "Family Relationships," 20.

9. James Lockhart offers this general sketch of two fates of mestizo children, abandoned or acknowledged by Spanish fathers, in sixteenth-century Peru. See Lockhart, "The Women of the Second Generation," in *People and Issues in Latin American History: The Colonial Experience*, ed. Lewis Hanke and Jane M. Rausch (Princeton, NJ: Marcus Wiener Publishing, 1997), 271.

10. Robert Burns, I., S.J., ed. *Las Siete Partidas*, trans. Samuel Parsons Scott, Vol. 4. (Philadelphia: University of Pennsylvania Press, 2001), 972.

11. Ida Altman, *Emigrants and Society: Extremadura and America in the Sixteenth Century* (Berkeley: University of California Press, 1989), 150–155; and Allyson Poska, "Elusive Virtue: Rethinking the Role of Female Chastity in Early Modern Spain," *Journal of Early Modern History* 8, no. 1/2 (2004): 143.

12. See Altman, *Emigrants and Society*, 9–10, 14–135.

13. Further, illegitimacy in Spain was higher than the rest of Europe, see Allyson Poska, "When Love Goes Wrong: Getting Out of Marriage in Seventeenth-Century Spain," *Journal of Social History* 29, no. 4 (Summer 1996): 873–874.

14. AGNP, 42 (1) Gascon, fols. 11–13v, Testamento de Diego Francisco, 3 enero 1554.

15. Lauren Benton describes how the colonial context was not unique for the legal pluralism that existed therein but rather how the colonial context high-lighted the struggles that emerged within a plural legal order. I borrow her concept and apply it to family structures. See Lauren Benton, *Law and Colonial Cultures: Legal Regimes in World History, 1400–1900* (Cambridge: Cambridge University Press, 2002), 9.

16. While her work focuses on the seventeenth century, this commonality of illegitimacy is developed convincingly in María Emma Mannarelli, *Private Passions and Public Sins: Men and Women in Seventeenth-Century Lima*, trans. Sidney Evans and Meredith D. Dodge (Albuquerque: University of New Mexico Press, 2007), *passim*. On the subject of *mestizaje* and the sixteenth-century, see Powers, *Women in the Crucible of Conquest*, pp. 68–92. For historical treatment of children in colonial Peru, see Bianca Premo, *Children of the Father King: Youth, Authority, and Legal Minority in Colonial Lima* (Chapel Hill, NC: University of North Carolina Press, 2005). For a wide-ranging geographical discussion of childhood for the Iberian world, see Ondina E. González and Bianca Premo, eds., *Raising an Empire: Children in Early Modern Iberia and Colonial Latin America* (Albuquerque: University of New Mexico Press, 2007). A collection on the history of children for Latin America, colonial and modern periods, is Tobias Hecht, ed., *Minor Omissions: Children in Latin American History and Society* (Madison: University of Wisconsin Press, 2002).

17. AGI, Lima 565, L.1, fol. 113, Queen to Peru, 8 marzo 1534.

18. Premo, *Children of the Father King*, 36.

19. AGI, Indiferente 737, N. 66, F. 2 [1551].

20. Kathryn Burns, "Gender and the Politics of Mestizaje: The Convent of Santa Clara in Cuzco, Peru," *Hispanic American Historical Review* 78, no. 1 (February 1998): 5–44, and Nancy van Deusen, *Between the Sacred and the Worldly: The Institutional and Cultural Practice of Recogimiento in Colonial Lima* (Stanford, CA: Stanford University Press, 2001).

21. AGNP, Protocolos 118, Moscoso, fol. 301, Poder Bartolomé Díaz to Joan Alvarez Maldonado and Barvola de Grado, 19 abril 1560.

22. AGI, Indiferente 737, N. 66, fol. 2 [1551].

23. ARA, Protocolos 57, García Muñoz, Carta de Poder, fol. 5, Pero Martín Barbera to Álvaro de San Miguel, 1556.

24. See ARA, Protocolos 100, Juan de Vera, R. 14, fol. 555v, 1 diciembre 1571. Will of Pedro Bernal de Cantalapiedra whose nine-month-old son Luis lived with his indigenous mother Ana. Law and custom intermingled in this practice; see *Las Siete Partidas*, Vol. 4, Title XIX, Law III, 973 which establishes three years of age as the period through which a mother should raise the child.

25. Premo, *Children of the Father King*, 26.

26. Premo, *Children of the Father King*, 26.

27. Nancy van Deusen focuses on the lives of these women and their Spanish owners in "Diasporas, Bondage, and Intimacy in Lima, 1535–1555," *Colonial Latin American Review* 19, no. 2 (August 2010): 247–277.

28. Lockhart, *Spanish Peru*, 231–232.

29. Kathryn Burns, *Colonial Habits, Convents and the Spiritual Economy of Cuzco, Peru* (Durham, NC: Duke University Press, 1999), 22. See also Burns, "Gender and the Politics of Mestizaje," 5–44, and on the treatment of mestiza daughters in Lima, van Deusen, *Between the Sacred and the Worldly*.

30. Joanne Rappaport, "El mestizo que desaparece: El género en la construcción de las redes sociales entre mestizos de élite en Santafé de Bogotá, siglos XVI y XVII," in Juan Camilo Escobar Villegas, Sarah de Mojica, and Adolfo León Maya, eds., *Celebraciones y crisis: Procesos independentistas en Iberoamérica y la Nueva Granada* (Bogotá: Editorial Pontificia Universidad Javeriana, 2012), 365–386.

31. Joanne Rappaport argues that to make sense of categories of identity in colonial Bogotá scholars must consider more carefully the location of the ethno-racial terms both in terms of geography and in the location where scholars find them. See "'Asi lo paresçe por su aspeto': Physiognomy and the Construction of Difference in Colonial Bogotá," *Hispanic American Historical Review* 91, no. 4 (2011): 631.

32. Rappaport, "Asi lo paresçe," 624–625.

33. Nancy van Deusen notes likewise that the use of the term "mestizo" did not occur in documents in Peru and Mexico until the 1550s. Van Deusen, "The

Intimacies of Bondage: Female Indigenous Servants and Slaves and Their Spanish Masters, 1492–1555," *Journal of Women's* History 24, no. 1 (2012): 14n6. On the use of the label mestizo versus *hijo natural* in colonial Bogotá, see Rappaport, "El mestizo que desaparece."

34. AGI, Lima 25, Petición Suelta, Lima, 1570. Juan de la Peña pide lixitimar ... "gozar de las premynencias que gocan los demas hijos lixitimos." On illegitimacy, see Ann Twinam, *Public Lives, Private Secrets, Gender, Honor, Sexuality, and Illegitimacy in Colonial Spanish America* (Stanford, CA: Stanford University Press, 1999).

35. On the relevance of social networks for shaping status and ethnic identity, see R. Douglas Cope, *The Limits of Racial Domination: Plebeian Society in Colonial Mexico, 1660–1720* (Madison: University of Wisconsin Press, 1994).

36. For another case in point, specifically how indigenous men and women identified as *criollos*, see Karen B. Graubart, "The Creolization of the New World: Local Forms of Identification in Urban Colonial Peru, 1560–1640." *Hispanic American Historical Review* 89, no. 3 (2009): 471–499.

37. Biblioteca Nacional del Perú (hereinafter BNP), A33, Protocolo of Diego Gutiérrez, fol. 60v, 8 septiembre 1548.

38. AGNP, Protocolos 36, Frías, R. 17, fols. 895v–896, 19 octubre 1560.

39. AGNP, Protocolos 4, Cristóbal de Aguilar Mendieta, fol. 960–960v, Poder Marcos Muñoz Ternero to Diego de Cimancas, 14 octubre 1597.

40. For an additional example of a father giving legal power to retrieve a mestizo son from New Spain, see AGNP, Protocolos 118, Moscoso, fol. 410, Poder Alonso Sánchez to Alvaro Muñoz, 12 marzo 1561.

41. AGNP, Protocolos 58, Fernan Gómez, fol. 252–252v, 9 agosto 1557.

42. AGNP, Protocolos 36, R. 5, Juan Cristóbal de Frias, fol. 715–715v, 1 abril 1559.

43. AGNP, Protocolos 28, Alonso de la Cueva, fol. 131r, Donación Antonio de Medina to María mestiza su hija natural, 12 junio 1577.

44. AGNP, Protocolos 28, Alonso de la Cueva, fols. 131–132v, Donación Antonio de Medina to María mestiza su hija natural, 12 junio 1577. Yanaguar is identified as being under the control of Sánchez's *repartimiento* but her specific labor obligation to him is not identified in more detail.

45. AGNP, Protocolos 28, Alonso de la Cueva, fol. 131–131v, Donación Antonio de Medina to María, 12 junio 1577.

46. AGNP, Protocolos 160, Sebastián Vázquez, fol. 271, Poder Mateo Veneciano to Pedro Tomas Griego, 15 febrero 1552. For similar cases not analyzed here, see AGNP, Protocolos 117, Moscoso, fols. 442v—443, Poder Gonzalo Gil to Álvaro de Yllescas to recover Catalina mestiza, 31 diciembre 1551; AGNP, Protocolos 118, Moscoso, fol. 268v, Poder Joan Ginoves to Bernaldo Bueno to recover Cristóbal mestizo, 29 diciembre 1559; AGNP, Protocolos 118, Moscoso, fol. 226v, Poder Juan Bejarano to Juan Mosquera to recover children, 4 septiembre

1559; AGNP, Protocolos 119, Moscoso, fol. 436, Poder Juan Machuca to Antonio de Oserin to recover Pedro, 24 septiembre 1575.

47. AGNP, Protocolos 84, Alonso Hernández, fols. 676–677v, Poder Pedro Rolón to Alvar Muñoz para pedir una hija natural, 6 julio 1571.

48. AGNP, Protocolos 58, Fernan Gómez, fol. 261–261v, 1557.

49. AGNP, Protocolos 93, Blas Hernández, fol. 1119—1119v, Poder Francisco Bobedo to Joan Fernández, 28 abril 1573. On the usage of the terms *morena*, to signify free, and *negra*, enslaved, in sixteenth-century Lima, see Karen B. Graubart, "'So color de una cofradía': Catholic Confraternities and the Development of Afro-Peruvian Ethnicities in Early Colonial Peru," *Slavery & Abolition* 33, no. 1 (2012): 43–64.

50. AGNP, Protocolos 114, Juan Martínez, fols. 213–215v, Testamento de Cristóbal Gómez, 5 mayo 1551.

51. AGNP, Protocolos 42 (1), Gascon, fols. 51v–53v, Testamento de Pedro de Çaera, 16 enero 1554. His will states "desposada por palabras" with Damiana. On "palabras" and the phases of the marriage ritual in sixteenth-century Spain, see Poska, "When Love Goes Wrong," 873. For additional analysis of Çaera, see van Deusen, "The Intimacies of Bondage," 27.

52. AGNP, Protocolos 33, Esquivel Franco, fol. 20v, Testamento de Loreynte Ponse de Cabrera, 7 diciembre 1569 ("en todo buena doctrina y policiada"). On this practice, see Lockhart, *Spanish Peru*, 185.

53. Robert I. Burns, S.J., ed. *Las Siete Partidas*, 975-976.

54. AGNP, Protocolos 64, Diego Gutiérrez, fol. 215, Donación Pedro Caxas to Mencia de Ayala, 6 julio 1554. For a similar case, see AGNP, Protocolos 64, Diego Gutiérrez, fols. 350v–351r, Juan de Fregenal, horro, gives power to Alonso Muñoz, 28 enero 1555 and AGNP, Protocolos 42 (1) Gascon, fols. 125v–128, Testamento de Pedro de la Hos, 31 enero 1554, the eleven-year-old mestiza daughter of Pedro de la Hos lived in the house of doña María de Valverde in Lima; AGNP, Protocolos 33, Esquivel Franco, fol. 264–264v, Testamento de Hernando Durán, 15 noviembre 1571, his *hija natural* Florencia Durán was in the home of doña Francisca Bolonya.

55. For instance, Elvira Hernández of Sevilla, whose husband is in the Indies, puts her ten-year-old son in apprenticeship with Fernando de Ocaña, a platero or silversmith, AHPS, Protocolos Notariales, Oficio 11, Signatura 6743, fol. 321, Aprendiz, 14 marzo 1560. For further information on these traditions in Iberia, see David Vassberg, *The Village and the Outside World in Golden Age Castile: Mobility and Migration in Everyday Rural Life* (Cambridge: Cambridge University Press, 1996).

56. For an analysis of child labor contracts in Lima, see Teresa C. Vergara, "Growing Up Indian, Migration, Labor, and Life in Lima (1570–1640)," in González and Premo, eds., *Raising an Empire*, 91–96.

57. AGNP, Protocolos 28, Alonso Cueva, fol. 104, Testamento de Diego García de Anteguera, 9 mayo 1578.

58. AGNP, Protocolos 160, Sebastián Vázquez, fol. 1156, Pedro de Emberes gives power to Juan de Ochandiano, 22 junio 1554.

59. AGNP, Protocolos 93, Blas Hernández, fol. 1150–1150v, Poder Pedro Rodríguez to Pedro de Guevara, 29 julio 1573.

60. AHPS, Protocolos, Signatura 7764, Francisco Díaz, Oficio 13, 1570, fol. 226, Asiento of Juan Gómez, 30 marzo 1570.

61. AHPS, Protocolos, Signatura 17613, Mateo de Almonacir, Oficio 9, Servicio Sebastián Rodríguez for his daughter Gerónima, 5 marzo 1570.

62. In sixteenth-century Seville, parents paid for others to raise their children including but not limited to wet-nursing. See AHPS, Protocolos, Signatura 1584, Baltasar de Godoy, Oficio 3, fol. 901, Carta de obligación Sebastián García to Isabel de Artega for "raising her daughter Elvira for 22 months," 6 mayo 1580. On the widespread nature of these practices in early modern Europe, see Cavallo, "Family Relationships," 29–32.

63. ARA, Protocolos 73, García Muñoz Madueno, fols. 37r–38v, Testamento de Doña Isabel de Zuñiga, 13 diciembre 1590.

64. Single or widowed women adapted to this practice quickly in Peru, likely drawing on Iberian precedent. See Lockhart, *Spanish Peru*, 175.

65. BNP, A 37, 1557, Protocolo de Alonso Hernández, fol. 59v–60r, Poder Hernando de Carrión to Miguel Ruíz y otros, 31 agosto 1557.

66. ARA, Protocolos 74, García Muñoz Madueno, fol. 76r–76v, Testamento de Beatriz Gutiérrez, 19 febrero 1592.

67. On the importance of *limpieza de sangre* in New World society, see María Elena Martínez, *Genealogical Fictions: Limpieza de Sangre, Religion and Gender in Colonial Mexico* (Stanford, CA: Stanford University Press, 2008).

68. AGNP, Protocolos 42 (1) Gascon, fols. 1–5v, Testamento de Alonso Descobar, 2 enero 1554. For the case of a Spaniard traveling in the company of his mestizo child and the child's mother, his indigenous partner, see Nancy E. van Deusen, *Global Indios, The Indigenous Struggle for Justice in Sixteenth-Century Spain* (Durham: Duke University Press, 2015), 95-96. Such cases were rare, but van Deusen provides pathbreaking analysis of extant cases to reveal the plight of indigenous men and women in Spain.

69. AGNP, Protocolos 117, Moscoso, fol. 544v, Testamento de Álvaro de Olmeda, 27 enero 1553 [mestiza girl from Potosí; he is taking her to Spain]; AGNP, 117, fols. 541–543, Testamento de Pedro Alvárez, 25 enero 1553. See also the case of Lima notary Salinas, who sends his mestizo son to Spain in 1543, as cited in Lockhart, *Spanish Peru*, 84.

70. Juan Gil, "Los primeros mestizos indios en España: Una voz ausente," in *Entre dos mundos: Fronteras culturales y agentes mediadores*, coord. Berta Ares Queija

and Serge Gruzinski (Sevilla: Escuela de Estudios Hispano-Americanos de Sevilla, 1997), 20–21.

71. For additional examples not analyzed in this chapter, see AGNP, Protocolos 153, Salinas, fols. 287–292v, Testamento de Domingo de Destre, 24 julio 1542 (sends his mestiza *hija natural* María to Aragon); ARA, Protocolos 60, García Muñoz, R. 2, fol. 192, Testamento de Baltasar Torres, 1561 (sends *hijos naturales* to Spain to live with his mother); AGNP, Protocolos 42 (1) Gascon, fols. 125v–128, Testamento de Pedro de la Hos, 31 enero 1554, orders that guardian of his eleven-year-old mestiza daughter can take her to his brothers in Lepe in Spain; AGNP, Protocolos 117, Moscoso, fols. 545–547, Testamento de Gaspar Hernández, 28 enero 1553, Gaspar Hernández orders the albaceas of Gaspar mestizo his *hijo natural* to take the boy to Spain to his brothers; AGNP, Protocolos 117, Moscoso, fols. 466v–476v, Poder Francisco Sánchez to Francisco de Ávalos, for guardianship and teaching of Juanico, mestizo *hijo natural* of Sánchez and Leonor of Cuzco, 24 febrero 1552; AGNP, Protocolos 109, Martel, fols. 609v—611v, Testamento de Juan Flores, 15 octubre 1557, to send mestizo children to Spain.

72. AGNP, Protocolos 64, Diego Gutiérrez, fols. 343v–354v, Testamento de Diego Martín Cabello, 26 enero 1555.

73. AGNP, Protocolos 117, Moscoso, fol. 435—435v, Poder Hernando de San Pedro to Ruy Díaz de Sigure and Cristóbal de Arenas, 28 enero 1553.

74. AGNP, Protocolos 33, Esquivel Franco, fol. 20v, Testamento de Loreynte Ponse de Cabrera, 7 diciembre 1569.

75. ARA, Protocolos 99, Juan de Vera, fols. l(v)–li, Testamento de Diego Hierro, 10 enero 1568.

76. AGNP, Protocolos 9, Simón de Alzate, fols. 631–634, Testamento de Alonso Muñoz, 13 agosto 1552.

77. AGNP, Protocolos 34, Esquival Franco, fols. 792–795v, fol. 795v, Testamento de Juan María de Abarreta del Cablo, diciembre 1580.

78. ARA, Protocolos 33, Gaspar Hernández, fol. xxxvi (vuelta), Testamento de Martín Díaz, 8 mayo 1556.

79. AGI, Seville, Contratación 242, N. 1, R. 15, fols. 23r–24r, Herederos de Ysabel Toto yndio sobre cobro de bienes, 1579.

80. Fols. 39r–40v. The *limpieza de sangre* regulations would have made it difficult for these young women to enter convents and take their vows, but their fathers made no mention of this potential problem.

81. AGNP, Protocolos 150, Juan Salamanca, fols. 430–433v, Testamento de Francisco Rodríguez, 17 enero 1575.

82. AGI, Contratación 476, N. 1, R. 1, Bienes de Manuel de Herrera.

83. AHPS, Protocolos, Oficio 6, Signatura 4063, Francisco de Soto, fol. 278, 24 noviembre 1569.

84. AGNP, Protocolos 114, Martínez, fol. 254–254v, Poder Juan Bautista Ginoves to Antonio Ginoves, 2 enero 1553.

85. AHPS, Protocolos, Oficio 13, Signatura 7764, Francisco Díaz, fol. 1035, 30 mayo 1570.

86. AHPS, Protocolos, Francisco de Almonte, Signatura 5383, Oficio 8, Companya Pedro de Mollinedo and Diego de Mollinedo, fol. 470, 11 octubre 1570.

CHAPTER 3

1. AGNP, Protocolos 9, Simón de Alzate, fols. 990v–991v, Poder Melchior Ximénez to Alonso Díaz and Gaspar Ximénez, 22 octubre 1551.

2. AGI, Indiferente General 421, L. 13, fols. 7–10v, 15 febrero 1528, Burgos.

3. ARA, Protocolos 45, Gaspar Hernández, 1581, R. 4, fol. 414r, Testamento de Juan Luis, 24 octubre 1581.

4. ARA, Protocolos 1, Diego de Aguilar, fols. 323v–328, Testamento de Diego Hernández de Talavara, 8 noviembre 1567.

5. Alexandra Parma Cook and Noble David Cook, *Good Faith and Truthful Ignorance: A Case of Transatlantic Bigamy* (Durham, NC: Duke University Press, 1991).

6. On marriages in colonial Charcas, see Ana María Presta, "Estados altera-dos: Matrimonio y vida maridable en Charcas temprano-colonial," *Población y Sociedad, Revista Regional de Estudios Sociales* 18, no. 1 (2011): 79–105.

7. The variety of responses by women to their husbands' absence in the Indies is analyzed by Mary Elizabeth Perry in *Gender and Disorder in Early Modern Seville* (Princeton, NJ: Princeton University Press, 1990), esp. 14–32. Ida Altman's transatlantic framework reveals family and kin adaptations to empire in Brihuega, Spain, and Puebla, Mexico. See Ida Altman, *Transatlantic Ties in the Spanish Empire: Brihuega, Spain & Puebla, Mexico, 1560-1620* (Stanford: Stanford University Press, 2000). Allyson Poska's study of women in Galicia views marriage in another region of Iberia and asserts that women's experiences were diverse, determined by factors such as class and local custom more so that the culture of honor that predominated in Church and prescriptive literature. See Allyson Poska, *Women and Authority in Early Modern Spain: The Peasants of Galicia* (New York: Oxford University Press, 2006), 9–10, 112–162.

8. The colonial *Recopilación de Leyes*, compiled in the late seventeenth century, offers some insights as well.

9. Enrique Otte, *Cartas privadas de emigrantes a Indias, 1540–1616* (México: Fondo de Cultura Económica, 1996).

10. María del Carmen Pareja Ortiz, *Presencia de la mujer Sevillana en Indias: Vida cotidiana* (Seville: Diputación Provincial de Sevilla, 1993), 30. See also

James Lockhart, *Spanish Peru, 1532–1560: A Social History*, 2nd ed. (Madison: University of Wisconsin Press, 1994), 175.

11. Konetzke, 125, citing *Colección de documentos inéditos relativos al descubrimiento, conquista y colonización de las antiguas posesiones españolas de Ultramar*. Women whose husbands had abandoned them for the Indies did become involved sexually with other men. In Rodriguez Sánchez's study of 1590s Coria, Extremadura, many women found to be cohabitating had husbands who were in the Indies or captive in Africa. See Angel Rodríguez Sánchez, *Hacerse nadie: Sometimiento, sexo y silencio en la España de finales del s. xvi* (Lleida: Editorial Mileno, 1998), 58 and 81.

12. Robert I. Burns, S.J., ed., *Las Siete Partidas*, trans. Samuel Parsons Scott, Vol. 4 (Philadelphia: University of Pennsylvania Press, 2001), Title IX, Law VIII, p. 920.

13. Heath Dillard offers a thorough discussion of how the tradition of *barraganía* differed throughout towns in Reconquest Spain. See Heath Dillard, *Daughters of the Reconquest: Women in Castilian Town Society, 1100–1300* (New York: Cambridge University Press, 1984), 128–134.

14. *Las Siete Partidas*, Title XIV, Concerning Other Women Whom Men Keep, and to Whom They are Not Married, p. 950.

15. For a definition of *vida maridable* articulated in Spain by a religious inspector (*visitador*), see Allyson Poska, "When Love Goes Wrong: Getting Out of Marriage in Seventeenth-Century Spain," *Journal of Social History* 29, no. 4 (Summer 1996): 877–878.

16. Richard Konetzke, "La emigración de mujeres españolas a America durante la epoca colonial," *Revista internacional de sociología* 3, no 9 (1945): 124.

17. AGI, Indiferente General 418, L. 2, fol. 166, 9 febrero 1511; AGI, Indiferente General 418, L. 3, fol. 110v, 21 junio 1511.

18. Perry, *Gender and Disorder*, 15–22.

19. AGI, Indiferente General 421, L. 13, fols. 7–10v, 15 febrero 1528, Burgos.

20. AGI, Indiferente General 421, L. 12, fols. 307v–308r, 13 marzo 1528, Madrid.

21. Konetzke, "La emigración de mujeres españolas," 134.

22. Konetzke, "La emigración de mujeres españolas," 126.

23. Konetzke, "La emigración de mujeres españolas," 126.

24. AGNP, Superior Gobierno, Legajo 1, Cuaderno 1, fol. 2. 16 Diciembre 1553.

25. Tamar Herzog, *Defining Nations: Immigrants and Citizens in Early Modern Spain and Spanish America* (New Haven, CT: Yale University Press, 2003), 43–45, and on Lima specifically, see 50–52.

26. AGNP, Superior Gobierno, Legajo 1, Cuaderno 1, fol. 1r, 16 Diciembre 1553.

27. AGNP, Superior Gobierno, Legajo 1, Cuaderno 1, fol. 1r, 16 Diciembre 1553. On the Reconquest practices that influenced the model for colonial Peru, see Dillard, *Daughters of the Reconquest*, 12–25.

28. AGNP, Superior Gobierno, Legajo 1, Cuaderno 1, fol. 1r, 16 Diciembre 1553.

29. AGNP, Superior Gobierno, Legajo 1, Cuaderno 1, fol. 1r, 16 Diciembre 1553.

30. This two-year limit for Tierra Firme, as opposed to a three-year limit for Peru, was probably because it was a closer distance and quicker travel time to Spain.

31. Ots de Capdequí, *Bosquejo histórico de los derechos de la mujer casada en la legislación de indias* 103.

32. Konetzke, "La emigración de mujeres españolas," 127.

33. Ots de Capdequí, *Bosquejo histórico de los derechos de la mujer casada en la legislación de indias,* 87.

34. For a listing of the encomenderos in the Viceroyalty of Peru in 1561, many of whom would have been appointed in the period under discussion here, see Teodoro Hampe, "Relación de los encomenderos y repartimientos del Perú en 1561," *Historia y Cultura* 12 (1979): 75–117. Five percent of those listed are women.

35. Ots de Capdequí, *Bosquejo histórico de los derechos de la mujer casada en la legislación de indias* 87.

36. Ots de Capdequí, 87, *Bosquejo histórico de los derechos de la mujer casada en la legislación de indias,* citing Palma citing the Cédula: "Ansí desaparecerá todo olor a barraganía, habrá la moral ganancia y se amansarán los genios turbulentos; que con viento se limpia el trigo y los vicios con castigo."

37. Pareja Ortiz, *Presencia de la mujer Sevillana,* 67, and James Lockhart, *Spanish Peru, 1532–1560: A Social History,* 2nd ed. (Madison: University of Wisconsin Press, 1994), 175.

38. BNP 1550 A 36, fols. 172r –173v, 30 mayo 1550.

39. BNP, 1550 A 36, fol. 173r.

40. AGNP, Protocolos 9, Simón de Alzate, fols. 764–765v, Poder Diego Maldonado to Francesco de Silva and Juan de Alamo, 14 abril 1551.

41. AGNP, Protocolos 9, Simón de Alzate, fols. 386–388, Poder Diego Maldonado de Alamos to Constanca Maldonado, 23 marzo 1552. For similar cases from 1564, see AGNP, Protocolos 41, García de Nogal, fol. 368–368v, Poder Diego Muñiz Farfán to Pedro Muñiz Farfán, 10 abril 1564; AGNP, Protocolos 41, García de Nogal, fol. 917–917v, Poder Francisco Muñiz to Alonso de Luque, 14 octubre 1564; AGNP, Protocolos 41, García de Nogal, fols. 603v—604v, Poder García Hernández de Medenilla to Ana Muñoz para vender casas, 23 mayo 1564.

42. AGNP, Protocolos 9, Simón de Alzate, fols. 990v–991v, Poder Melchior Ximénez to Alonso Díaz and Gaspar Ximénez, 22 octubre 1551.

43. AGNP, Protocolos 9, Simón de Alzate, fol. 397, Poder Alonso Hernándes to Diego Maldonado Altamirano, 28 marzo 1552. Note: Diego the son had recently agreed, before a notary, to marry according to his father's wishes Catalina de Ojeda, an *hija natural* of an unnamed mother, daughter of Juan Julio de Ojeda, regidor of the city of Cuzco. See same volume of protocolos, fol. 388–388v.

44. AGNP, Protocolos 109, Martel, fol. 783v, Poder Fabian Blanco to Pedro Bermúdez, 28 febrero 1558 (muchos negocios and ynpedimientos). For another 1560s example, see AGNP, Protocolos 127, Esteban Pérez, fols. 409v–411, Poder Diego Herres to Diego Flores, 8 abril 1562.

45. Otte, *Cartas privadas*, 538, letter 603.

46. Herzog does suggest some adaptations in the case of Lima, especially for encomenderos, but those develop later in the sixteenth century. See Tamar Herzog, *Defining Nations, Immigrants and Citizens in Early Modern Spain and Spanish America* (New Haven, CT: Yale University Press, 2003), 50–59.

47. Another example is AHPS, Signatura 2355, Ref. 1259, Juan Pérez, Oficio IV, Libro II, Obligación de Juan Pérez, fol. 837, 25 octubre 1580. In this case, Rodríguez Perete did not make good on his claims, spent the money, and landed in a Seville jail.

48. AGNP, Protocolos 150, Juan Salamanca, fols. 44–46, Concierto Miguel Gerónimo con Jorge Dote, 5 marzo 1574.

49. Dote died before leaving port and the power went to another man. See AGNP, Protocolos 150, Juan Salamanca, fols. 62–63, Poder Miguel Gerónimo to Simón Rodrígues, 6 marzo 1574.

50. AGNP, Protocolos 36, Juan Cristóbal Frias; R. 5, fols. 716–717v; R. 6, fols. 726v–728; R. 6, fol. 730—730v. For additional examples of *poderes* to have a third party bring a wife back from Spain, see AGNP, Protocolos 9, Simón de Alzate, fols. 347v—348 [1550]; AGNP, Protocolos 36, Juan Cristóbal de Frias, R. 17, fols. 867v—868 [155?]; AGNP, Protocolos 9, Simón de Alzate, fols. 232v–233, Poder Alonso Sánchez to Francisco Vázquez and Diego de Yllescas, 23 enero 1552; AGNP, Protocolos 122, Padilla, fols. 121–122, Poder Tome Gallego to Alonso de Yllescas, 26 marzo 1558; AGNP, Protocolos 37, Juan Cristóbal de Frias, fol. 348—348v [1561]; AGNP, Protocolos 38, Juan García, fols. 773–774v [1566]; AGNP, Protocolos 38, Juan García, fol. 758—758v [1566]. Examples from Seville notary archives of plans for wives to join husbands in Peru to *hacer vida maridable:* AHPS, Signatura 2366, Oficio IV, Libro II, Juan Pérez, fol. 837–837v, 25 Octubre 1580; AHPS, Protocolos Notariales, Signatura 5383, Oficio 8, Francisco de Almonte, R. 27, fol. ivdcrxxxii, Petition of Juana de Çamorana, abril 1569; AHPS, Signatura 12451, Gaspar de León, Oficio 19, Petition of Francisca Rodríguez, fol. 655, 22 octubre 1580.

51. AGNP, Protocolos 39, Juan García Tomino, R. 3, 1567, fols.. 1357v—1359. See also variations on this, as in Joan Pérez, fisherman and resident of Callao, who gives a ship captain legal power to bring his wife to Lima from Tierra Firme. AGNP, Protocolos 36, Juan Cristóbal de Frias, R. 3, fol. 1347–1347v, 1550. See also AGNP, Protocolos 36, Juan Cristóbal de Frias, R. 17, fols. 867v—868.

52. AGNP, 114, Juan Martínez, fols. 101v—102, Poder Marcos de Sosa to María Fernández, 16 agosto 1549. For other examples of husbands moving wives in the Indies/colonies (as opposed to from Spain to the Indies), see AGNP, Protocolos

117, Moscoso, fol. 413—413v, Poder Ruy García to Pero Sánchez Espinan and others, 5 noviembre 1552. AGNP, Protocolos 150, Juan Salamanca, fols. 158–159, concierto Gaspar de Agular con Francisco Hernández, 3 mayo 1573. For a similar example with a wife in Tierra Firme, see AGNP, Protocolos 127, Estevan Pérez, fols. 822–823, Poder Diego Hernández to Antón de Rodas, 30 junio 1562.

53. Otte, *Cartas privadas*, 492, letter 554. Rebecca Earle's analysis of 361 letters from the sixteenth through the eighteenth centuries suggests that the primary reason men wrote to their wives was to convince them to make the voyage to the New World. See Rebecca Earle, "Letters and Love in Colonial Spanish America," *The Americas* 62, no. 1 (July 2005): 26.

54. Otte, *Cartas privadas*, 416.

55. Otte, *Cartas privadas*, 416.

56. Otte, *Cartas privadas*, 410–411, letter Roberto de Burt to his wife Ana Franca, Los Reyes, 20 febrero 1583.

57. See Carlos Alberto González Sánchez, *Dineros de Ventura: La varia fortuna de la emigración a Indias (siglos XVI–XVII)* (Seville, Spain: Universidad de Seville, 1995).

58. In 1619 the Crown recognized a solution to help those "poor" Spaniards in the Indies return home to their wives: a new royal decree ordered that married men in this situation be given a spot in the Royal Armada, replacing any soldiers who had died on the voyage over. See Ots de Capdequí, *Bosquejo histórico de los derechos de la mujer casada en la legislación de indias*, 104, citing Cédula, 16 febrero 1619.

59. Otte, *Cartas privadas*, 413–414, letter of Hernando Gónzalez to su mujer Leonor Gómez, en Trujillo, Los Reyes, 15 abril 1585.

60. Otte, *Cartas privadas*, 414.

61. Konetzke, "La emigración de mujeres españolas," 129, citing Juan Solórzano, *Política Indiana*, libro 5, cap. 5, núm. 22.

62. Otte, *Cartas privadas*, 452.

63. Otte, *Cartas privadas*, 452, letter 510.

64. Otte, *Cartas privadas*, 452, letter of Cristóbal Páez de Becerril to Agustina de Vara, Lima, 30 abril 1599. Lockhart summarizes the potential for a pampered life for Spanish women in *Spanish Peru*, 180.

65. Otte, *Cartas privadas*, 452, letter 510.

66. Otte, *Cartas privadas*, 415–416, letter of Francisco de Meza Matamoros to su mujer Gregoria de Meza, Lima, 28 octubre 1586.

67. Otte, *Cartas privadas*, 396, letter of Doña María de Córdoba to her sister, Lima, 27 marzo 1578.

68. Otte, *Cartas Privadas*, 485, letter of Bartolomé de Saldaña to his wife Elvira Pérez, 1 febrero 1570.

69. In 1539, Carlos V ordered that anyone who held Indians in encomienda had to marry within three years. By 1551, women who inherited encomiendas were

also required to marry. Ots de Capdequí, *Bosquejo histórico de los derechos de la mujer casada en la legislación de indias*, 86.

70. Ots de Capdequí, *Bosquejo histórico*, 87.

71. AGI, Justicia 1071, N. 1, R. 4, fol. 4r. The original reads "persona libre no obligada en matrimonyo."

72. AGI, Justicia 1071, N. 1, R. 4, fols. 1r–6v, *Vida Maridable*, 1551–1556.

73. AGI, Charcas 415, L. 1, fol. 232v. On Pendones, see also Presta, "Estados Alterados," 85. For an analogous case from 1570, see AHPS, Signatura 19716, Andres de Herrera, Oficio 12, fol. 1560v, Poder Doña Melchiora Bezerril to Sebastián de Santander for Consejo de Indios to compel her husband Juan de Tardajos to return from Peru to *hacer vida maridable*, 18 agosto 1570. The most complete analysis of such petitions to date is María José de la Pascua Sánchez, *Mujeres solas: Historias de amor y de abandono en el mundo hispánico* (Málaga, Spain: Centro de Ediciones de la Diputación de Málaga, 1995), who focuses on eighteenth-century Cádiz. That this same problem and process continue suggests a long-standing trend in women's attempts to track down husbands lost in the Indies. Bianca Premo has found reference to similar cases for eighteenth-century Oaxaca; personal communication, June 2012.

74. AHPS, R. 1444, Signatura 1100, 1580 Oficio II, libro 1, Gaspar de Toledo, fols. 1027–1029, 10 diciembre. Testamento de Leonor de Egas, fol. 1029.

75. Perry, *Gender and Disorder*, 14–32.

76. AHPS, Protocolos, Francisco Díaz, Signatura 7764, Oficio 13, fol. 51, Slave sale María Dona to Alonso González de Tapia, 3 marzo 1570. For an example of a married woman representing herself in a legal pardon when her husband was in the Indies, see AHPS, Protocolos, Signatura 15992, Oficio 23, Libro 2, fol. 730, Perdón Catalina Gómez to Antón Martín, 3 agosto 1555.

77. AHPS, Protocolos, Signatura 6743, Oficio 11, fol. 321, Francisco Roman, Aprendiz of Esteban to Fernando de Ocaña, 14 marzo 1560.

78. AHPS, Signatura 17613, Oficio 9, fol. 1547, Mateo de Almonacir, 31 marzo 1570.

79. AGI, Lima 565, L. 3, fol. 10, 08 julio 1538, Real Cédula.

80. For another case where a wife alleged she wrote her husband many times to request he return home, see AGI, Contratación 4881, fol. 46r, 1599, Inés Hernándes de Losangeles.

81. AGI, Indiferente General 2094, N. 22, fols. 1–6, enero 1584. Francisca Manrique, *vida maridable*.

82. AGI, Indiferente General 2094, N. 22, fols. 1–6, enero 1584. Francisca Manrique, *vida maridable*, fols. 4–5. Testimony of Luisa Goncález.

83. AGI, Contratación 4881, fol. 35r, Antonia Hernández. For another example of a petition with physical description, see AGI, Contratación 4881, fol. 38r, 1595, María Gallegos con Francisco Ruíz. On analysis of similar descriptions in applications for travel licenses, see Joanne Rappaport, "'Asi lo paresçe por su

aspeto': Physiognomy and the Construction of Difference in Colonial Bogotá,"
Hispanic American Historical Review 91, no. 4 (2011): esp. 610–615.

84. AGI, Contratación 4881, fol. 18r, 1587, Inés de Barbona.

85. AGI, Contratación 4881, fol. 27r, 1590, Catalina Martín. She had witnesses confirm her marriage.

86. AGI, Contratación 4881, fol. 8r, 1583, Ana de Sanabria. See also ARA, Protocolos 60 García Muñoz, R. 1, fols. 132v–133v, Testamento de Xayme Salazar, 6 marzo 1561.

87. AGNP, Protocolos 127, Estevan Pérez, fol. 368r–368v, Testamento de Hernan Gómez, 2 abril 1562.

88. AGNP, Protocolos 42, Gascon (1), fols. 203–205v, Grisostomo de Hontiberos deshereda a su hija Catalina de Hontiberos, 1554. Because I did not locate Hontiberos's final testament, it is not clear if the action to disinherit Catalina held.

89. Latin American historians have a lively debate on parents' role in marriage during the colonial era. See Patricia Seed, *To Love, Honor, and Obey in Colonial Mexico* (Stanford, CA: Stanford University Press, 1988).

90. AGI, Indiferente General 421, L. 11, fol. 355, Digital image 713, 26 noviembre 1526.

91. AGI, Lima 565, L. 3, fol. 24r, 08 julio 1538. The word *calidad* is in the original, and I have translated it as rank.

92. AGI, Contratación 4881, fol. 12r, 1584, Madalena Hernández. Both Hernández and Pérez were described as "de color negro."

93. AGI, Contratación 4881, fol. 41r, 1590, Goncalo Martín.

94. AGI, Contratación 4881, fols. 49r–51v, Sebastián Correa.

95. AGNP, Protocolos 127, Estevan Pérez, fol. 368–368v, Obligación Bernaldino de Castro to el Virrey Conde de Nieva, 9 julio 1561.

96. AGI, Contratación 4881, fols. 131r–133r, Diego Fernández de Cabrera, undated, probably early seventeenth century [1610s] based on location in the archives.

97. AGNP, Protocolos 93, Blas Hernández, fol. 885, Bartolomé Rodrígues fianza for Diego Amandor. I have not located a similar cluster of *vida maridable* imprisonments. All eight records are in AGNP, Protocolos 93 on the following fols.: 888v, 885, 880–880v, 879–879v, 851–851v, 850—850v, 849—849v, and 845.

98. Ana María Presta has explored women's challenges to colonial norms in "Portraits of Four Women: Traditional Female Roles and Transgressions in Colonial Elite Families in Charcas, 1550–1600," *Colonial Latin American Review* 9, no. 2 (2000): 237–262.

99. AGI, Justicia 790, N. 3, 1. Cathalina de Palma (aka Catalina de Mendoça) vezina de Seville sobre que se declare no ser obligada a ir hazer vida con Diego de Orca su marido, 1565.

100. AGI, Justicia 790, N. 3, 1. Cathalina de Palma vezina de Seville sobre que se declare no ser obligada a ir hazer vida con Diego de Orca su marido, 1565, fol. 1 (paper)/5 (digital).

101. AGI, Justicia 790, N. 3, 1. Cathalina de Palma vezina de Seville sobre que se declare no ser obligada a ir hazer vida con Diego de Orca su marido, 1565, fol. 1 (paper)/5 (digital).

102. On women's work during this era, see Perry, *Gender and Disorder*, 16.

103. Luis Romera Iruela y María del Carmen Galbis Díez, *Catálogo de Pasajeros a Indias durante los siglos XVI, XVII, y XVIII*, Vol. IV (Madrid: Ministerio de Cultura, Dirección General de Bellas Artes, Archivos y Bibliotecas, Subdirección General de Archivos, 1980), Record no. 947, 6 febrero 1561, II-129.

104. AGI, Justicia 698, N. 7, María García viuda y Cristobal Morán Promotor Fiscal de esta causa con Francisco García Comitre Vezino de Triana y maestre de nao sobre que le ascusa de cierta fuera que en su nao quiso hacer a ha dha María García que benia de pasajera. Seville, 1527. See discussion of this case in chapter 4 as well as in Altman, "Spanish Women of the Caribbean."

105. AGI, Justicia 790, N. 3, fol. 49, digital. "Sin abrigo mas que el dho Francisco Arco."

106. AGI, Justicia 790, N. 3, fol. 49, digital.

107. AGI, Justicia 790, N. 3, 1. Cathalina de Palma vezina de Seville sobre que se declare no ser obligada a ir hazer vida con Diego de Orca su marido, 1565, fol. 49.

108. AGI, Justicia 790, N. 3, fol. 55, digital, 24r, on original.

109. Ots de Capdequí, *Bosquejo histórico de los derechos de la mujer casada en la legislación de indias*, 104–105.

110. Catalina de Erauso, *Memoirs of a Basque Lt. Nun: Transvestite in the New World* (Boston: Beacon Press, 1996).

111. AGI, Justicia 1083, N. 1, R. 3, fols. 1–6r, Consexo Año de 1565, El Fiscal de SM y Juan Vizcaino con doña Mencia Baltodano.

112. This encomienda and its transfer from Origuela to Baltodano through the widow is in Hampe, "Relación de Encomenderos," 90.

113. AGI, Justicia 1083, N. 1, R. 3, fol. 3r [1565].

114. AGI, Justicia 1084, N. 1, R. 2, fol. 16v, Segovia, 18 septiembre 1565.

115. Karen B. Graubart, *With Our Labor and Sweat: Indigenous Women and the Formation of Colonial Society in Peru, 1550–1700* (Stanford, CA: Stanford University Press, 2007), ch. 5.

116. Ots de Capdequí, *Bosquejo histórico de los derechos de la mujer casada en la legislación de indias*, 138.

117. Ots de Capdequí, *Bosquejo histórico de los derechos de la mujer casada en la legislación de indias*, citing Solórzano, III, Cap. 6, p. 126.

118. Ots de Capdequí, *Bosquejo histórico de los derechos de la mujer casada en la legislación de indias*, 139.

119. AGI, Justicia 1084, N. 1, R. 2. Con Francisco Acuña, vecino de la Ciudad del Cuzco, sobre la posesión de unos indios que había tenido en el Peru, 1568.

120. AGI, Justicia 1084, N. 1, R. 2, fol. 22r, Con Francisco Acuña, vecino de la Ciudad del Cuzco, sobre la posesión de unos indios que había tenido en el Peru, 1568.

121. AGI, Justicia 1084, N. 1, R. 2, fol. 12r [*aprendi* possession].

122. AGNP, Protocolos 117, Moscoso, fol. 150–150v, Poder Alonso de León to Andrea de Campo, 17 noviembre 1551.

CHAPTER 4

1. AGI, Contratación 5219, N. 4, R. 5, fol. 2v, Relación de pasageros, 16 abril 1561.

2. On how siblings facilitated the New World journey, see Amelia Almorza Hidalgo, "Sibling Relations in Spanish Emigration to Latin America, 1560–1620," *European Review of History* 17, no. 5 (October 2010): 735–752. Allyson Poska has studied an eighteenth-century set of Crown-sponsored family voyages between Galicia and Argentina. See Allyson Poska, "Babies on Board: Women, Children and Imperial Policy in the Spanish Empire," *Gender and History* 22, no. 2 (August 2012): 269–293.

3. Letters collected by Enrique Otte, *Cartas privadas de emigrantes a Indias, 1540–1616* (México: Fondo de Cultura Económica, 1996), provide excellent documentation of these links. Less explored, however, is the notarial evidence from Peru and Seville of these rich connections.

4. Auke Pieter Jacobs, "Legal and Illegal Emigration from Seville, 1550–1650," in *"To Make America": European Emigration in the Early Modern Period*, eds. Ida Altman and James Horn (Berkeley: University of California Press, 1991), 59–84.

5. See Pablo E. Pérez-Mallaína, *Spain's Men of the Sea: Daily Life on the Indies Fleets in the Sixteenth Century*, trans. Carla Rahn Phillips (Baltimore: Johns Hopkins University Press, 1998).

6. Amelia Almorza Hidalgo, "Sibling Relations in Spanish Emigration to Latin America, 1560–1620," *European Review of History* 17, no. 5 (October 2010): 736.

7. Pablo E. Perez-Mallaína, *Spain's Men of the Sea: Daily Life on the Indies Fleets in the Sixteenth Century*, trans. Carla Rahn Phillips (Baltimore: Johns Hopkins University Press, 1998), 9.

8. Peter Boyd-Bowman, *Patterns of Spanish Emigration to the New World (1493–1580)* (Buffalo, NY: SUNY Buffalo, 1973), 40. To obtain his figures about emigration from the city of Seville, Boyd-Bowman factored into his analysis whether or not people were "visiting" Seville en route to the Indies or had natural or vecino status.

9. Boyd-Bowman, *Patterns of Spanish Emigration*, 67.

10. Boyd-Bowman, *Patterns of Spanish Emigration*, 94.

11. Boyd-Bowman, *Patterns of Spanish Emigration*, 52.

12. Boyd-Bowman, *Patterns of Spanish Emigration*, 52.

13. Boyd-Bowman, *Patterns of Spanish Emigration*, 81.

14. Peter Boyd-Bowman, "Patterns of Spanish Emigration to the Indies, 1579–1600," *The Americas* 33, no. 1 (July 1976): 85.

15. Boyd-Bowman, *Patterns of Spanish Emigration*, 47.

16. Boyd-Bowman, *Patterns of Spanish Emigration*, 23, 49. Jose Luis Martínez, *Pasajeros de Indias: Viajes transatlánticos en el siglo XVI* (Madrid: Alianza Editorial, 1983), 163–165.

17. Boyd-Bowman, *Patterns of Spanish Emigration*, 79.

18. AHPS, Protocolos, Signatura 7764, Francisco Díaz, Oficio 13, 1570, Testamento de doña Isabel de Villa, fol. 346.

19. AHPS, Protocolos, Signatura 1558, Baltasar de Godoy, Libro I, fol. 1023, 10 agosto 1566.

20. AHPS, Protocolos, Signatura 7764, Francisco Díaz, Oficio 13, 1570, Testamento de Francisca Segura, fol. 148v.

21. AHPS, Protocolos, Signatura 16037, Alonso Fernández de Carmona Oficio 23, Libro 1, fols. 552–553, Testamento de Inés de Cordova, 23 febrero 1570.

22. AGNP, Protocolos 64, Diego Gutiérrez, fols. 847–849v, Poder para arrendar casas, 2 diciembre 1555.

23. AHPS, Protocolos, Signatura 10608, Diego de Portes, Oficio 17, fol. 243, Poder Juan de Maqueda to Pedro de Castro, 27 enero 1560. Further examples of business between Peruvian cities and Seville, see AHPS, Protocolos, Signatura 10608, Diego de Portes, Oficio 17, fol. 228, Obligación Diego de Galdo to Isabel Mendes, 4 enero 1560; AHPS Protocolos, Signatura 6774, Gaspar de Torres, Oficio 11, s/f, Poder para cobrar Martín Lopez de Aguilar to Captain Juan Díaz de Valejera, marzo 1580.

24. Daviken Studnicki-Gizbert, *A National upon the Ocean Sea: Portugal's Atlantic Diaspora and the Crisis of the Spanish Empire, 1492–1640* (New York: Oxford University Press, 2007), 67–89.

25. AHPS, Protocolos, Signatura 5383, Francisco de Almonte, Oficio 8, fol. 470, Companya Pedro de Mollinedo and Diego de Mollinedo, 11 octubre 1570.

26. ARA, Protocolos 57, Garci Muñoz, fols. 19r–21r, Testamento de Leonor Ortiz, 8 noviembre 1557.

27. AGNP, Protocolo 68, Juan Gutiérrez, fols. 847–848, Donación Juan de Fuentes to Beatriz de Fuentes, 22 noviembre 1566.

28. AGNP, Protocolo 68, Juan Gutiérrez, fols. 888v–889v, Poder Juan de Fuentes to Leonor del Yelmo, 3 enero 1567.

29. AHPS, Protocolos, Signatura 6743, Francisco Roman, Oficio 11, fol. 858v, Testamento de Álvaro Fernández, 26 abril 1560.

30. AHPS, Signatura 10608, Diego de Portes, Oficio 17, fol. 152, 3 enero 1560. For other examples of siblings claiming inheritance across the ocean, see AHPS

Signatura 10608, Diego de Portes, Oficio 17, fol. 299, Carta de recibo Lope de Mendieta por doña Maria de Carate, 12 enero 1560.

31. AGNP, Protocolos 127, Estevan Pérez, fols. 1167r–1167v, Testamento de Cosma Munoz, 1561 [NB: badly deteriorated]. For further discussion of the ties between Seville and Peru, esp. trade ties, see Lockhart, *Spanish Peru*, 91–92, 102–103.

32. AGNP, Protocolos 160, Sebastián Vázquez, fols. 83–85v, Testamento de Leonor Sánchez, 20 noviembre 1551.

33. AGNP, Protocolos 160, Sebastián Vázquez, 11 mayo 1554, fols. 1149v–1150.

34. AGNP, Protocolos 64, Diego Gutiérrez, Testamento de Agueda Cornejo, fols. 157r–159r, 10 junio 1553.

35. AGNP, Protocolos 68, Juan Gutiérrez, fols. 662–665v, Testamento de Madalena de la Paz, 14 septiembre 1556.

36. Luis Martínez, *Pasajeros de Indias*, 179.

37. AGI, Justicia 1081, N. 1, R. 2, Consejo Año de 1560, El senor Fiscal y Ana de Pero Sánchez y su hija yndia, naturales de la Ciudad del Cuzco con doña Elvira de Guzmán vezina de Toledo sobre la libertad de dhas indias. This example is one of many *libertad de indios* cases heard by the courts in Seville during this era and studied by Nancy van Deusen in *Global Indios: The Indigenous Struggle for Justice in Sixteenth-Century Castile* (Durham, NC: Duke University Press, 2015).

38. Juan Gil, "Los primeros mestizos Indios en España: Una voz ausente," in *Entre dos mundos: Fronteras culturales y agentes mediadores*, coord. Berta Ares Queija and Serge Gruzinski (Seville: Escuela de Estudios Hispano-Americanos de Sevilla, 1997), 18.

39. José Carlos de la Puente, "Into the Heart of Empire: Indian Journeys to the Hapsburg Royal Court," Ph.D. dissertation, Texas Christian University, 2010.

40. *Catálogo de pasajeros a Indias durante los siglos XVI, XVII, y XVIII*, comp. Archivo General de Indias, Instituto Gonzalo Fernández de Oveido (Sevilla: Imprenta editorial de la Gavidia, 1940–), Vol. III, no. 3579, I-211, v. 5219, no. 15.

41. *Catálogo de pasajeros a Indias*, Vol. III, no. 3783, I-238v, p. 288.

42. *Catálogo de pasajeros a Indias*, Vol. III, no. 3506, I-202, p. 266. See also the mestizo brothers Juan and Hernando Castellón traveling from Spain to Callao, *Catálogo de pasajeros a Indias*, Vol. III, no. 4088, II-21, p. 310.

43. On family networks and merchants in Peru, see Lockhart, *Spanish Peru*, 91–92.

44. AHPS, Protocolos Signatura 10608, Diego de Portes, Oficio 17, fol. 283, Obligation Diego Sánchez to Diego Sánchez the elder, 12 enero 1560. "y por me se buena obra por ende por esta presente comprometido me obligo de dar y pagar."

45. Luis Martínez, *Pasajeros de Indias*, 66.

46. AGNP, Protocolos 128, Estevan Pérez, fols. 193r–195r, Testamento de Simón de Ortega, 1571.

47. Jacobs, "Legal and Illegal Emigration," 70.

48. AGNP, Protocolos 93, Blas Hernández, fol. 535, Fianza Antonio de Yllescas for Juan Dexio, 5 julio 1571.

49. Jacobs, "Legal and Illegal Emigration," 59–84.

50. AGI, Lima 592, folios sueltos, 6 junio 1591.

51. Otte, *Cartas privadas*, Inés Alonso Cervera to her son García de Escobar, 387, "que por ésta serán esos señores servidos darte licencia."

52. AHPS, Protocolos, Signatura 6743, Francisco Roman, Oficio 11, fol. 636, Testamento de Juan de Ayala, 9 marzo 1560.

53. AHPS, Protocolos, Signatura 6743, Francisco Roman, Oficio 11, 9 marzo 1560.

54. AGI, Lima 1, N. 243, Doña Bernardina de Arellano a su magestad, 22 agosto 1602.

55. AGI, Lima, Suelto, s/f, Petition María Varas to the Commisario Real de las Indias, 1586.

56. "Remediar una hija mya."

57. AGI, Contratación 5219, N. 1, R. 15, fol. 1r–1v, Relación de pasajeros, 1557. For another married passenger given a three-year timeframe, see *Catálogo de Pasajeros*, Vol. IV, Record no. 1824, II-318, 4 febrero 1562.

58. *Catálogo de Pasajeros*, Vol. IV, Record no. 4138, III-475v, 11 septiembre 1565. See the orders for Alonso de Loaysa to send for his wife on the first available flota, *Catálogo de Pasajeros*, Vol. V, Tomo 2, Record no. 3789 [N. 3, R. 4, fol. 28v, 5222, N. 4, R. 67], 28 febrero 1575.

59. Otte, *Cartas privadas*, 27.

60. Carlos Martínez Shaw, *La emigración española a América (1492–1824)* (Asturias, Spain: Fundación Archivo de Indianos, 1994), 34–35.

61. *Catálogo de Pasajeros*, Vol. IV, Record no. 254, II-77, 9 enero 1560.

62. BNP, A299, 1553, 2ff. Prontuario de las informaciones de nobleza y limpieza dadas por Alonso Muñoz Martínez Rengifo para pasar a estos reynos del Peru, 18 diciembre 1553.

63. For more detail on the process to prove limpieza, see José Luis Martínez, *Pasajeros de Indias, Viajes transatlánticos en el siglo XVI*, tercera ed. (México: Fondo de Cultura Económica, 1999), 31–34. The dissertation of Karoline Cook treats the subject of those *moriscos* and *conversos* who, notwithstanding these prohibitions, reached the Indies. See Cook, "Forbidden Crossings: Morisco Emigration to Spanish America, 1492 – 1650." Ph.D. dissertation, Princeton University, 2008.

64. AGI, Justicia 909, N. 7, El fiscal de SM con Juana Bautista vecina de la Ciudad de Sevilla sobre cierto fraude que hizo para pasar a un hijo suyo a Yndias bistiendo en havito de muger y haciendo ynformacion de que lo hera.

65. Bautista's other son Pedro was never part of the plan to go to the Indies. If we consider other family experiences in Seville at this moment, it is reasonable to suspect that he was old enough to be apprenticed somewhere and would not travel with his mother. The separation of parents from children for apprenticeship or travel to the Indies was common, the former all over Spain and the latter in Seville.

66. AGI, Justicia 909, N. 7, El fiscal de SM con Juana Bautista vecina de la Ciudad de Sevilla sobre cierto fraude que hizo para pasar a un hijo suyo a Yndias bistiendo en havito de muger y haciendo ynformacion de que lo hera "posava en su casa."

67. AGI, Justicia 909, N. 7, El fiscal de SM con Juana Bautista vecina de la Ciudad de Sevilla sobre cierto fraude que hizo para pasar a un hijo suyo a Yndias bistiendo en havito de muger y haciendo ynformacion de que lo hera, fol. 24. "que no avia menester licencia."

68. AGI, Justicia 909.

69. Perez-Mallaína, *Spain's Men of the Sea*, 181.

70. Allyson Poska, *Women and Authority in Early Modern Spain: The Peasants of Galicia* (New York: Oxford University Press, 2006).

71. AGI, Lima 1, N. 83, Ldo. Esteban Marañon to Consejo de Inidas, 17 diciembre 1586.

72. Otte, *Cartas privadas*, 491, María Alfonso to Juana Gutiérrez.

73. Otte, *Cartas privadas*, 540–541, Francisco de Ortega to su mujer Jerónimoa de Loaysa, Potosí, 16 diciembre 1594.

74. Pérez-Mallaína, *Spain's Men of the Sea*, 9.

75. Luis Martínez, *Pasajeros de Indias*, 112.

76. Perez-Mallaína, *Spain's Men of the Sea*, 14.

77. AGNP, Protocolos 28, Alonso de la Cueva, fol. 339, Poder Hernán Goncáles to Alonso Rodrígues, 22 octubre 1577.

78. Otte, *Cartas privadas*, 538, letter 603.

79. Otte, *Cartas privadas*, 442, Diego Hurtado to his sister Juana Hurtado.

80. Jacobs, 67.

81. Perez-Mallaína, *Spain's Men of the Sea*, 130.

82. Perez-Mallaína, *Spain's Men of the* Sea, 131.

83. AHPS, Protocolos, Signatura 16037, Alonso Fernández de Carmona, Oficio 23, Libro 1, fols. 123–124, Codicilio de Rodrigo de Cantillana, 7 enero 1570.

84. For detailed descriptions of food amounts, see Perez-Mallaína, *Spain's Men of the Sea*, 141, and Luis Martínez, *Pasajeros de Indias*, 58–62.

85. Otte, *Cartas privadas*, 442, Diego Hurtado to his sister Juana Hurtado. Arnold Bauer discusses in further detail how travelers brought coveted items with them from Spain to Peru in *Goods, Power, History, Latin America's Material Culture* (Cambridge: Cambridge University Press, 2001), 75.

86. Perez-Mallaína, *Spain's Men of the Sea*, 167.

87. On the subject of honor as understood by non-elites, see Lyman Johnson and Sonia Lipsett-Rivera, *The Faces of Honor: Sex, Shame and Violence in Colonial Latin America* (Albuquerque: University of New Mexico Press, 1998).

88. AHPS, Protocolos, Signatura 5383, Francisco de Almonte, Oficio 8, R. 27, fol. ivdcrxxxii, Petition of Juana de Çamorana, abril 1569. Husband is an entallador.

89. Otto, *Cartas privadas*, 379, Hernando del Río to sus hijas doña Catalina y doña Isabel Sarmiento.

90. Otte, *Cartas privadas*, 130, Juan Cabeza de Vaca a Elvira de Cantalejos, en Osuna, "que las mujeres que son honradas, honradas van y vienen."

91. AGI, Justicia 698, N. 7, fol. 7 digitized, "quytaos de mi." For more detail on this case of María García, see Ida Altman, "Spanish Women of the Caribbean, 1493-1540," in *Women in the Iberian Atlantic*, eds. Sarah E. Owens and Jane E. Mangan (Baton Rouge: Lousiana State University Press, 2012), p. 72.

92. *Catálogo de Pasajeros a Indias*, Vol. III, 3378, I-238v, 288.

CHAPTER 5

1. The records analyzed in this chapter date primarily from the 1560s through the 1580s.

2. ARA, Protocolos 98, Juan de Vera, Will of Leonor López yndia palla, R. 5, fol. 81, 5 febrero 1564. For a similar case from Lima, see AGNP, Protocolos 29, Alonso de la Cueva, fols. 234–235r, Testamento de Leonor yndia natural del Cuzco, 5 julio 1579. Leonor alleged that Luis Villareal of Guamanga, with whom she had a daughter, promised a dowry of a bar of silver and a *solar*.

3. On the significance of *cocos* (the silver version of *keros*), see Thomas B. F. Cummins, *Toasts with the Inca: Andean Abstraction and Colonial Images on Quero Vessels* (Ann Arbor: University of Michigan, 2002).

4. On this topic, see Paul Charney, *Indian Society in the Valley of Lima, Peru, 1532–1821* (Lanham, MD: University Press of America, 2001), see esp. 147–159, "Holding together the Indian Family." Charney's source base uses 123 wills from a very broad chronological period, which may explain the slight variations in interpretation that I have found with regard to families' compositions and identity. My analysis focuses squarely on the century prior to most of Charney's research. For additional analysis on family change in Lima and Trujillo, see Karen B. Graubart, *With Our Labor and Sweat: Indigenous Women and the Formation of Colonial Society in Peru, 1550–1700* (Stanford, CA: Stanford University Press, 2007), ch. 5.

5. When he noted, "there was no such thing as a mestizo family," historian James Lockhart referred specifically to identity suggesting that families either drifted toward Spanish identity or toward indigenous identity. See James Lockhart, *Spanish Peru, 1532–1560: A Social History*, 2nd ed. (Madison: University of Wisconsin Press, 1994), 191.

6. The experience of mestizos of the uppermost echelons of colonial society in New Granada has been analyzed expertly in Joanne Rappaport, *The Disappearing Mestizo: Configuring Difference in the Colonial New Kingdom of Granada* (Durham, NC: Duke University Press, 2014).

7. Tom Cummins, "Forms of Andean Colonial Towns, Free Will, and Marriage," in *The Archeology of Colonialism*, eds. Claire Lyons and John Papadopoulos (Los Angeles: Getty Press, 2002): 199–240.

8. ARA, Protocolos 5, Diego de Aguilar, Will of Alonso Cama, fol. 227 (v), 14 mayo 1571.

9. ARA, Protocolos 6, Diego de Aguilar, Cuaderno no.1, fol. 215 (v).

10. For additional examples, see the married couple don Juan Rimache of Cuzco and Catalina Nusta from Porco who never had children together, though Rimache had one natural son with another woman. ARA, Protocolos 81, Diego Navarro, fols. 10r–11v, Testamento de Don Juan Rimache, 6 marco 1579. For a similar family structure with an indigenous couple, see ARA, Protocolos 81, Diego Navarro, fols. 162v–165v, Testamento de don Juan Guaca Condori, 27 mayo 1586. See the Royal Cédula on caciques in Peru keeping more than one wife, Richard Konetzke, ed., *Colección de documentos para la historia de la formacón social de Hispanoamérica, 1493–1910* (Madrid: Consejo Superior de Investigaciones Científicas, 1953), 1:295.

11. Michelle A. McKinley argues that unmarried women in seventeenth-century Lima had certain freedoms that married women did not. See McKinley, "Illicit Intimacies: Virtuous Concubinage in Colonial Lima," *Journal of Family History* 39, no. 3 (2014): 204–221.

12. Ann Twinam, *Public Lives, Private Secrets: Gender, Honor, Sexuality, and Illegitimacy in Colonial Spanish America* (Stanford, CA: Stanford University Press, 1999).

13. AGNP, Protocolos 41, García de Nogal, fols. 949v–951, Testamento de Catalina Anpo, 11 septiembre 1564. Anpo was a native of Yanac de la Merced and daughter of the indigenous Carua and an unknown father.

14. AGNP, Protocolos 150, Juan Salamanca, fols. 197–198v, Testamento de Francisca india, 29 marzo 1574.

15. Kathryn Burns's work on notaries reveals the existence of indigenous notaries; many families might have used indigenous notaries if available. Those records are not extant. On land litigation in the courts by indigenous individuals or families, see Karen Graubart, *With Our Labor and Sweat: Indigenous Women and the Formation of Colonial Society in Peru, 1550–1700* (Stanford, CA: Stanford University Press, 2007), Steve J. Stern, *Peru's Indian Peoples and the Challenge of Spanish Conquest, Huamanga to 1640* (Madison: University of Wisconsin Press, 1982), as well as Susan Ramirez, *The World Upside Down: Cross-Cultural Contact and Conflict in Sixteenth-Century Peru* (Stanford, CA: Stanford University Press, 1996).

16. AGNP, Protocolos 122, Padilla, fol. 62–62v, Poder Felipe Manasca to Hernando Vica Alaya, 30 enero 1558.

17. On the practice of customary law, which could include both indigenous custom and Iberian custom, under colonial rule, see Lauren Benton, *Law and Colonial Culture: Legal Regimes in World History, 1400–1900* (Cambridge: Cambridge University Press, 2002), 83–84.

18. ARA, Protocolos 3, Diego de Aguilar, fols. xxxli (v)–xxxlii (r), 2 agosto 1569

19. ARA, Protocolos 2, Diego de Aguilar, R. 6, fol. 337r, Asiento Beatriz india con Joan de Quiros, 24 septiembre 1568.

20. ARA, Protocolos 44, Gaspar Hernández, R. 4, fol. 82–82v, Francisco de Santandar, protector de naturales, servicio a Angelina yndia, 27 mayo 1578.

21. The late colonial era brought a more explicit change to fathers' obligations and rights, for indigenous as well as Spanish fathers, see Bianca Premo, *Children of the Father King: Youth, Authority, and Legal Minority in Colonial Lima* (Chapel Hill: University of North Carolina Press, 2005), 193–196.

22. ARA, Protocolos 81, Diego Navarro, fol. 32v, Asiento between Ysabel india and Antonio de Balderrama, 11 febrero 1581. See also ARA, Protocolos 81, Diego Navarro, fol. 72r, Asiento between María Pacna india, daughter of Juan and Inés, and doña María Xaramillo for one year of service, 8 febrero 1583.

23. Scholars have argued that indigenous women used dowries to influence future generations in marriage. Frank Salomon, "Indian Women of Early Quito as Seen through Their Testaments," *Americas* 44, no. 3 (1988): 325–341. The practice Salomon identified through the Quiteño will was probably more widespread than other scholarship has suggested.

24. ARA, Protocolos 12, Diego Aguilar, R. 10, fol. 385v, Carta de Venta (con cabeça de testamento) Ysabel yndia Chachapoya to Diego Martínez yndio, 3 octubre 1565.

25. ARA, Protocolos 57, García Muñoz, fol. 169,Promesa de dote Lorenco de León to Diego Pérez indio ladino, 2 septiembre 1557.

26. Nancy van Deusen discusses this practice in, "The Intimacies of Bondage Female Indigenous Servants and Slaves and Their Spanish Masters, 1492–1555," *Journal of Women's History* 24, no. 1 (2012): 25. The possibility for such dowries was identified in the seminal work by Lockhart, *Spanish Peru*, 244–245.

27. AGNP, Protocolos 34, Esquivel Franco, fols. 11–12v, Testamento de Francisco Mostare, 14 abril 1578.

28. AGNP, Protocolos 41, García de Nogal, fols. 353–354, Testamento de Isabel Quispe Rimache, 20 marzo 1564.

29. AGNP, Protocolos 109, Martel, fols. 313–314, Testamento de Gonzalo de Vega, 4 agosto 1556.

30. ARA, Protocolos 59, Garcia Muñoz, R. 12, fol. xxciii, 24 octubre 1560.

31. ANGP, Protocolos 34, Esquivel Franco, fols. 50–51v, Recibo de dote Juana de los Reyes from Elvira Hernández, 29 April 1578. For a similar case in Arequipa, see ARA, Protocolos 99, Juan de Vera, fol. cvi (vuelta), Testamento de Francisco Ramirez, 30 mayo 1568, wherein de Vera provides a dowry for mestiza Leonor Gomez who was raised in his household. This practice of the bequest to a servant girl in the household for a dowry had parallels in sixteenth-century Seville. See, e.g., AHPS, Protocolos, Signatura 12461, Gaspar de León, Oficio 19, fol. 749, Will of Pedro Pablo, 24 de octubre,

"Mando a Ysabel hija de María my esclava morisca 20 ducados para ayuda a su casamiento."

32. On the obligation of men to children raised in his house who are not his biological offspring, see Title XX in Robert I. Burns, S.J., ed. *Las Siete Partidas,* 975–976.

33. ARA, Protocolos 37, Gaspar Hernández, Cuaderno 6, fol. 186 (v), Dote Catalina Hernández de Olea, 29 mayo 1564. She was marrying Cuzco native, mestizo Alonso Martín.

34. See ARA, Protocolos 99, Juan de Vera, fol. cvi (vuelta), Testamento de Francisco Ramírez, 30 mayo 1568, wherein de Vera provides a dowry for mestiza Leonor Gomez who was raised in his household.

35. AGNP, Protocolos 29, Alonso de la Cueva, fols. 4r–5r, Dowry of Ana de Pineda, 8 enero 1580.

36. AGNP, Protocolos 68, Juan Gutiérrez, fols. 940v–941v, Dote de Madalena Hernández de Lorono, 18 diciembre 1566. For another example of young female servants who received noteworthy sums from their mistresses for years of service, see AGNP, Protocolos 3, Cristóbal de Aguilar Mendieta, fols. 231v–244v, Testamento de María de Messa, 16 abril 1596.

37. The tradition of *arras*, both why it was awarded and how much control women had over it, had varying customary practices in different regions of Spain. See Heath Dillard, *Daughters of the Reconquest: Women in Castilian Town Society, 1100–1300* (New York: Cambridge University Press, 1984), 48–54.

38. AGNP, Protocolos 68, Juan Gutiérrez, fols. 662–665v, Will of Madalena de la Paz, 14 septiembre 1566.

39. AGNP, Protocolos 128, Esteban Pérez, fols. 1r–5r, Testamento de doña Elvira de Orellana, 1 enero 1572.

40. AHPS, Protocolos, Signatura 4063, Francisco de Soto, Oficio 6, fol. 153v, Testamento de Francisca Pérez, 1570. The 6,000 maravedis was worth about 22 pesos. Pérez also made bequests of 100 ducats to the boy Melchior, and to two nieces, Pérez gave 400 and 250 ducats, respectively, for "the love" she had for them.

41. Sandra Cavallo, "Family Relationships," in *A Cultural History of Childhood and Family in the Early Modern Age,* ed. Sandra Cavallo and Silvia Evangelisti (Oxford: Berg, 2010), 30.

42. AGNP, Protocolos 29, Alonso de la Cueva, Carta de promesa, fol. 196v, 28 mayo 1580.

43. AGNP, Protocolos 160, Sebastian Vázquez, fol. 1097–1097v, Will of María de Rojas, 26 enero 1554. Rojas also gave a 100-peso dowry to a mestizo named Juana.

44. Here the work of Douglas Cope on seventeenth-century Mexico City is useful. Cope's focus on class and networks of occupation and residence as trumping strict ethnic identities is suggestive of the way I view sixteenth-century Andean families which show people of supposed or real status differences linked—by

law, obligation, and custom which they themselves shaped. See Douglas Cope, *The Limits of Racial Domination, Plebeian Society in Colonial Mexico City, 1660–1720* (Madison: University of Wisconsin Press, 1994), esp. 68–85.

45. Studies suggest that some 15% to 20% of unions between Spaniards and indigenous women were marriages. See van Deusen, "The Intimacies of Bondage," 24.

46. AGNP, Protocolos 109, Martel, fols. 915–916v, Testamento de Simon Ginovés, 29 agosto 1558.

47. A rich literature exists on Andean textiles. John Murra was a leading early voice on the subject for the pre-Columbian era in "Cloth and its Functions in the Inca State," *American Anthropologist* 64, no. 4 (1962): 710–728. Frank Salomon discusses the significance for women in colonial times, see Frank Salomon, "Indian Women of Early Quito," *The Americas* 44, no. 3 (1988): 334–336.

48. Here I frame these not as anecdotal cases, but as networks, and this emphasis differs slightly from Lockhart, *Spanish Peru*, 6.

49. María Emma Mannarelli, *Private Passions and Public Sins: Men and Women in Seventeenth-Century Lima*, trans. Sidney Evans and Meredith D. Dodge (Albuquerque: University of New Mexico Press, 2007), 9.

50. AGNP, Protocolos 29, Alonso de Cueva, fols. 125r–128r, Testamento de Francisco de Aguilera, 6 diciembre 1580. Aguilera dictated his will after Pedro de Bocanegra gave Aguilera inflicted a fatal wound in the neck, allegedly without provocation, on the road to Callao.

51. AGNP, Protocolos 33, Esquivel Franco, fols. 303–304, Testamento de Elvira, 15 abril 1572.

52. On the significance of *cocos* (the silver version of *keros*), see Thomas B. F. Cummins, *Toasts with the Inca: Andean Abstraction and Colonial Images on Quero Vessels* (Ann Arbor, MI: University of Michigan, 2002).

53. ARA, Protocolos 98, Juan de Vera, R. 5, fol. 32, power to testate from doña Elvira india to her husband Marcos Baez, 31 julio 1564

54. ARA, Protocolos 98, Juan de Vera, R. 5, fols. 309–311, Will of doña Elvira india as dictated by her husband, 31 julio 1564. For other examples of indigenous material culture in indigenous–Spanish marriages, see ARA, Protocolos 32, Gaspar Hernández, fol. lxxli (r)–lxxli, Testamento de Baltasar Godines, 6 noviembre 1555, as well as AGNP, Protocolos 4, Cristóbal de Aguilar Mendieta, fols. 595r–596r, 13 junio 1597, where Diego Hernández married the indigenous Isabel circa 1560 and the two had a daughter Juana.

55. ARA, Protocolos 39, Gaspar Hernández, fol. xciii, Testamento de Leonor india guanca, 6 march 1567.

56. See, for instance, the will of Isabel Tocto, AGI, Contratación 242, N. 1, R. 15, fols. 23r–24r, Herederos de Isabel Tocto yndia sobre cobro de bienes, 1579. For additional analysis of urban indigenous women's wills, see Mangan, *Trading Roles*, 134–158.

57. ARA, Protocolos 62, García Muñoz, R. 3, fols. 83–84, Testamento de Alonso de Escoba, 17 febrero 1562. If Escoba dictated a will in 1562, he must have been born by 1540 at the latest, so he was a child of the early contact period.

58. Stern, *Peru's Indian Peoples*, 171.

59. Nancy van Deusen refers to these connections as "thin blue lines." See "The Intimacies of Bondage," 24–26.

60. ARA, Protocolos 81, Diego Navarro, fols. 148r–150v, Testamento de doña Ana Palla, 18 febrero 1586

61. ARA, Protocolos 81, Diego Navarro, fol. 149v, Testamento de doña Ana Palla, 18 febrero 1586.

62. ARA, Protocolos 81, Diego Navarro, fol. 149v, Testamento de doña Ana Palla, 18 Febrero 1586. The *mejora* allowed a testator to bequeath one-fifth of their property to anyone they wished, thereby getting around the legal requirement that all children inherit equally if a parent wished to "favor" one child over another. The fifth could also be used for bequests to non-relatives.

63. ARA, Protocolos 66, García Muñoz, fols. 135v–137, Testamento de Beatriz Cisa Ocul, 16 mayo 1571.

64. AGNP, Protocolos 128, Estevan Pérez, fols. 786v–789v, Testamento de María Beltrán, 28 septiembre 1571.

65. AGNP, Protocolos 127, Estevan Pérez, fols. 881v–882 [no paso], Servicio Antón Sánchez and Gaspar de Herrera, 21 julio 1572.

66. AGNP, Protocolos 34, Esquivel Franco, fols. 733–734v, Testamento de Elvira Hernández de Herrera, 26 noviembre 1582.

67. AGNP, Protocolos 33, Esquivel Franco, fols. 298v–300v, Testamento de María de Carvajal, 17 enero 1572.

68. ARA, Protocolos 11, Diego de Aguilar, fol. 933r, Carta de Compania, 1 octubre 1581.

69. Legal age of majority was 25. See Premo, *Children of the Father King*, 22.

70. ANB, Escrituras Públicas Vol. 144, Cuaderno no.7, fol. 805, Testamento de Diego de Rojas, 1 marco 1618. The usage of these titles might not have reflected Inca nobility since late sixteenth-century commoners adopted practices once reserved for the elite. Ana María Presta argues this point in "Undressing the *Coya* and Dressing the Indian Woman: Market Economy, Clothing, and Identities in the Colonial Andes, La Plata (Charcas), Late Sixteenth and Early Seventeenth Centuries," *Hispanic American Historical Review* 90, no. 1 (February 2009): 41–46.

71. Note that most dowries in Lima and Arequipa, with a few exceptional ones valued close to 20,000, amounted to 1,000. The 4,000 peso dowry, then, was impressive. Diego de Rojas had another child, a mestizo son, seemingly later in life. This boy, Juan de Rojas, also received a plot of land from his father and went on to marry and start his own family.

72. AGNP, Protocolos 118, Moscoso, fols. 237–238v, Testamento de Diego Hernández, 16 septiembre 1559.

73. AGNP, Protocolos 160, Sebastian Vázquez, fol. 1030–1030v, Testamento de Francisca Cambero, 25 noviembre 1553. The exact year of her departure is unclear, but she made her will in 1553 and was well settled in Lima by that date.

74. AGNP, Protocolos 159, Pedro de Valverde, fol. 1032v, codicilio Francisca Cambero, 29 noviembre 1553.

75. AGNP, Protocolos, 109, Martel, fols. 853–854, Testamento de Hernando del Salto, 1 julio 1558. Two details are notable in the naming of the mestiza daughter: first, Salto uses the term "mestiza," which many documents do not use at this time, and second, the girl has a double name "Sica del Salto" presumably using the Sica name from her mother. Mestizo children were rarely identified by two last names.

76. AGNP, Protocolos 29, Alonso de la Cueva, fols. 117r–120v, Testamento de Álvaro de Solano, 12 enero 1580.

77. AGNP, Protocolos 29, Alonso de la Cueva, fol. 119v, Testamento de Álvaro de Solano, 12 enero 1580.

CHAPTER 6

1. ARA, Protocolos 1, Diego de Aguilar, R. 10, fol. 328r, Testamento de Diego Hernández de Talavera, 8 noviembre 1577. For an in-depth overview of wills and the practice of testing in colonial Latin America, see Susan Kellogg and Matthew Restall, eds., *Dead Giveaways: Indigenous Testaments in Colonial Mesoamerica and the Andes* (Salt Lake City: University of Utah Press, 1998), 1–12.

2. ARA, Protocolos 1, Diego de Aguilar, R. 10, fols. 323v–328r, Testamento de Diego Hernández de Talavera, 8 noviembre 1577.

3. ARA, Protocolos 1, Diego de Aguilar, R. 10, fol. 327r, Testamento de Diego Hernández de Talavera, 8 noviembre 1577.

4. ARA, Protocolos 1, Diego de Aguilar, R. 10, fol. 325r, Testamento de Diego Hernández de Talavera, 8 noviembre 1577.

5. ARA, Protocolos 1, Diego de Aguilar, R. 10, fol. 356v, Codicil of Diego Hernández de Talavera, 8 noviembre 1577.

6. For one discussion of mestizos and deviancy, see F. E. Ruan, "Andean Activism and the Reformulation of Mestizo Agency and Identity in Early Colonial Peru," *Colonial Latin American Review* 21, no. 2 (2012): 209–237. A contrasting discussion of mestizos more along the lines of my findings for Lima and Arequipa is Joanne Rappaport, *The Disappearing Mestizo: Configuring Difference in the Colonial New Kingdom of Granada* (Durham, NC: Duke University Press, 2014).

7. The seminal work on this point is Kathryn Burns, "Gender and the Politics of Mestizaje: The Convent of Santa Clara in Cuzco, Peru," *Hispanic American Historical Review* 78, no. 1 (February 1998): 5–44.

8. Lauren Benton refers to this practice of accommodation to fit a circumstance in *Law and Colonial Cultures: Legal Regimes in World History, 1400–1900* (Cambridge: Cambridge University Press, 2002), 27–28. Brian Owensby gestures similarly to using law to create order in the challenging circumstances of the sixteenth century, see *Empire of Law and Indian Justice in Colonial Mexico* (Stanford, CA: Stanford University Press, 2008), 13.

9. On how images of St. Joseph as father in the post–Council of Trent world influenced society, see Charlene Villaseñor Black, *Creating the Cult of St. Joseph: Art and Gender in the Spanish Empire* (Princeton, NJ: Princeton University Press, 2006), 13.

10. AGNP, Protocolos 28, Alonso de Cueva, fol. 131r–131v, Donación Antonio de Medina to María, 12 junio 1577.

11. AGNP, Protocolos 84, Alonso Hernández, fols. 676–677v, Poder Pedro Rolón to Alvar Muñoz para pedir una hija natural, 6 julio 1571.

12. She was born to Pizarro and Ynguill, who may have been descended from the Inca dynasty on both the maternal and paternal sides. Juan received Ynguill from Manco Capac, probably in 1534. See Catherine Julien, "Francisca Pizarro, la cuzqueña, y su madre, la *coya* Ynguill," *Revista del Archivo Regional del Cuzco* 15 (June 2000): 53–74.

13. Julien, "Francisca Pizarro, la cuzqueña," 53–54, citing the will of Juan Pizarro. Julien argues that sufficient proof exists to call Juan Pizarro the father of this Francisca.

14. Julien, "Francisca Pizarro, la cuzqueña," 60.

15. Julien, "Francisca Pizarro, la cuzqueña," 55. For a discussion of how physical appearance was described, categorized, and utilized in this period, see Joanne Rappaport, "'Asi lo paresçe por su aspeto': Physiognomy and the Construction of Difference in Colonial Bogotá," *Hispanic American Historical Review* 91, no. 4 (2011): 631.

16. Julien, "Francisca Pizarro, la cuzqueña," 66, citing "Provanca."

17. Julian, "Francisca Pizarro, la cuzqueña," 72, testimony of Lorenzo Yngles.

18. Julien, "Francisca Pizarro, la cuzqueña," 68, citing "Provanca," witness Sancho Hortiz de Orue.

19. Julien, "Francisca Pizarro, la cuzqueña," 60, citing "Provanca de doña Francisca Picarro."

20. For a discussion of colonial inheritance law, see Matthew Mirow, *Latin American Law* (Austin: University of Texas Press, 2005). Much of the legal code used in the sixteenth century came from the Siete Partidas and the Leyes de Toro.

21. See Karen B. Graubart, *With Our Labor and Sweat: Indigenous Women and the Formation of Colonial Society in Peru, 1550–1700* (Stanford, CA: Stanford University Press, 2007), 103–105. Ann Twinam's work on eighteenth-century illegitimacy analyzes the legal and social realities associated with children's out-of-wedlock birth status as seen in the *gracias al sacar* petitions. The

entire book is relevant, but for legal definitions, see Ann Twinam, *Public Lives, Private Secrets: Gender, Honor, Sexuality, and Illegitimacy in Colonial Spanish America* (Stanford, CA: Stanford University Press, 1999), 26, 37–41, 47–48.

22. AGNP, Protocolos 41, García de Nogal, fols. 61–63v, Testamento de Diego de Herrera, 3 mayo 1564.

23. ARA, Protocolos 60, Garcia Muñoz, fols. 132v–133, Testamento de Xayme de Salazar, 6 marzo 1561.

24. On illegitimate children and inheritance practices in Extremadura, see Ida Altman, *Emigrants and Society: Extremadura and America in the Sixteenth Century* (Berkeley: University of California Press, 1989), 150–155.

25. For examples, see ARA, Protocolos, Garcia Muñoz 60, fol. 405 (v), Codicil of Lázaro Rodríguez, 19 de noviembre 1561, as well as ARA, Protocolos 98, Juan de Vera, fol. 20, Will of Juan de Mediano, 14 abril 1564; AGNP, Protocolos 35, Marco Esquivel Franco, fol. 828–828v, Will of Pedro Gomez, 26 enero 1583; AGNP, Protocolos 153, Pedro de Salinas, fols. 382–383, Will of Diego Castano, 16 agosto 1542.

26. ARA, Protocolos 41, Gaspar Hernández, fol. 145, Donación Diego de Ojedo to Francisca de Ojeda, 9 septiembre 1570. For a similar recognition and donation to a mestiza natural daughter in Arequipa, see ARA, Protocolos 45, fol. 230r, Donación Gerónimo de Vidgal to María Gómez, 3 junio 1581, and for Lima, see AGNP, Protocolos 28, Alonso Cueva, fols. 131–132v, donación of Antonio de Medina to María, 12 junio 1577, as well as AGNP, Protocolos 160, Sebastián Vázquez, fols. 1008–1009, 5 noviembre 1553. Çaera makes a new will in 1554 after the child is born (a son) when he becomes engaged to marry a Spanish woman. See discussion in Nancy van Deusen, "The Intimacies of Bondage: Female Indigenous Servants and Slaves and Their Spanish Masters, 1492–1555," *Journal of Women's History* 24, no. 1 (2012): 27. AGNP, Bartolomé Gascón 42, fols. 51v–53v, 15 enero 1554.

27. BNP, 1550 A 36, Testamento de Domingo de Otre, fols. 212v–218v, 26 junio 1550. Note: he declares four additional *hijos naturales* in this will.

28. AGNP, Protocolos 153, Salinas, fols. 287–292v, Testamento de Domingo de Destre, 24 julio 1542. For another example of "natural" inserted above the line, see ARA, Protocolos 5, Diego Aguilar, Cuaderno no.7, Carta de Dote, fol. 1057.

29. Altman refers to references to "amor" and deep emotional bonds in the documents on sixteenth-century Extremaduran society. See *Emigrants and Society*, 143.

30. ARA, Protocolos 43, R. 7, fol. 357, donación Nicolás del Benino to María del Benino, 20 octubre 1570. Benino was a well-known Florentine who prospered in Potosí. Reform is from "remediar." See Nancy E. van Deusen, *Between the Sacred and the Worldly, The Institutional and Cultural Practice of* Recogimiento

in Colonial Lima (Stanford: Stanford University Press, 2001), 56, on reforming mestizas through life in convents.

31. ARA, Protocolos 62, García Muñoz, R. 4, fol. 106v, 1562.

32. ARA, Protocolos 49, Gaspar Hernández, fol. 279r, Donation Felipe de León to Gomez Felipe, 3 junio 1573.

33. ARA, Protocolos 41, Gaspar Hernández, fol. 129r, Donation Pedro García de la Cuerda to María de la Cuerda, 14 agosto de 1570.

34. AGNP, Protocolos 2, Simón de Alzate, fols. 206–210v, Testamento de María Alonso, 9 marzo 1554. "Estoy confiada del que como es obligado mirar e procurar por las dhas mys hijas y en desle encargola conciencia."

35. AGNP, Protocolos 127, Estevan Pérez, fols. 734r–737r, Testamento de Martín de Aguirre, 9 mayo 1561. See also, AGNP, Protocolos 109, Martel, fol. 916v, Testamento de Simón Ginovés, 28 agosto 1558.

36. ARA, Protocolos 99, Juan de Vera, fol. page numbers ripped, Testamento de Pedro de Castilla, 26 julio 1569.

37. AGNP, Protocolos 160, Sebastián Vázquez, fol. 1124, Codicilio of Alexos Goncales Galego, 5 abril 1554. See also AGNP, Protocolos 93, Hernández, fol. 520, Donation Joan Ramírez Quintero clerigo to Leonor mestiza, 2 mayo 1571. "for love and affection."

38. ARA, Protocolos 99, Juan de Vera, fol. 106v, Testamento de Francisco Ramírez, 30 mayo 1568.

39. Will of Pedro Çaera, AGNP, Protocolos 42, Bartolomé Gascon, fols. 51v–53v, 16 enero 1554, as cited in van Deusen, "The Intimacies of Bondage," 27.

40. ARA, Protocolos 66, García Muñoz, fol. 212, 227, 228, Testamento de Diego de Hojeda, 13 agosto, 1571

41. AGNP, Protocolos 35, Esquivel Franco, fol. 972–974, Testamento de Juan Garabito, 14 abril 1583.

42. The wills are taken from my sample of notarial records in ARA and AGNP. See the bibliography for the volumes consulted in each archive.

43. Karen Graubart posed the question of how parents treated natural children when naming heirs in her study of Lima and Trujillo for the 1550 through 1700 period. Her results revealed a miniscule percentage of natural children being named as heirs. Her sample differs from mine in two regards: the focus on indigenous women's wills in the study as well as the emphasis on the seventeenth century. See Graubart, *With Our Labor and Sweat*, 104–105.

44. The percentage of those with children in Arequipa is slightly higher than the Lima sample, but both samples confirm that many people testated even in the absence of children (the reasons for this were both spiritual and material).

45. AGNP, Protocolos 42 (1) Gascon, fols. 149–153, Testamento de Lázaro Cabeça, 2 septiembre 1554.

46. AGNP, Protocolos 160, Sebastián Vázquez, fols. 258–263, Testamento de Sebastián Bernal, 11 febrero 1552.

47. See also AGNP, Protocolos 160, Sebastián Vázquez, fols. 810–810v, 26 noviembre 1552, codicilio Sebastián Bernal.

48. ARA, Protocolos 99, Juan de Vera, fols. 19v–20v [extant; remainder is missing], Testamento de Martín López, 1568 or 1569.

49. ARA, Protocolos 33, Gaspar Hernández, fol. 80v–83r, Testamento de Francisco de Quiros, 2 marzo 1556.

50. For another example of an agricultural donation in Arequipa, see ARA, Protocolos 29, Gaspar Hernández, R. 6, No. 296, Donation from Francisco de Ávila Figueroa to his three hijos naturales, 11 junio 1550, wherein Ávila Figueroa donated thirty goats to mestizo children Gracia Ana de Figueroa, Sancho de Figueroa, and Isabel de Figueroa Ávila.

51. On the colonial kurakas, see Karen Spalding, *Huarochirí, An Andean Society under Inca and Spanish Rule* (Stanford, CA: Stanford University Press, 1984), 219 – 38. See Susan Ramirez, *The World Upside Down: Cross-Cultural Contact and Conflict in Sixteenth-Century Peru* (Stanford, CA: Stanford University Press, 1996), on how rules for *cacicazgos* become more strict in the Toledan era.

52. ARA, Protocolos 81, Diego Navarro, fols. 162v–165v, Testamento de don Juan Guaca Condori, 27 mayo 1586.

53. ARA, Protocolos 81, Diego Navarro, fol. 164r, Testamento de don Juan Guaca Condori, 27 mayo 1586.

54. ARA, Protocolos 81, Diego Navarro, fol. 164v, Testamento de don Juan Guaca Condori, 27 mayo 1586.

55. ARA, Protocolos 81, Diego Navarro, fols. 10r–11v, 6 marzo 1579.

56. AGNP, Protocolos 9, Simón de Alzate, fols. 1009–1011, Testamento de Alonso Hernández de Valderrama [no date—around noviembre 1553]. See also the case of Francisco de Figueroa, who designated his son and daughter, Isabel and Alonso, born out of wedlock to different indigenous mothers, as his heirs: AGNP, Protocolos 128, Estevan Pérez, fols. 948r–951v, Testamento de Francisco de Figueroa, 13 noviembre 1571.

57. AGNP, Protocolos 160, Sebastián Vázquez, fols. 864v–865, 6 marzo 1553.

58. ARA, Protocolos 100, Juan de Vera, R. 14, fol. 555v, Testamento de Pedro Bernal de Cantalapiedra, 1 diciembre 1571.

59. ARA, Protocolos 73, García Muñoz Madueno, fols. 98v–101r, Testamento de Xpoval de Quiros, 21 abril 1591.

60. AGI, Contratación 256A, N. 1, R. 4.

61. AGNP, Protocolos 28, Alonso de la Cueva, fols. 69–70v, Testamento de Eugenio de Gudiel, 20 mayo 1578.

62. AGNP, Protocolos 28, Alonso de la Cueva, fol. 71–71v, Codicilio of Eugenio de Gudiel, 22 mayo 1578.

63. See Jane Mangan, *Trading Roles: Gender, Ethnicity and Urban Economy in Colonial Potosí* (Durham, NC: Duke University Press, 2005).

64. Brian Owensby articulates this kind of practice for the way legal participants in colonial Mexico understood the pursuit of justice. See Owensby, *Empire of Law*, 11–12. Bianca Premo argues for a practice of accommodation with regard to laws as applied to children in colonial Lima, what she calls a "politics of the child"; see Bianco Premo, *Children of the Father King: Youth, Authority, and Legal Minority in Colonial Lima* (Chapel Hill: University of North Carolina Press, 2005), 59–77.

65. So argues Benton, *Law and Colonial Cultures*, 22.

66. ARA, Protocolos 99, Juan de Vera, fols. 319v–321, Donation of Nicolás de Almacan to Luisa de Almacan, 9 septiembre 1568.

67. ARA, Protocolos 99, Juan de Vera, fols. 319v–321, Donation of Nicolás de Almacan to Luisa de Almacan, 9 septiembre 1568, Stipulations on fol. 321r.

68. ARA, Protocolos 99, Juan de Vera, fol. 320r, Donation of Nicolás de Almacan to Luisa de Almacan, 9 septiembre 1568.

69. ARA, Protocolos 99, Juan de Vera, fol. 319v, Donation of Nicolás de Almacan to Luisa de Almacan, 9 septiembre 1568.

70. ARA, Protocolos 99, Juan de Vera, fol. 320v, Donation of Nicolás de Almacan to Luisa de Almacan, 9 septiembre 1568.

71. ARA, Protocolos 99, Juan de Vera, fol. 319v, Donation of Nicolás de Almacan to Luisa de Almacan, 9 septiembre 1568.

72. ANP, Protocolos 64, Diego Gutiérrez, fol. 190–191r, Testamento de Jorge Palomino, 15 julio 1553.

73. AGNP, Protocolos 9, Simón de Alzate, fols. 994–995v, Testament de Francisco Martínez, 26 augusto 1553. Angelina is natural Nicaragua; Francisca natural Guamanga.

74. AGI, Contratación 249, N. 1, R. 14, Bienes difuntos Domingo Carvallo.

75. His case is a good example of Carlos Alberto González Sánchez's argument in *Dineros de Ventura: La varia fortuna de la emigración a Indias (siglos XVI–XVII)* (Seville: Universidad de Sevilla, 1995).

76. The *bienes de difuntos* cases for Peru are analyzed extensively by González Sánchez in his *Dineros de Ventura*. González Sánchez used these cases to argue against the commonly held belief that all Spaniards become rich in Peru, and he shows instead that only a few enjoyed financial success while a majority lived at much the same status as they had in Spain or even worse off, dying penniless.

77. AGI, Contratación 265A, N. 1, R. 2.

78. AGI, Contratación 265A, N. 1, R. 2.

79. BNP, A542, 1556, Alonso Hernández, fol. 42 [extant numeration, original is 243].

80. See Graubart, *With our Labor and Sweat*, 103–105.

81. AGNP, Protocolos 127, Esteven Pérez, fols. 647v–649r, Testamento de Beatriz Hernández, 20 mayo 1562.

82. AGNP, Protocolos 9, Simón de Alzate, fol. 996–996v, Testamento de Leonor Martín, 5 septiembre 1553. For a similar case of a Spanish woman who had a *hija natural* before marriage, see AGNP, Protocolos 128, Estevan Pérez, fols. 398r–399r, Testamento de Isabel Ximénez de Bohorques, 24 abril 1571.

83. AGNP, Protocolos 28, Alonso de la Cueva, fols. 350–355v, Testamento de Beatriz de Bives, 23 noviembre 1577. For an example from Arequipa, see ARA, Protocolos, Diego de Aguilar 7, fol. 336v–340, Will of Elvira Ruiz, 5 septiembre 1575.

84. AGI, Contratación 279B, N. 1, R. 9. Autos sobre bienes de difuntos: Catalina Rodríguez, natural de Las Garrovillas, difunta en Potosí, 249 folios.

85. AGI, Contratación 279B, N. 1, R. 9, fol. 43v, Autos sobre bienes de difuntos: Catalina Rodríguez, natural de Las Garrovillas, difunta en Potosí.

86. ANGP, Protocolos 68, Juan Gutiérrez, fols. 50–51, Testamento de Francisca Rodríguez, 15 diciembre 1565.

87. Graubart, *With our Labor and Sweat*, p. xx.

88. Owensby, *Empire of Law*, 7.

CONCLUSION

1. See, e.g., Richard Boyer, *Lives of the Bigamists: Marriage, Family and Community in Colonial Mexico* (Albuquerque: University of New Mexico Press, 1995); María Emma Mannarelli, *Pecados Públicos, La ilegitimidad en Lima, siglo XVII* (Lima: Ediciones Flora Tristán, 1993); Bianca Premo, *Children of the Father King: Youth, Authority, and Legal Minority in Colonial Lima* (Chapel Hill: University of North Carolina Press, 2005).

2. James Lockhart, *Spanish Peru, 1532–1560: A Social History*, 2nd ed. (Madison: University of Wisconsin Press, 1994).

3. Mannarelli, *Pecados Públicos*, is an excellent example of this trend.

4. Elizabeth Kuznesof, "Ethnic and Gender Influences on 'Spanish' Creole Society in Colonial Spanish America," *Colonial Latin American Review* 4, no. 1 (1995): 153–176.

5. This does not imply I am accessing the family experiences of the most impoverished or destitute women, as they rarely appear in the record in any detail.

6. ANB.EP, Vol. 63, Castro, fol. 389, Letter of donation, 29 enero 1607.

7. ANB.EP, Vol. 63, Castro, fol. 389, Letter of donation, 29 enero 1607, "granjerias e ynteligencias."

8. AGI, Justicia 1088, Autos Fiscales Lima, N. 4, R. 1, fol. 1r. Emphasis added.

9. AGNP, Protocolos 9, Simón de Alzate, fols. 631–634, Testamento de Alonso Muñoz, 13 agosto 1552.

10. Enrique Otte, *Cartas privadas de emigrantes a Indias, 1540–1616* (México: Fondo de Cultura Económica, 1996), 381.

11. On the Quechua language concept of being without family as being poor, see Cynthia Milton, *The Many Meanings of Poverty: Colonialism, Social Compacts, and Assistance in Eighteenth-Century Ecuador* (Stanford, CA: Stanford University Press, 2007), 49–50.

Bibliography

ARCHIVAL SOURCES

Archivo General de Indies, Seville, Spain (AGI)
    Contratación
    Justicia
    Lima
Archivo General de la Nación, Lima, Peru (AGNP)
    Sección Superior Gobierno, Cabildo Civil, Causas Civiles
    Sección Protocolos:
    Cristóbal de Aguilar Mendieta [3, 4, 5]
    Francisco Adrada; Francisco Alejandro; Diego Álvarez; Francisco de Avendaño [8]
    Simón Alzate [9]
    Pedro de Castañeda [18]
    Alonso de la Cueva [28, 29, 30]
    Pedro de Estrena [32]
    Marcos Esquivel Francos [33, 34]
    Juan Cristóbal de Frías [36, 37]
    Juan García Tomino [39]
    Juan García de Nogal [41]
    Bartolomé Gascón [42]
    Rodrigo Gómez de Baeza [43]
    Fernan Gómez [58]
    Nicolas de Grados [62]
    Juan Gutiérrez [63, 64, 67, 68]
    Juan Martínez [114]
    Ambrosio de Moscoso [118]
    Estevan Pérez [127, 128]
    Pedro de Salinas [153, 154]
Archivo Histórica Provincial de Sevilla, Spain (AHPS)
    Sección Protocolos:
    Gaspar de Toledo [1444]

Baltasar de Godoy [1558, 1584]

Francisco de Soto [4063]

Francisco de Almonte [5383]

Andrés de Herrera [19716]

Juan Pérez [1259]

Francisco Roman [6743]

Gaspar de Torres [6774]

Diego de Portes [10608]

Gaspar de León [1404]

Alonso Fernández de Carmona [16037]

Mateo de Almonacir [17613]

Francisco Díaz [7664]

Archivo Regional de Arequipa, Peru (ARA)

Sección Protocolos:

Diego de Aguilar [1, 2, 3, 4, 5, 6, 7, 8, 9, 10, 11, 12]

García Muñoz [57, 58, 59, 60, 62, 66]

García Muñoz Madueno [73, 74]

Juan de Vera [98, 99, 100, 101]

Gaspar Hernández [29, 30, 31, 32, 33, 35, 36, 37, 39, 40, 41]

Diego Navarro [81]

Juan de Torres [83]

Alonso de Valdecabras [97]

Biblioteca Nacional del Perú (BNP)

Sección Protocolos:

Diego Gutiérrez (A32, A33, A34, A36, A402)

Alonso Hernández (A37, A542)

Esteban Pérez (A334)

Alonso de Luque (A632)

OTHER SOURCES

Altman, Ida. *Emigrants and Society: Extremadura and America in the Sixteenth Century.* Berkeley: University of California Press, 1989.

Altman, Ida. *Transatlantic Ties in the Spanish Empire: Brihuega, Spain & Puebla, Mexico, 1560-1620.* Stanford: Stanford University Press, 2000.

Altman, Ida. "Spanish Women in the Caribbean, 1493-1540." In *Women in the Iberian Atlantic*, edited by Sarah E. Owens and Jane E. Mangan. Baton Rouge: Lousiana State University Press, 2012.

Anghie, Anthony. *Imperialism, Sovereignty and the Making of International Law.* Cambridge: Cambridge University Press, 2005.

Baber, R. Jovita. "Categories, Self-Representation and the Construction of the *Indios.*" *Journal of Spanish Cultural Studies* 10, no. 1 (March 2009): 31–32.

Bauer, Arnold. *Goods, Power, History: Latin America's Material Culture*. Cambridge: Cambridge University Press, 2001.

Benton, Lauren. *Law and Colonial Cultures: Legal Regimes in World History, 1400–1900*. Cambridge: Cambridge University Press, 2002.

Black, Charlene Villaseñor. *Creating the Cult of St. Joseph: Art and Gender in the Spanish Empire*. Princeton, NJ: Princeton University Press, 2006.

Bowser, Frederick. *The African Slave in Colonial Peru, 1524–1650*. Stanford, CA: Stanford University Press, 1974.

Boyd-Bowman, Peter. "Patterns of Spanish Emigration to the Indies, 1579–1600." *The Americas* 33, no. 1 (July 1976): 78–95.

Boyd-Bowman, Peter. *Patterns of Spanish Emigration to the New World (1493–1580)*. Buffalo, NY: SUNY Buffalo, 1973.

Boyer, Richard. *Lives of the Bigamists: Marriage, Family and Community in Colonial Mexico*. Albuquerque: University of New Mexico Press, 1995.

Burns, Kathryn. *Colonial Habits, Convents and the Spiritual Economy of Cuzco, Peru*. Durham, NC: Duke University Press, 1999.

Burns, Kathryn. "Gender and the Politics of Mestizaje: The Convent of Santa Clara in Cuzco, Peru." *Hispanic American Historical Review* 78, no. 1 (February 1998): 5–44.

Burns, Kathryn. *Into the Archive: Writing and Power in Colonial Peru*. Durham, NC: Duke University Press, 2010.

Burns, Kathryn. "Unfixing Race." In *Rereading the Black Legend: The Discourses of Religious and Racial Different in the Renaissance Empires*, edited by Margaret R. Greer, Maureen Quilligan, and Walter D. Mignolo. Chicago: University of Chicago Press, 2008.

Burns, Robert I., S.J., ed. *Las Siete Partidas*. Translated by Samuel Parsons Scott, Vol. 4. Philadelphia: University of Pennsylvania Press, 2001.

Cahill, David. "Colour by Numbers: Racial and Ethnic Categories in the Viceroyalty of Peru, 1532–1824." *Journal of Latin American Studies* 26, no. 2 (1994): 325–346.

Carrasco, Pedro. "Indian–Spanish Marriages in the First Century of the Colony." In *Indian Women of Early Mexico*, edited by Susan Schroeder, Stephanie Wood, and Robert Haskett. Norman: University of Oklahoma Press, 1997.

Cavallo, Sandra. "Family Relationships." In *A Cultural History of Childhood and Family in the Early Modern Age*, edited by Sandra Cavallo and Silvia Evangelisti. Oxford: Berg, 2010.

Charney, Paul. *Indian Society in the Valley of Lima, Peru, 1532–1824*. Lanham, MD: University Press of America, 2001.

Chipman, Donald. *Moctezuma's Children: Aztec Royalty under Spanish Rule, 1520–1700*. Austin: University of Texas Press, 2005.

Cook, Alexandra Parma, and Noble David Cook, *Good Faith and Truthful Ignorance: A Case of Transatlantic Bigamy*. Durham, NC: Duke University Press, 1991.

Cook, Karoline. "Forbidden Crossings: Morisco Emigration to Spanish America, 1492 – 1650." Ph.D. dissertation. Princeton University, 2008.

Cope, R. Douglas. *The Limits of Racial Domination: Plebeian Society in Colonial Mexico, 1660–1720.* Madison: University of Wisconsin Press, 1994.

Cummins, Thomas. "Forms of Andean Colonial Towns, Free Will, and Marriage." In *The Archeology of Colonialism,* edited by Claire Lyons and John Papadopoulos. Los Angeles: Getty Press, 2002.

Cummins, Thomas B. F. *Toasts with the Inca: Andean Abstraction and Colonial Images on Quero Vessels.* Ann Arbor: University of Michigan, 2002.

Cusicanqui, Silvia Rivera. "La raíz: colonizadores y colonizados." In *Violencias encubiertas en Bolivia,* coord. Xavier Albó and Rául Barrios Morón (La Paz: CIPCA, 1993).

Davies, Keith. *Landowners in Colonial Peru.* Austin: University of Texas Press, 1984.

de la Fuente, Alejandro. *Havana and the Atlantic in the Sixteenth Century.* Chapel Hill: University of North Carolina Press, 2011.

De la Puente Luna, José Carlos. "A costa de Su Majestad: Indios viajeros y dilemas imperiales en la corte de los Habsburgo." *Allpanchis: Historia y Sociedad* 39, no. 72 (2008): 11–60.

De la Puente Luna, José Carlos. "Into the Heart of Empire: Indian Journeys to the Hapsburg Royal Court," Ph.D. dissertation, Texas Christian University, 2010.

Dillard, Heath. *Daughters of the Reconquest: Women in Castilian Town Society, 1100–1300.* New York: Cambridge University Press, 1984.

Earle, Rebecca. "Letters and Love in Colonial Spanish America." *The Americas* 62, no. 1 (July 2005): 17–46.

de Erauso, Catalina. *Memoirs of a Basque Lt. Nun: Transvestite in the New World.* Boston: Beacon Press, 1996.

Gaudermann, Kimberly. *Women's Lives in Colonial Quito: Gender, Law and Economy in Spanish America.* Austin: University of Texas Press, 2003.

Gil, Juan. "Los primeros mestizos indios en España: Una voz ausente." In *Entre dos mundos: Fronteras culturales y agentes mediadores,* coord. Berta Ares Queija and Serge Gruzinski. Seville: Escuela de Estudios Hispano-Americanos de Sevilla, 1997.

Gonzalbo, Pilar. *Familias novohispanas: Siglos XVI al XIX.* México, DF: El Colegio de México, Centro de Estudios Históricos, 1991.

González, Ondina E., and Bianca Premo, eds. *Raising an Empire: Children in Early Modern Iberia and Colonial Latin America.* Albuquerque: University of New Mexico Press, 2007.

González Sánchez, Carlos Alberto. *Dineros de Ventura: La varia fortuna de la emigración a Indias (siglos XVI– XVII).* Seville: Universidad de Sevilla, 1995.

Gose, Peter. *Invaders as Ancestors: On the Intercultural Making and Unmaking of Spanish Colonialism in the Andes.* Toronto: University of Toronto Press, 2008.

Gose, Peter. "The State as a Chosen Woman: Brideservice and the Feeding of Tributaries in the Inka Empire." *American Anthropologist* 102, no. 1 (March 2000): 84–97.

Graubart, Karen B. "The Creolization of the New World: Local Forms of Identification in Urban Colonial Peru, 1560–1640." *Hispanic American Historical Review* 89, no. 3 (2009): 471–499.

Graubart, Karen B. "Indecent Living: Indigenous Women and the Politics of Representation in Early Colonial Peru." *Colonial Latin American Review* 9, no. 2 (2000): 213–235.

Graubart, Karen B. "'So color de una cofradía': Catholic Confraternities and the Development of Afro-Peruvian Ethnicities in Early Colonial Peru." *Slavery & Abolition* 33, no. 1 (2012): 43–64.

Graubart, Karen B. *With Our Labor and Sweat: Indigenous Women and the Formation of Colonial Society in Peru, 1550–1700*. Stanford, CA: Stanford University Press, 2007.

Guaman Poma de Ayala, Felipe. *The First New Chronicle and Good Government*, translated and annotated by David Frye. Indianapolis: Hackett Publishing Company, Inc., 2006.

Guaman Poma de Ayala, Felipe. *Nueva Coronica y Buen Gobierno*, transcripción, prólogo, notas y cronología por Franklin Pease. 2 Vol. Caracas: Biblioteca Ayacucho, 1980.

Guengerich, Sara Vicuña. "Capac Women and the Politics of Marriage in Early Colonial Peru." *Colonial Latin American Review* 24, no. 2 (2015): 147–167.

Hampe, Teodoro. "Relación de los encomenderos y repartimientos del Perú en 1561." *Historia y Cultura* 12 (1979): 75–117.

Hecht, Tobias, ed. *Minor Omissions: Children in Latin American History and Society*. Madison: University of Wisconsin Press, 2002.

Hemming, John. *The Conquest of the Incas*. New York: Harcourt, Brace, Jovanovich, 1970.

Herzog, Tamar. *Defining Nations, Immigrants and Citizens in Early Modern Spain and Spanish America*. New Haven, CT: Yale University Press, 2003.

Hidalgo, Amelia Almorza. "Sibling Relations in Spanish Emigration to Latin America, 1560–1620." *European Review of History* 17, no. 5 (October 2010): 735–752.

Jacobs, Auke Pieter. "Legal and Illegal Emigration from Seville, 1550–1650." In *"To Make America": European Emigration in the Early Modern Period* edited by Ida Altman and James Horn. Berkeley: University of California Press, 1991.

Johnson, Lyman, and Sonia Lipsett-Rivera. *The Faces of Honor: Sex, Shame and Violence in Colonial Latin America*. Albuquerque: University of New Mexico Press, 1998.

Julien, Catherine. "Francisca Pizarro, la cuzqueña, y su madre, la *coya* Ynguill." *Revista del Archivo Regional del Cuzco* 15 (June 2000): 53–74.

Julien, Catherine. *Reading Inca History*. Iowa City: University of Iowa Press, 2002.

Kellogg, Susan, and Matthew Restall, eds. *Dead Giveaways: Indigenous Testaments in Colonial Mesoamerica and the Andes*. Salt Lake City: University of Utah Press, 1998.

Konetzke, Richard, ed. *Colección de documentos para la historia de la formación social de Hispanoamérica, 1493–1910*. Vol. 1. Madrid: Consejo Superior de Investigaciones Científicas, 1953.

Konetzke, Richard. "La emigración de mujeres españolas a America durante la época colonial." *Revista internacional de sociologia* 3, no. 9 (1945): 123–150.

Kuznesof, Elizabeth. "Ethnic and Gender Influences on 'Spanish' Creole Society in Colonial Spanish America." *Colonial Latin American Review* 4, no. 1 (1995): 153–176.

Lamana, Gonzalo. *Domination without Dominance: Inca–Spanish Encounters in Early Colonial Peru*. Durham, NC: Duke University Press, 2008.

Liang, Yuen-Gen. *Family and Empire: The Fernández de Córdoba and the Spanish Realm*. Philadelphia: University of Pennsylvania Press, 2011.

Lockhart, James. *Spanish Peru, 1532–1560: A Social History*. 2nd ed. Madison: University of Wisconsin Press, 1994.

Lockhart, James. "The Women of the Second Generation." In *People and Issues in Latin American History: The Colonial Experience*, edited by Lewis Hanke and Jane M. Rausch. Princeton, NJ: Marcus Wiener Publishing, 1997.

MacCormack, Sabine. "History, Historical Record, and Ceremonial Action: Incas and Spaniards in Cuzco." *Comparative Studies of Society and History* 43, no. 2 (2001): 329–363.

Mangan, Jane. "A Market of Identities: Women, Trade, and Ethnic Labels in Colonial Potosí." In *Imperial Subjects, Race and Identity in Colonial Latin America*, edited by Andrew B. Fisher and Matthew O'Hara. Durham, NC: Duke University Press, 2009.

Mangan, Jane. *Trading Roles: Gender, Ethnicity and Urban Economy in Colonial Potosí*. Durham, NC: Duke University Press, 2005.

Mannarelli, María Emma. *Pecados Públicos, La ilegitimidad en Lima, siglo XVII*. Lima: Ediciones Flora Tristán, 1993.

Mannarelli, María Emma. *Private Passions and Public Sins: Men and Women in Seventeenth-Century Lima*. Translated by Sidney Evans and Meredith D. Dodge. Albuquerque: University of New Mexico Press, 2007.

Martínez, José Luis. *Pasajeros de Indias: Viajes transatlánticos en el siglo XVI*. Madrid: Alianza Editorial, 1983.

Martínez, María Elena. *Genealogical Fictions: Limpieza de Sangre, Religion and Gender in Colonial Mexico*. Stanford, CA: Stanford University Press, 2008.

Martínez Shaw, Carlos. *La emigración española a América (1492–1824)*. Asturias, Spain: Fundación Archivo de Indianos, 1994.

McKinley, Michelle. "Illicit Intimacies: Virtuous Concubinage in Colonial Lima." *Journal of Family History* 39, no. 3 (2014): 204–221.

Milanich, Nara. *Children of Fate: Childhood, Class, and State in Chile, 1850–1930.* Durham, NC: Duke University Press, 2009.

Milanich, Nara. "Whither Family History? A Road Map from Latin America." *American Historical Review* 112, no. 2 (April 2007): 439–458.

Milton, Cynthia. *The Many Meanings of Poverty: Colonialism, Social Compacts, and Assistance in Eighteenth-Century Ecuador.* Stanford, CA: Stanford University Press, 2007.

Mirow, Matthew. *Latin American Law.* Austin: University of Texas Press, 2005.

Murra, John. "Cloth and its Functions in the Inca State." *American Anthropologist* 64, no. 4 (1962): 710–728.

Nowack, Kerstin. "Aquellas señoras del linaje real de los incas, vida y supervivencia de las mujeres de la nobleza inca el en Perú en los primeros años de la Colonia." In *Elites indígenas en los andes, nobles, caciques y cabildantes bajo el yugo colonial,* edited by David Cahill and Blanca Tovías. Quito: Ediciones Abya-Yala, 2003.

O'Toole, Rachel Sarah. *Bound Lives: Africans, Indians, and the Making of Race in Colonial Peru.* Pittsburgh: University of Pittsburgh Press, 2012.

Ortiz, María del Carmen Pareja. *Presencia de la mujer Sevillena en Indias: Vida cotidiana.* Seville: Diputación Provincial de Seville, 1993.

Otte, Enrique. *Cartas privadas de emigrantes a Indias, 1540–1616.* México: Fondo de Cultura Económica, 1996.

Owensby, Brian. *Empire of Law and Indian Justice in Colonial Mexico.* Stanford, CA: Stanford University Press, 2008.

Pascua Sánchez, María José de la. *Mujeres solas: Historias de amor y de abandono en el mundo hispánico.* Málaga, Spain: Centro de Ediciones de la Diputación de Málaga, 1995.

Pérez-Mallaína, Pablo E. *Spain's Men of the Sea: Daily Life on the Indies Fleets in the Sixteenth Century.* Translated by Carla Rahn Phillips. Baltimore: Johns Hopkins University Press, 1998.

Perry, Mary Elizabeth. *Gender and Disorder in Early Modern Seville.* Princeton, NJ: Princeton University Press, 1990.

Poska, Allyson. "Babies on Board: Women, Children and Imperial Policy in the Spanish Empire." *Gender and History* 22, no. 2 (August 2012): 269–293.

Poska, Allyson. "Elusive Virtue: Rethinking the Role of Female Chastity in Early Modern Spain." *Journal of Early Modern History* 8, no. 1/2 (2004): 135–146.

Poska, Allyson. "When Love Goes Wrong: Getting Out of Marriage in Seventeenth-Century Spain." *Journal of Social History* 29, no. 4 (Summer 1996): 871–882.

Poska, Allyson. *Women and Authority in Early Modern Spain: The Peasants of Galicia.* New York: Oxford University Press, 2006.

Powers, Karen. "The Battle for Bodies and Souls in the Colonial North Andes." *Hispanic American Historical Review* 75, no. 1 (February 1995): 31–56

Powers, Karen. *Women in the Crucible of Conquest: The Gendered Genesis of Spanish American Society, 1500–1600*. Albuquerque: University of New Mexico Press, 2005.

Premo, Bianca. *Children of the Father King: Youth, Authority, and Legal Minority in Colonial Lima*. Chapel Hill: University of North Carolina Press, 2005.

Premo, Bianca. "Familiares: Thinking beyond Lineage and across Race in Spanish Atlantic Family History." *William and Mary Quarterly* 70, no. 2 (April 2013): 295–316.

Premo, Bianca. "An Old Father in a New Tragedy: Fatherhood in the Legal Theater of the Spanish Atlantic, 1770–1820." *Clio* 40, no. 1 (2010): 109–130.

Presta, Ana María. "Estados alterados: Matrimonio y vida maridable en Charcas Temprano-Colonial." *Población y Sociedad, Revista Regional de Estudios Sociales* 18, no. 1 (2011): 79–105.

Presta, Ana María. "Portraits of Four Women: Traditional Female Roles and Transgressions in Colonial Elite Families in Charcas, 1550–1600." *Colonial Latin American Review* 9, no. 2 (2000): 237–262.

Presta, Ana María. "Undressing the *Coya* and Dressing the Indian Woman: Market Economy, Clothing, and Identities in the Colonial Andes, La Plata (Charcas), Late Sixteenth and Early Seventeenth Centuries." *Hispanic American Historical Review* 90, no. 1 (February 2009): 41–46.

Ramirez, Susan. *The World Upside Down: Cross-Cultural Contact and Conflict in Sixteenth-Century Peru*. Stanford, CA: Stanford University Press, 1996.

Rappaport, Joanne. "'Asi lo paresçe por su aspeto': Physiognomy and the Construction of Difference in Colonial Bogotá." *Hispanic American Historical Review* 91, no. 4 (2011): 602–631.

Rappaport, Joanne. *The Disappearing Mestizo: Configuring Difference in the Colonial New Kingdom of Granada*. Durham, NC: Duke University Press, 2014.

Rappaport, Joanne. "El mestizo que desaparece: El género en la construcción de las redes sociales entre mestizos de élite en Santafé de Bogotá, siglos XVI y XVII." In *Celebraciones y crisis: Procesos independentistas en Iberoamérica y la Nueva Granada*, edited by Juan Camilo Escobar Villegas, Sarah de Mojica, and Adolfo León Maya. Bogotá: Editorial Pontificia Universidad Javeriana, 2012.

Romera, Luis Iruela y María del Carmen Galbis Díez. *Catálogo de pasajeros a Indias durante los siglos XVI, XVII, y XVIII*. Vol. IV. Ministerio de Cultura, Dirección General de Bellas Artes, Archivos y Bibliotecas, Subdirección General de Archivos, 1980.

Rostworowski de Diez Canseco, María. *Doña Francisca Pizarro, una ilustre mestiza, 1534–1598*. Lima: Instituto de Estudios Peruanos, 1989.

Ruan, F. E. "Andean Activism and the Reformulation of Mestizo Agency and Identity in Early Colonial Peru." *Colonial Latin American Review* 21, no. 2 (2012): 209–237.

Salomon, Frank. "Indian Women of Early Quito as Seen through Their Testaments." *Americas* 44, no. 3 (1988): 325–341.

Sánchez, Angel Rodríguez. *Hacerse Nadie: Sometimiento, sexo y silencio en la España de finales del s. xvi.* Lleida: Editorial Mileno, 1998.

Schwartz, Stuart. "Colonial Identities and the Sociedad de Castas." *Colonial Latin American Review* 4, no. 1 (1995): 185–201.

Schwartz, Stuart, and Frank Salomon. "New Peoples and New Kinds of People: Adaptation, Readjustment, and Ethnogenesis in South American Indigenous Societies (Colonial Era)." In *The Cambridge History of the Native Peoples of the Americas*, vol. 3 *South America*, Part 2, edited by Frank Salomon and Stuart B. Schwartz. Cambridge: Cambridge University Press, 1999.

Seed, Patricia. *To Love, Honor, and Obey in Colonial Mexico.* Stanford, CA: Stanford University Press, 1988.

Shelton, Laura. "Like a Servant or Like a Son? Circulating Children in Northwestern Mexico (1790–1850)." In *Raising an Empire: Children in Early Modern Iberia and Colonial Latin America*, edited by Ondina E. González and Bianca Premo. Albuquerque: University of New Mexico, 2007.

Stavig, Ward. *The World of Tupac Amaru: Conflict, Community, and Identity in Colonial Peru.* Lincoln: University of Nebraska Press, 1999.

Stern, Steve J. *Peru's Indian Peoples and the Challenge of Spanish Conquest, Huamanga to 1640.* Madison: University of Wisconsin Press, 1982.

Stolcke, Verena, and Alexandre Coello, eds. *Identidades ambivalentes en America Latina (siglos XVI–XXI).* Barcelona: Ediciones Bellaterra, 2008.

Stoler, Ann Laura. *Carnal Knowledge and Imperial Power: Race and the Intimate in Colonial Rule.* Berkeley and Los Angeles: University of California Press, 2002.

Stoler, Ann Laura. "Tense and Tender Ties: The Politics of Comparison in North American History and (Post) Colonial Studies." *Journal of American History* 88 (2001): 829–865.

Stone, Lawrence. *The Family, Sex and Marriage in England, 1500–1800.* New York: Harper & Row, 1977.

Studnicki-Gizbert, Daviken. *A Nation upon the Ocean Sea: Portugal's Atlantic Diaspora and the Crisis of the Spanish Empire, 1492–1640.* New York: Oxford University Press, 2007.

Townsend, Camila. *Malintzin's Choices: An Indian Woman in the Conquest of Mexico.* Albuquerque: University of New Mexico Press, 2006.

Twinam, Ann. "Honor, paternidad e ilegitimidad: Los padres solteros en América Latina durante la Colonia." *Estudios Sociales* 3 (September 1988): 9–32.

Twinam, Ann. *Public Lives, Private Secrets: Gender, Honor, Sexuality, and Illegitimacy in Colonial Spanish America.* Stanford, CA: Stanford University Press, 1999.

van Deusen, Nancy E. *Between the Sacred and the Worldly: The Institutional and Cultural Practice of Recogimiento in Colonial Lima.* Stanford, CA: Stanford University Press, 2001.

van Deusen, Nancy E. "Diasporas, Bondage, and Intimacy in Lima, 1535–1555." *Colonial Latin American Review* 19, no. 2 (August 2010): 247–277.

van Deusen, Nancy E. *Global Indios: The Indigenous Struggle for Justice in Sixteenth-Century Castile.* Durham, NC: Duke University Press, 2015.

van Deusen, Nancy E. "The Intimacies of Bondage: Female Indigenous Servants and Slaves and Their Spanish Masters, 1492–1555." *Journal of Women's History* 24, no. 1 (2012): 13–43.

Varón Gabai, Rafael. *Francisco Pizarro and his Brothers: The Illusion of Power in Sixteenth-Century Peru.* Translated by Javier Flores Espinoza. Norman: University of Oklahoma Press, 1997.

Vassberg, David. *The Village and the outside World in Golden Age Castile: Mobility and Migration in Everyday Rural Life.* Cambridge: Cambridge University Press, 1996.

Vergara, Teresa C. "Growing Up Indian: Migration, Labor, and Life in Lima (1570–1640)." In *Raising an Empire: Children in Early Modern Iberia and Colonial Latin America,* edited by Ondina E. González and Bianca Premo. Albuquerque: University of New Mexico, 2007.

Yupanqui, Titu Cusi. *History of How the Spaniards Arrived in Peru.* Translated with an introduction by Catherine Julien. Cambridge, MA: Hackett, 2006.

Zamora, Margarita. *Language, Authority, and Indigenous History in the Comentarios reales de los Incas.* New York: Cambridge University Press, 1988.

Index

Made in the USA
San Bernardino, CA
01 September 2017